Library of
Davidson College

ENDGAMES OF EMPIRE
Studies of Britain's Indian Problem

By the same author

Sir Charles Wood's Indian Policy, 1853–66
Liberalism and Indian Politics, 1872–1922
The Crisis of Indian Unity, 1917–1940
Churchill, Cripps, and India, 1939–1945
Escape from Empire: The Attlee Government and the Indian Problem
Making the New Commonwealth
Edited, *Tradition and Politics in South Asia*

ENDGAMES OF EMPIRE
Studies of Britain's Indian Problem

R. J. MOORE

DELHI
OXFORD UNIVERSITY PRESS
BOMBAY CALCUTTA MADRAS
1988

Oxford University Press, Walton Street, Oxford OX2 6DP
NEW YORK TORONTO
DELHI BOMBAY CALCUTTA MADRAS KARACHI
PETALING JAYA SINGAPORE HONG KONG TOKYO
NAIROBI DAR ES SALAAM
MELBOURNE AUCKLAND
and associates in
BERLIN IBADAN

© Oxford University Press 1988

SBN 19 562143 3

Phototypeset by Graphic Letters (P) Ltd., New Delhi 110015
printed at Rekha Printers (P) Ltd., New Delhi 110020
and published by S.K. Mookerjee, Oxford University Press
YMCA Library Building, Jai Singh Road, New Delhi 110001

Preface

All the studies presented here have been published previously in collective volumes or learned journals. I have not attempted to revise them, apart from correcting errors and imposing uniformities of exposition and citation. Nor have I attempted to take account of the work of others, for I have recently surveyed elsewhere historical writing on the transfer of power in the last twenty years.* The point of bringing the studies together here is that they form a coherent series (though to supplement Chapter 5 as a bridge between the Cripps Mission and the Mountbatten viceroyalty the Introduction paraphrases some of the arguments of my *Escape from Empire. The Attlee Government and the Indian Problem*). They span a significantly longer period than any of my monographs on the later Raj. Moreover, while they continue to be cited some of them are not readily available. Several of them emerged from privileged access to private papers and revised accepted interpretations, often perpetrated by members of the governing circles at Whitehall or New Delhi. I hope that, with the writer, the reader will still be engaged by the excitement of viewing events against the grain of the received, though by now many of the findings have become conventional.

I wish to acknowledge the original editors and publishers of the following studies:

1. D. A. Low (ed.), *Congress and the Raj: Facets of the Indian Struggle, 1917–47*, Heinemann, London, 1977.
2. and 3. C. H. Philips and Mary Doreen Wainwright (eds), *The Partition of India: Policies and Perspectives, 1935–1947*, George Allen and Unwin Ltd., London, 1970.
4. *The Journal of Commonwealth Political Studies*, 11.3 (1973).
5. *Modern Asian Studies*, 17.4 (1983).
6. *The Journal of Commonwealth and Comparative Politics*, 19.1 (1981).

---

* 'The Transfer of Power: An Historiographical Survey', *South Asia*, XI (1986), 83–95. An important volume subsequently published is Amit Kumar Gupta (ed.), *Myth and Reality: The Struggle for Freedom in India, 1945–47* (New Delhi, 1987), esp. ch. 1, Partha Sarathi Gupta, 'Imperial Strategy and the Transfer of Power, 1939–51'.

7. A. Jeyaratnam Wilson and Dennis Dalton (eds), *The States of South Asia, Problems of National Integration: Essays in Honour of W. H. Morris-Jones*, C. Hurst & Company, London, 1982.

I also wish to record a continuing debt to Kenneth Ballhatchet, teacher, colleague and friend, who has helped to sustain the interest and confidence that the prolonged investigation of the remarkable case of British India requires.

Flinders University of South Australia   R. J. Moore
1988

Contents

Preface	v
Introduction	1
1 The Problem of Freedom with Unity	9
2 The Making of India's Paper Federation, 1927–35	37
3 British Policy and the Indian Problem, 1936–40	67
4 The Mystery of the Cripps Mission	86
5 Jinnah and the Pakistan Demand	106
6 Mountbatten, India and the Commonwealth	134
7 India in 1947: The Limits of Unity	174
Abbreviations used in the notes	202
Notes	203
Index	225

Introduction

> It will be found that for a generation past the stress in Indian politics has been all on freedom, but that now, when the full attainment of freedom is in sight, the balance has swung over and unity has become again, as it was when British rule began, the major Indian problem.
>
> Sir Reginald Coupland, 1942

Coupland's three-volume *Report on the constitutional problem in India, submitted to the Warden and Fellows of Nuffield College, Oxford* (1942–3) was a worthy successor to the Montagu-Chelmsford and Simon Reports, on which the constitutions of 1919 and 1935 were so largely based. Coupland, in good Whiggish fashion, viewed those steps to freedom as culminating in the Cripps 'Declaration of Indian Independence' on 29 March 1942. With the objective of freedom at last enshrined in an unequivocal promise of post-war dominionhood and the right to secede from the Commonwealth, Coupland devoted his final volume to an analysis of the means of its fulfilment consistently with the unity of India. His solution, the grouping of provinces and princely states in regions, with an 'agency' centre, was an attempt to come to terms with both the movement for Pakistan and the states' internal autonomy. It bears some resemblance to the Cabinet Mission's ill-fated three-tier scheme, with its provincial groups, and three-subject all-India centre. The convolutions to which first Coupland and later the Cabinet Mission resorted to give effect to the promise of freedom cast doubts upon his thesis that for the generation to 1942 the stress of British policies had been upon Indian freedom.

In general terms, this series of studies in the high politics of empire suggests that from 1917 to 1945 British constitutional strategies and viceregal diplomacy were concerned primarily with underpinning imperial governance with Indian collaborative structures. In the process legitimacy was accorded to blocks in the Congress path to national freedom with unity. Policy trends were directed in essentials by non-Labour governments and there is evidence to suggest that they would have persisted into the post-war period if the Conservatives had won the 1945 general election. Instead, from its accession to office, Attlee's Government viewed the Indian problem from a post-imperial perspective, seeking a nationalist succession compatible with British economic interests, the stability of the subcontinent, and the security of the Indian Ocean area. In consequence, an overriding value was placed upon the co-operation of the Congress and maximizing Indian unity.

I

The first study in the series measures the successive British promises of 'responsible government' and 'Dominion status' with the gauge of equality. It traces a trail of tergiversation in which, until the Cripps declaration, the objective was always qualified, or contingent upon the achievement of unity. It finds, too, that the principles and schemes of the 1919 and 1935 constitutions emphasized the separateness of princely and Muslim India from the Hindu provinces on which the national pretensions of the Congress mainly depended. Where the India Act of 1935 gave the princes a veto over the emergence of a responsible central government, the August Declaration of 1940 blocked any constitutional advance to which the powerful Muslim minority objected. Again the Cripps declaration cut the Gordian knot, serving fifteen years' notice on the princes of their need to adhere to an Indian Union, and allowing separate dominionhood to provinces that wished to secede from the Union.

The first study was prepared in 1975 as an attempt to draw general conclusions from such specific findings as those of the three following studies. The paper on the putative all-India federation argues that neither by intention nor potentiality was it the viable alternative to eventual partition that the well-meaning former Viceroy, Lord Halifax, supposed. For the devious former Secretary of State, Lord Templewood, with Simon its principal architect, it was the means of retaining in imperial hands the threads of effective control, while buying off Congress nationalism with the loaves and fishes of provincial office. The 'paper federation' would have been an incompatible mixture of provincial democrats and princely autocrats, satisfying the minimum requirements of neither. The study rejects Templewood's attempt to place the blame for the federation's failure upon viceregal ineptitude. However, the following paper, on British policy from the passing of the Act to the 'August offer' of 1940, suggests that Lord Linlithgow lacked the insight and the will to pursue means of resolving the crisis of Indian unity in the fresh context created by the crisis of world freedom. Successive Conservative secretaries of state, Lord Zetland and Leopold Amery, were then disposed towards liberal initiatives. Winston Churchill, who had gone into the political wilderness rather than support even the qualified and contingent responsibility of the 1935 Act, opposed them implacably, now viewing the Congress-League conflict as a pillar of the Raj. In 1942, as the paper on the Cripps Mission shows, he was the senior member of the triumvirate, embracing Linlithgow and Amery, that aborted Cripps's attempt to bring the Indian parties together in a reconstructed Viceroy's executive council.

The 1975 study of freedom and unity therefore rejected the thesis that for a generation the emphasis of British policy had been upon freedom. Yet it accepted Coupland's argument that the Cripps offer was, in spite of the Mission's failure, a decisive victory for the principle of freedom. The promise of full post-war Dominion status was reaffirmed in Parliament and its fulfilment seemed consonant with Britain's own interests. It is clear in retrospect that the study underestimated the endurance of imperialist attitudes, and the sustenance that developments on the subcontinent and shifts in the international situation might afford them. The Cripps offer required the agreement of the Indian parties to enter a constituent assembly, and only when the Union constitution was made could a province opt out as a separate Dominion. When, soon after VE day, Lord Wavell tried to negotiate the entry of the Indian parties to his executive as a step towards setting up a constituent assembly, Jinnah made recognition of the Muslim right to separate national status—encapsulated in the principle of Congress-League parity—the precondition of co-operation. It became clear that the condition of the Cripps offer, which the League had seemed to acknowledge in 1942, was no longer acceptable to it. In effect, the League vetoed the procedure of the Cripps offer, and the Attlee Government was obliged to find an alternative route to Indian freedom. At the same time, while the war against Hitler was won the Cold War with Russia had begun. The Labour Cabinet soon apprehended the perils of quitting the subcontinent unless and until stable successors could be established, which implied agreement between the Indian parties. Even with Labour in power, India faced a post-war crisis of freedom.

II

The study of Jinnah and the demand for Pakistan suggests that until the end of the war Jinnah's conception of Pakistan was in harmony with ideas that leading Conservatives expressed at the time of the Cripps Mission. As early as February 1940 the National Labour Organization had argued for bridging the constitutional impasse by extending a form of Dominion status to parts of the subcontinent. In March 1942 Amery wrote of the concession of 'local option', the right of a province to choose dominionhood: 'This is after all only what has happened in the case of every Dominion, where provinces have stuck out for a time, or, as in the case of Newfoundland, New Zealand, and Southern Rhodesia, stood out permanently.'* R.A. Butler recorded that 'the powers-that-be are reconciled to the idea of a Moslem Confederation in the north'. He was critical of the Cripps declaration's failure to mention any 'central government': its 'new constitution' for a Union would include only the Hindu provinces and 'no mention is made of a constitution which will tie up at the centre Pakhistan, the Hindu world, and the Indian states'. Perhaps such a clarification would be 'too blunt an expression of the view that the British influence must and shall remain, in some capacity, in India'. In private Amery left no doubt that 'the Viceroy will have to remain, not merely as constitutional Governor-General, but as a representative of broader imperial aspects of government for a good long time to come, to be equipped with the instruments of power required to carry out his functions'. Delhi and a considerable area around it must not pass into the hands of any of the ' "Dominions" that may temporarily emerge', but be retained 'as the ultimate federal territory of an eventual united India'. Churchill envisaged that in 'the Central government we might sit on top of a tripos—Pakistan, Princely India and the Hindus'.

In February 1942 the U.P. Leaguer, Choudhry Khaliquzzaman, set a similar proposal before Coupland:

The Moslem demand is that Britain, after the war, should by Act of Parliament, establish the zonal system, before considering further Swaraj. British control would be still required at the Centre—apparently for an indefinite period—since Defence and Foreign Policy (which is practically all the Centre would deal with) should still be in British hands. The zones would have fiscal autonomy. If they couldn't agree on tariff policy, the British at the

---

*Amery to Sir S. Hoare, 11 March 1942, Templewood P., Cambridge Univ. Lib.,XIII.19.

Centre would settle it. Pakistan, moreover, would require British aid and capital for its development before it would be able to stand alone.

Throughout the war Jinnah's own statements contemplated the post-war emergence of Pakistan and Hindustan dominions, subordinate, with the princely states, to Britain for defence and foreign affairs.

It would be too much to speak of a Conservative-Muslim League accord, but after March 1946, when Attlee removed dominionhood as a step prerequisite to full freedom, both the Conservative leaders and Jinnah insisted upon the right of Muslim India, or Pakistan, to remain in the Commonwealth. Churchill and, remarkably, Templewood upheld that right—the right, in effect, ultimately to divide India. For Churchill, too, a Pakistan Dominion (and princely dominions as the last study in this series shows) would be subordinate within the Commonwealth, even if a Hindustan were outside it. Under the auspices of a Churchill government the post-war transfer of power would assuredly have sundered subcontinental unity by encouraging several successor states and limited the freedom of at least some of them by a restrictive conception of dominionhood.

The Labour Government's policy of seeking the Indian parties' agreement upon a scheme for transferring power at a stroke was a blow to Jinnah's hopes of consolidating the Muslim provinces within zones under British suzerainty. Labour favoured an early withdrawal not only because the party was pledged to it, but because it would best serve Britain's own interests. The co-operation of Congress, which demanded independence, seemed necessary to the preservation of the now uncertain internal order and the security of the Indian Ocean area. Agreement between the major parties was desirable for the same reasons. Labour favoured a unitary transfer of power, mainly in the interests of the co-ordination of defence. But agreement was the desideratum and an agreed partition would be acceptable. In any event, a defence treaty was to be required. The interests of the services could be negotiated later, and after an amicable transfer of power the new national authorities would no doubt wish to retain some British civil and military officers. The best security for commercial and financial interests lay in an orderly transfer and the continuation of the collaborative arrangements that had prospered before and during the war (when leading magnates were associated with government).

Labour's Cabinet Mission foundered on the Pakistan issue. The tangled tale of its negotiations must tell of Jinnah's initial acceptance of a scheme that gave promise of accommodating the Pakistan demand at a subnational group level within a weak central Union; of progressive British concessions to Congress that undermined the promise; of Jinnah's alienation in the face of Congress violations of the spirit of the scheme and British acquiescence in them.

In mid-1946 the Labour Cabinet resolved that in the context of the Cold War it must retain imperial control over an India whose main parties could not agree on the terms of a transfer of power. In the months that followed resolution faded, until in February 1947 Attlee declared that Britain would quit by June 1948, if necessary without achieving agreement between the Indian parties and without a defence treaty. Power would be transferred to the best successor authorities available at that time.

Attlee's somewhat revolutionary time-limit statement sets the scene for an assessment of Mountbatten's viceroyalty, the main achievements of which are examined in the last two studies in this series. The circumstances in India that contributed to the policy shift and the change of viceroys included: the steady rundown of the administration, which Wavell's 'breakdown plan' emphasized; the communal carnage that followed Jinnah's rejection of constitutionalism; the emergence of para-military forces; and the paralysis of Nehru's communally divided Interim Government. In that freezing British winter of discontent, however, the policy shift was part of a larger imperial endgame. A strategy of early withdrawal was driven by an over-extension of imperial military commitments that were no longer supportable by a bankrupt metropolitan power.

III

The ultimate solution to the problem of freedom with unity involved the partition of British India between two Dominions, and the accession of the princely states to one or other of them. The unity that the Raj had achieved about a century earlier was dissolved in the transfer of power. In the context of Congress-League disputation, communal disorder, and anti-imperialist sentiment, the agreement on dual dominionhood appears as an achievement. There were even shortlived hopes that joint agencies might emerge for matters of common concern, that a defence treaty might be negotiated, or that as continuing members of the Commonwealth India and Pakistan might resolve their differences. Such hopes were dashed by the massacres that attended the partition of the Punjab and the hostilities over Kashmir, which had failed to decide its accession before the British withdrawal.

The last two studies in this series acknowledge the centrality of Mountbatten's diplomacy to such successes and failures. At the same time, they seek to place the extravagant claims of (and for) the royal fabulist in historical perspective. Whilst the most recent official biographer perpetuates aspects of the Mountbatten myth he concedes that Mountbatten 'sought to rewrite history with cavalier indifference to the facts to magnify his own achievements'.* He appears to accept much of the penultimate study's answer to the notorious puzzle of the plans, expressing for example surprise that Mountbatten should ever have expected Nehru to agree to his staff's 'Plan Balkan'. Against the background of Jinnah's demand and the Conservative affirmation that Pakistan must remain in the Commonwealth, and of Congress demands for the immediate concession of Dominion status to the Interim Government so that it could counter 'fissiparous tendencies', the deal for dual Dominions seems less of a viceregal policy breakthrough than a clever diplomatic coup. Again, Mountbatten's *realpolitik* flowed from his recognition of Congress goodwill as essential to Britain's post-imperial interests. To a greater degree than has been acknowledged Congress called the cards in the last rubber of the endgame: in the accelerated transfer of power; in the severe treatment of Jinnah and his claims; in the persuasion of the princes to accede to a dominion, which the final study describes as 'a *de facto* policy of unification' and Mountbatten's major contribution to the subcontinent's unity.

IV

In the Introduction to his *Report* Coupland carried out into the world at large his emphasis upon the interplay of the principles of freedom and unity in India. He recorded that he had already 'urged the need for combining unity with freedom and illustrated his theme from the history of the British Commonwealth'. In 1942, with the United Nations engaged in a war for survival, he argued that 'the freedom which our victory will save or restore to all nations will be

---

*Philip Ziegler, *Mountbatten: The Official Biography* (London, 1985), 701. See also my 'Putting the Viceroy in his place', *South*, August 1985, 93; and review articles 'Towards Partition and Independence in India' and 'The Mountbatten Viceroyalty', *Journal of Commonwealth and Comparative Politics*. 20 (1982), 189–99 and 22 (1984), 204–15.

unfruitful or precarious unless it is combined with the greatest practicable measure of international unity'. Whilst the transfer of power relieved Britain of an onerous and hazardous burden the Labour Government continued for some years to play for the engagement of the successor nations in a new Commonwealth.* That game was won when India and Pakistan agreed to 'remain united as free and equal members of the Commonwealth of Nations, freely co-operating in the pursuit of peace, liberty and progress'. In that sense, the endgames of empire in South Asia culminated in the celebrated London Declaration of 28 April 1949, rather than the midnight revels of 14 August 1947.

* See my *Making the New Commonwealth* (Oxford, 1987).

1
The Problem of Freedom with Unity

The demission of empire in India was the greatest transfer of power in modern times. The process, inaugurated in 1917 largely as a means of rallying support in war-time, was only completed thirty years later, when a second war had exposed the palpable inadequacy of Britain's resources to sustain an empire. In the end Britain quit quickly, for only in 1946 was there any devolution of responsibility in the Central Government of India. The consequence of Britain's unwillingness or inability to transfer central authority earlier was that when the main Indian parties confronted the problem of governing the old united empire they could not agree upon a solution. The price of freedom became partition.

The problem of demission may be defined in terms of reconciling the principles of freedom and unity, of preserving in freedom the unity that empire had imposed. Whilst the Indian adversaries of the Raj claimed that Britain's real object during the ostensible age of devolution was *divide et impera*, British statesmen and officials held that their constant purpose was to transfer power progressively by constitutional steps designed to bring together the disparate elements of a deeply divided dependency.

It is important to trace the development of Britain's commitment to the principle of freedom and to consider the bearing of the series of devolutionary stages upon the problem of unity. In fact, Britain's intentions with regard to India's eventual status remained obscure until the Second World War. Declarations of purpose were never until then unequivocal on the key question of equality. Moreover, at both of the major stages in the devolution of responsibility, the Montagu-Chelmsford reforms of 1919 and the India Act of 1935, the constitutional arrangements exacerbated the dualities in Indian political society, between the princely states and the British Indian provinces, and between the Hindu majority and the Muslim majority provinces. Until 1939 Britain's vague purpose of freedom awaited clarification, while the collapse of the putative all-India federation in that year left Britain bereft of a policy for giving effect to it.

It is also important to discover how and when the consequent constitutional impasse was bridged. British responses to the early wartime Congress demands for a clarification of purpose and for the immediate concession of appropriate rights and reforms were not constructive. The Cripps Mission to India in March 1942 marks the point in time at which Britain's declared purpose clearly became complete freedom, within or without the empire as India wished, as soon as the war was over. It also marks the revision of Britain's policy that freedom should be granted only to a united India, by accepting that freedom might be achieved either through unity or partition. Even so, decisive action awaited the return of a Labour Government in July 1945.

I

The earliest official statement on India's eventual status was the declaration of Edwin Montagu (Secretary of State, 1917–22) on 20 August 1917 that Britain's policy was 'the progressive realization of responsible government'.[1] It was incorporated in the Preamble to the India Act of 1919, with the condition that Parliament was to decide the time and nature of each successive advance. For some five years after Montagu's declaration the full range of policies, external as well as internal, was referred to the purpose that it avowed. The Indianization of the civil and military services, the tolerable level of political dissent and the determination of appropriate tariffs; Indian representation at the Versailles Peace Conference, at Dominions' conferences, in London and at the League of Nations; all reflected the glow of eventual freedom. It was commonly assumed that the 1917 declaration promised dominionhood. In 1929 the Reforms Branch of the Government of India submitted that Britain's own actions supported the assumption.[2]

However, in 1924 the assumption was repudiated. In a statement to the Indian Legislative Assembly that had been vetted by the Secretary of State, the Home Member of the Government of India (Sir Malcolm Hailey) argued that 'full self-governing Dominion status' might be a step beyond responsible self-government.[3] The obstacles to the step were Britain's responsibilities for defence, the minorities, and the princely states. Later, Hailey insisted that his main concern had been to deny the possibility of the step being taken at the time of the decennial review for which the 1919 Act had provided.[4] Still, it came at a time when there was evidence of tergiversation in London. The Viceroy, Lord Reading (1921–6), who had himself equated Montagu's purpose and Dominion status, had been rebuffed for his liberal intentions towards further constitutional change and the Indianization of the services.

Three years later, the all-white complexion of the decennial review body, the Statutory Commission (1927–30), revealed only too clearly Britain's persistent assumption of superiority. In recollection, Hailey's statement seemed sinister, and in 1928–9 Indian Liberals, Congressmen and Muslims pressed Lord Irwin (Viceroy, 1926–31) hard for a clarification of Britain's purpose.

In July 1929 Irwin came to London with the intention of securing the British parties' imprimatur for the equation of responsible self-government with Dominion status. His announcement of 31 October did affirm the equation, but it was not the definitive statement upon equality that he intended. The difficulty was not so much its lack of a time limit to British control as the extraordinary context in which it was made. For though it was upheld by the minority Labour Government it was contested vigorously by the Liberal and Conservative leaders, save only Baldwin. The evidence requires a brief rehearsal.[5]

The Prime Minister, Ramsay MacDonald, supported Irwin's initiative but he referred it to Baldwin and Lloyd George, partly because he lacked a parliamentary majority but mainly because India was not then a party issue. The 1919 Act had been framed by a coalition and the Statutory Commission was deliberating as an all-parties parliamentary inquiry. When Baldwin received MacDonald's notice of Irwin's initiative he was at Bourges, *en route* to Aix-les-Bains. Without reference to his colleagues he approved the plan (Irwin was not only a friend but had gone to India at his own nomination) on the understanding that the Statutory Commission agreed. The Commission had not seen the draft statement, but as its chairman, Sir John Simon, knew of it the Government assumed its acquiescence. Similarly, when the Government proceeded with the initiative Simon assumed Baldwin's approval. During the week preceding the announcement Baldwin was made aware that the Conservative experts on India abominated the initiative, and that their dislike was shared by the Liberals' Indian expert, Lord Reading, and his leader,

Lloyd George, as well as by all but the Labour members of the Statutory Commission, Baldwin demanded the postponement of the declaration pending all-party consultation, but as copies of it had already been released to Indian leaders the Government remained obdurate. On 31 October Irwin's announcement would have commanded the support of only the Labour Party if it had been put to the vote in Parliament.

The opposition leaders' objection was based upon an apprehension that Dominion status was an advance upon responsible self-government. On 25 October, after luncheon with two recent Secretaries of State (Lords Birkenhead and Peel), Lord Winterton, himself a former Under-Secretary, noted:

Now 'Dominion Status' has a very special meaning (especially since the Imperial Conference of 1926), and use of the term would be in advance of any definitions hitherto attempted, such as 'self-government within the Empire', because of that meaning.[6]

Before 1926 'Dominion status' had still implied a measure of subordination to the British Parliament, but then Balfour had explicitly defined the Dominions as 'autonomous communities within the British Empire, equal in status, in no way subordinate one to another in any aspect of their domestic or external affairs, though united by a common allegiance to the Crown, and freely associated as members of the British Commonwealth of Nations'.[7] Birkenhead therefore described the Irwin declaration as making 'an indication never made before'.[8] Reading, adhering to his Government's statement of 1924, objected to the declaration chiefly because Indians would view it as an advance in policy and demand its early implementation.

The parliamentary debates on the declaration in November did not bring down the Government. For reasons of their own, neither Baldwin nor Simon joined the opposition chorus. Simon was now fighting to preserve his Commission, which party warfare must destroy. Baldwin was personally in favour of Irwin's policy, and he became committed to defending it when his leadership was challenged by a coalition of Conservative and Liberal leaders that charged him with jettisoning the empire. In the event, the Irwin line was held against a combined assault from the foremost constitutional experts of the day.

However, the opposition forced Baldwin to require, and MacDonald to concede, a written assurance that the declaration marked no advance on the Preamble to the 1919 Act.[9] In effect, the rearguard action was intended to establish that notwithstanding Balfour's definition of 1926, in 1929 Dominion status meant no more than had responsible self-government within the empire ten years previously. This face-saving dodge could scarcely erase the purport of the Irwin announcement: that the Montagu declaration implied that India should enjoy Dominion status as defined in 1929. The opposition leaders' awareness of the weakness of their ground is revealed by their refusal to countenance the repetition of the Dominion status pledge in Parliament when Irwin requested it in June 1930 (although he was allowed to make the reaffirmation in India as a quid pro quo for MacDonald's agreement to opposition representation at the impending Round Table Conference).

During the decade that followed Irwin's announcement, the term 'Dominion status' was sedulously avoided in official documents and speeches on the constitution. The reports of the Statutory Commission and the Joint Parliamentary Committee on the India Bill were silent on the matter. The opposition delegations to the Round Table Conference refused to contemplate the use of the expression, even 'with safeguards', which Simon considered a contradiction in terms. At the close of the first Conference session MacDonald spoke merely of 'central responsibility with safeguards'. Dissension within the National Government prevented the preparation of a Preamble to the 1935 Act, for unless it simply repeated that of 1919 it could, in the words of the Secretary of State, Sir Samuel Hoare (1931–5), 'possibly prejudice the whole passage of the Bill'.[10] At the Bill's second reading Hoare proposed to speak of the goal of 'self-government within the Empire'.[11] Only after the Viceroy, Lord Willingdon (1931–6)), objected did he state that India would 'ultimately... take her place among the fully self-governing members of the British Commonwealth of Nations',[12] but without defining what 'her place' was. In December 1939 Lord Linlithgow, chairman of the Joint Parliamentary Committee on the 1935 Bill and now Viceroy (1936–43), described the spirit of the legislation:

> ... we framed the constitution as it stands in the Act of 1935, because we thought that way the best way ... of maintaining British influence in India. It is no part of our policy, I take it, to expedite in India constitutional changes for their own sake, or gratuitously to hurry the handing over of the controls to Indian hands at any pace faster than that which we regard as best calculated, on a long view, to hold India to the Empire.[13]

Certainly until after the outbreak of the Second World War British cabinets shrank from defining in unequivocal terms their intention to extend to India Dominion status of the Balfour declaration or Statute of Westminster variety.

II

Whatever their intentions towards India's eventual status, British statesmen applied them to all India, to the united India of the Raj.[14] The Montagu declaration spoke of 'the progressive realization of responsible government in India as an integral part of the British Empire'. In 1929 the Reforms Branch of the Government of India observed that since 1917 British policies in the international field assumed an eventual single Dominion of provinces and princely states. However the difficulty of conveying a united India towards dominionhood was formidable. In 1917 the states were virtual autocracies whereas the provinces enjoyed representative government. Moreover the political development of the disparate elements in provincial societies was highly uneven, and, in particular, the relatively backward Muslim minority of British India apprehended that democratic rule by the Hindu majority would leave it permanently subject. The 1919 Preamble's provision for advance by 'progressive successive stages' was a logical approach to the problem of constitutional and social heterogeneity. Responsibility must be devolved gradually, for Britain was obliged to protect the princes and the minorities until they were prepared to entrust their interests to a self-governing Dominion. From 1917 the future unity of India turned on the question whether the princes and the Muslims could be accommodated to a polity acceptable to the increasingly dominant party of British India, the essentially Hindu and ostensibly democratic Congress. The first stage of devolution set up severe strains.

Under the Montagu-Chelmsford constitution the separateness of the princely states was emphasized by their exclusion. Nothing was done to encourage the princes to bring their states into constitutional harmony with the provinces. Their response to the reforms was to seek freedom from the operation of paramountcy, or British intervention in their affairs, and assurance that the paramount power would never transfer its sovereignty to a responsible Indianized central authority. By the late 1920s 'two Indias' had emerged, and, in the judgment of the Government of India, the Statutory Commission and the Indian States Committee (1928–9), there was little prospect of bringing them together in the near future.

In relation to British India the Montford reforms left the Central

Government intact, with the Governor-General presiding over a predominantly official executive, the Indian members of which were no more than 'responsive' to the overwhelmingly Indian and elected legislature. At the centre the principle of unitary government was retained, and though there were separate electorates to protect certain minority interests and communities the generality of legislative members were returned through direct territorial, not indirect provincial, electorates. However, the provinces divided along communal lines. Aided by separate electorates even in their majority provinces, Muslim parties were able to enjoy ministerial power, most notably in the Punjab and Bengal. In so doing they soon realized the advantage to them of a federal form of constitutional development. By the late 1920s Muslim leaders had subscribed to a strong-province-but-weak-federation strategy. Their platform included: separate electorates; strong sovereign provinces; the separation of Sind and its elevation, together with the reformed North-West Frontier Province and Baluchistan, to full provincial status; the cession, on a voluntary basis, of appropriate provincial powers to a federal government in which Muslims enjoyed weighted representation and guarantees of their separate identity.

By 1929, when the decennial revision of the Montford constitution was in progress, the princes had emerged as opponents of a fully responsible self-governing Dominion, and the Muslims as enemies of a unitary self-governing British India. At the same time these powerful antagonists of Congress-style democratic freedom (as expressed, say, in the Nehru Report's essentially unitary constitution in 1928) had become natural allies of their trustee, the British Raj. From 1920 Congress had rejected devolution by stages and demanded immediate *Swaraj*. Britain was prepared neither to recognize Congress as the representative of India at large, nor to accept the possibility of India providing for its own defence, nor to jettison its own financial and commercial interests. The stability, security, and solvency of India continued to demand a gradual demission of empire. As the Congress would not co-operate the Raj must look to the minorities and the princes to help with the work of constitutional devolution.

In the absence of the Congress, the constitution that was made between 1930 and 1935 favoured the princes and the Muslims. It seemed to take India a step closer to responsible self-government but it really contributed to disunity. While it did provide for central responsibility within a strong federation (except that defence and political relations were reserved, and finance, the services, commerce, the minorities, and the safety, tranquillity, and interest of British India were subject to safeguards), it allowed the princes to veto this step and the Muslims to entrench themselves against it.

In the first place, the India Act of 1935 replaced the unitary central legislature of British India with a federal all-India legislature. The princes and the Muslims were both to receive weighted representation, so that Congress could hope to secure only about a third of the seats. British statesmen believed tht the experience of the princes and their ministers would stabilize an assembly that might otherwise be dominated by popular demagogues. The accession of sufficient princes to fill half of the states' seats was therefore made a condition of the advance to central responsibility with reserves and safeguards. The princes had flirted with federation at the first Round Table Conference in order to further their own concerns: the enhancement of their sovereignty through the reduction of paramountcy, the redress of some of their grievances, and the reaffirmation by the Crown of its treaty obligations to protect them. As they came to realize that Britain would not bargain away paramountcy in return for their co-operation with the federal scheme, and that any all-India federation involved the diminution of their sovereignty and the revision of their treaty rights, their reluctance to accede became increasingly manifest. On the eve of the war their substantial rejection of the federal offer was apparent. It had been confirmed by a Congress campaign for the return of the states' federal representatives by popular election rather than princely nomination.

Secondly, the 1935 Act provided for the introduction of provincial autonomy prior to the creation of federation. In consequence, when provincial elections were held in 1937 Muslim parties were able to consolidate their control over the Punjab, Bengal and Sind. Moreover, Congress was able to secure control of the Muslim minority provinces and to deny the Muslim population any say in their government. A sense of exclusion and even persecution drove the Muslims into hostility against the Act for the scope that it afforded to Hindu raj. The experience of Hindu provincial government stimulated the growth of Muslim separatism. Congress attempts to overturn the balance of the federal constitution, first by bringing pressure to bear on the princes, and secondly by seeking to impose uniform policies upon the Congress provinces through the Working Committee, had the same effect. By the outbreak of war the resurgent Muslim League was calling for the reconsideration of the constitution *de novo*. The League's secretary, Liaqat Ali Khan, argued the need for a constitutional structure that would prevent Congress from governing India alone. He expounded three alternatives: Pakistan, or the partition of India; Dominion status for each province, with the option of acceding to or abstaining from a federation; a confederation of Muslim provinces and Hindu provinces.[15] The League now condemned responsible self-government as a constitutional ideal unsuited to the realities of Indian politics.

The devolution of power by stages, coupled with the uncooperative or unconciliatory policies of the Congress, enlarged the obstacles to the achievement of dominionhood by a united India. Between 1917 and 1939 the phased demission of empire produced a crisis of unity. As Britain had never contemplated dominionhood for any entity other than a united India the collapse of the paper federation in 1939 precipitated a crisis of freedom.

III

It was the Second World War that drove Whitehall to clarify its intentions with regard to Indian freedom, and to decide the bearing that the problem of unity should have upon their implementation.[16] The relationship between events and the making of policy must now be traced in some detail.

On 14 September 1939, a few days after Linlithgow committed India to the war, the Congress Working Committee demanded a declaration of Britain's 'war aims in regard to democracy and imperialism', and of how these aims would 'apply to India and so be given effect to in the present'.[17] Congress sought the right of Indians to frame their own constitution through a Constituent Assembly and to participate in the war effort through representation in the Viceroy's Executive Council. Linlithgow recommended and the Cabinet approved the reiteration of the purpose of Dominion status, an intimation that after the war Britain would consult Indians about modifying the 1935 Act, and the offer of Indian membership of an advisory war committee. The statement was issued on 18 October. Four days later the Congress Working Committee, rejecting it as a reiteration of 'the old Imperialist policy', called for the resignation of the Congress provincial ministries. On 26 October, Hoare, speaking for the Government in the House of Commons, argued that Britain's pledge of Dominion status 'did not mean some system of government that deprived India of the full status of equality within the British

Commonwealth'. It meant 'the Dominion status of 1926'. On 7 November the Secretary of State, Lord Zetland (1935-40), reaffirmed in the House of Lords that Britain meant India to have Dominion status of the Statute of Westminster variety. At the same time, Linlithgow secured Cabinet approval to offer the enlargement of his executive to accommodate representative Indians. Congress was unconvinced by these new promises of eventual equality and aggrieved by the denial of India's right to make its own constitution at the end of the war. By mid-November all of the provincial Congress ministries had resigned.

Though dominionhood had been interpreted as equality of status the Cabinet still distinguished it from independence. Early in 1940 the Cabinet required Linlithgow to substitute the phrase 'self-government within the Empire' for 'independence within the Empire' in a speech to the Orient Club, Bombay, that explained the meaning of Dominion status. Zetland conveyed to him the opinion of Sir Thomas Inskip, as the Attorney-General during the making of the 1935 Act, that Dominion status assumed membership of the empire and carried no right to repudiate the allegiance to the Crown.[18] Linlithgow's speech, which repeated Zetland's earlier reference to 'Dominion status of the Statute of Westminster variety', led Gandhi to request further discussions. Early in February Linlithgow offered him the following package: a reaffirmation of the object to grant Dominion status at the earliest possible date; the addition of representative politicians to the central executive; the inauguration of federation as soon as the necessary princely accessions were secured; 'at some time in the future, at all events after the war, consultation with Indians on the revision of the constitution'.[19] The offer fell too far short of self-determination to induce Congress to negotiate.

Linlithgow's three offers during the first six months of the war did not amount to a new approach to the constitutional problem. Neither he, nor the Chamberlain Cabinet that approved them, would go beyond the policy of Dominion status within the empire, all-India federation, and consultation (but without responsibility) through a body set up to revise the 1935 Act and in the existing central government. Democratic concessions were inhibited by the continued defence of the princes and the minorities. Trusteeship remained. Linlithgow insisted that even the admission of the Indian parties to his executive must be conditional upon their prior agreement to a reconstitution of the provincial governments.

Almost from the beginning of the war a non-official initiative began to develop in London. On 3 October 1939 Clement Attlee criticized the Viceroy's lack of tact in not seeking to bring India into the war 'on a level with us'.[20] He called for 'more imaginative insight in dealing with the Indian people'. A deputation of Labour and Liberal Members of Parliament waited on Zetland to secure a debate that would elicit an official statement, going as far as possible to meet Congress claims and enlist it as a willing partner in the war. When the debate occurred on 26 October the most remarkable speech was delivered by Sir Stafford Cripps.

Cripps had first encountered the Indian problem in 1932, when he was briefed by a firm of London solicitors to advise the Nizam of Hyderabad on the implications of the federal scheme for his sovereignty. In 1938 he met Nehru in London. The two socialists had much in common. Cripps sympathized with Congress aspirations to democratic self-government. He corresponded sporadically with Nehru, was in touch with Krishna Menon, and wrote articles on Indian freedom for the *Tribune*. At the outbreak of war he was an independent Member of Parliament and had given up his bar practice to devote himself to public affairs. On 28 September he visited the Foreign Secretary, Lord Halifax (formerly Lord Irwin), about a proposed tour of Russia and the East. He argued that Nehru was not unreasonable and Halifax, somewhat impressed, arranged for him to visit Zetland the next day. Claiming 'a very close knowledge of Nehru' (derived from conversation with Menon), he told Zetland that with regard to immediate reform Nehru would settle for a reconstitution of the Central Assembly (which was still operating under the 1919 Act) and the association of selected members of it with the Viceroy's executive.[21] On 11 October he advised Nehru that Congress should 'stand firm as a rock upon its demands', accepting nothing short of 'action which proves conclusively the faith behind words'.[22] On 23 October, the day after Congress rejected Linlithgow's offer of a consultative war committee, he saw Halifax again. Whereas Halifax argued that Congress was not the only Indian party and that Britain could not go beyond its first offer, Cripps held that Congress spoke for the majority of British India and that to concede consultation on war matters alone was insulting.

In his Commons speech of 26 October Cripps claimed that the 'new circumstances which have inevitably arisen with the coming of the struggle in Europe' made India 'a test question in the eyes of the world'. The war object of freedom must be applied to India. He expounded a bold plan to win India's co-operation 'in our effort to establish democracy and freedom in the world'. Britain should pledge itself to grant 'full self-government after the war'; all-India federation should be abandoned, as it was anathema to both the Congress and the League; a new Central Legislative Assembly should be elected on the basis of the existing provincial registers; the Viceroy should then ask the majority party in the Assembly to form a government and appoint it as his executive. Cripps's proposed reconstitution of the Viceroy's Executive is of particular interest, for it bears upon his negotiations in 1942:

It is true that, technically and in accordance with the constitution, the Executive Council would not be a Cabinet, but there is no reason on earth why our Government should not give an undertaking that the Viceroy would deal with the Executive Council... as if it were a Cabinet on all major matters; that is to say he would accept their advice as the Crown here accepts the advice of the Cabinet when duly tendered to it.

During November Cripps's proposed private tour of India won moral support from several members of Parliament who favoured sending out a non-parliamentary mission to explore the demands of the Indian parties. They included Halifax, R. A. Butler (a former Under-Secretary of State for India), Lord Snell (Labour's leader in the Lords), Wedgwood Benn (Labour Secretary of State for India, 1929–31), R.W. Sorensen (Labour), Sir Stanley Reed (Unionist), Sir George Schuster (Liberal, Finance Member of the Viceroy's Executive, 1928–34), and even Zetland himself (to whom the elder statesman, Raghavendra Rao, commended the notion). At a dinner party to which Schuster invited a number of them, as well as Lord (formerly Sir Malcolm) Hailey, Cripps's explanation of his ideas 'made a considerable impression'. Encouraged by the apparent receptiveness to his proposed new initiative, Cripps wrote to Nehru on 16 November of 'a quite remarkable change of opinion even among Conservatives, which is most remarkable, and may have its influence on Government action'.[23] This was wishful thinking. Only ten days earlier the Cabinet had agreed unanimously that Britain should not make a statement such as Congress demanded. Nehru assessed Cripps correctly at this stage as a man whose 'judgment is not always to be relied upon'.[24] Cripps probably mistook interest for agreement. This was certainly the case a little later when, at the behest of Schuster and Butler (the latter urging 'the unity of India is at stake'[25]), Sir Findlater Stewart, Permanent Under-Secretary for India, saw him twice for discussions.[26]

By about 22–4 November Cripps had decided upon the heads of a scheme that he would take to India.[27] Britain should declare its willingness to grant 'Dominion status', by which it meant 'complete self-government and absolute liberty to terminate partnership in the British Commonwealth of Nations'. This involved deciding 'to implement forthwith its promises of Dominion status in the form of complete self-government for India', and carried the right of Indians to frame their own constitution through a Constituent Assembly. As an Act of Parliament was necessary to set up the Assembly some delay was unavoidable, but the Government would bind itself to introduce a bill 'immediately the war is over, or before that time if opportunity occurs'. Cripps envisaged an Assembly of some 2000 members, chosen on the basis of the existing provincial electorates and with the proportional representation of the states' peoples. But he was prepared to accept any alternative Assembly agreeable to the Indian parties. Britain would endorse decisions taken by the Assembly on a three-fifths vote, provided only that the Assembly agreed to enter into a fixed term treaty (he suggested fifteen years), whereby Britain could discharge its obligations to the princes, the minorities, and the services, and for defence, finance, and commerce. Consistently with its avowed purpose, Britain would immediately 'do its utmost in association with the representatives of the Indian people to arrange such expedients as are possible under the existing constitution to give the Indian people a larger measure of self-government during the war'.

During December Cripps met Gandhi, Nehru, A. K. Azad, and many other Congressmen both at Allahabad and Wardha, Liaqat Ali Khan at Delhi, Jinnah at Bombay, and the Viceroy at Calcutta. The Congress leaders were sceptical of Britain promising complete independence by any particular date, while the Muslims were opposed to the democratic machinery of a Constituent Assembly. The Viceroy listened without confiding his views, but his letters to Zetland reveal his hostility. He thought that in the existing conditions of communal animosity it would be hopeless to get the Muslims into any Hindu-dominated assembly. He abominated Cripps's acceptance of the central Congress demands and advised persevering with his own more limited courses. After meeting Linlithgow Cripps concluded that there was no hope of the Hindus and the Muslims being brought together while he was Viceroy. As far as Cripps personally was concerned this first private initiative lapsed when he left India at the end of the year.

However, first Zetland and later his successor, L. S. Amery (May 1940–July 1945), pressed the Viceroy and the Cabinet to accept some of the major aspects of the scheme, until in almost unrecognizably adulterated form it appeared as the August offer of 1940. These aspects included allowing a Constituent Assembly to make a Dominion constitution as soon as the war was over, the negotiation of a fixed term treaty for the discharge of Britain's remaining obligations, and the admission of representative Indians to the Viceroy's executive. Neither Zetland nor Amery advocated two other aspects of the scheme: the definition of Dominion status in terms of the right to secede, and the conversion of the Viceroy's executive into a quasi-responsible Cabinet.

The attraction of the immediate post-war date for Dominion status was that it established Britain's bona fides with regard to freedom. The advantage of the Constituent Assembly plan was that it placed upon Indians themselves the responsibility of removing the main obstacle to post-war freedom: disunity. If the Indian parties could agree upon the form of a constituent body to settle safeguards for the Muslims and terms of accession for the princes then instant dominionhood was theirs. Congress would have to realize that the way to freedom lay through their accommodation of the Muslims and the princes. Britain would neither impose a constitution agreeable to the majority but anathema to the minorities and the princes, nor interfere to secure its own interests under the constitution. A treaty for a relatively short transitional period, and negotiated by a co-equal Indian Dominion, was the only condition.

Zetland urged the merits of the scheme upon the Prime Minister in December and put it before the Cabinet in January 1940. However, Linlithgow scotched advance along such 'radical' lines by insisting upon his own conservative approaches. He was highly sceptical of the prospect of a post-war communal agreement, and believed that Britain must stay on 'for many years'. Further concessions to Congress would only encourage their recalcitrance over the communal problem, at the same time alienating important Muslim collaborators. Britain could not bind itself to accept the decisions of a Constituent Assembly as long as it desired a connection with India. After Linlithgow's February talks with Gandhi failed, Zetland again put the scheme to the Cabinet. Like independent observers of the Indian scene at the time he was appalled at the hardening of the divisions between Congress and League, and Congress and Government.[28] India was sliding toward disunity and civil disobedience. While the Government could suppress satyagraha, its methods would expose our motives in the war to the most effective criticism'.

Before he could budge the Cabinet, both Congress (by claiming complete independence at Ramgarh on 20 March) and the League (by claiming Pakistan at Lahore on 24 March) adopted unapproachable postures.

Almost as soon as the Churchill Government was formed Amery peppered Linlithgow to take up the scheme. Then, on 17 June, he urged him 'most strongly' to support its incorporation in an invitation to the party leaders to reconstitute the provincial Governments and join the central executive.[29] Though Linlithgow was still unconvinced of the case for change, the gravity of the war situation after the fall of France induced him to arrange meetings with Gandhi and Jinnah. At this time, a Congress Working Committee resolution at Wardha recognized that, with the fall of France, 'the problem of the achievement of national freedom has now to be considered along with the one of its maintenance and the defence of the country'.[30] Gandhi was effectively set aside as leader. On 1 July Linlithgow proposed the 'somewhat revolutionary scheme' that he had resisted for months.[31] On 7 July the Congress Working Committee added a plank to its complete independence platform that might facilitate its cooperation with the war effort: '... a provisional National Government should be constituted at the Centre, which, though formed as a transitory measure, should be such as to command the confidence of all the elected elements in the Central Legislature, and secure the closest cooperation of the responsible Governments in the Provinces'.[32]

On 12 July Amery placed before Cabinet a draft declaration, based on Linlithgow's cabled proposals. Briefly, it promised: membership of the Commonwealth as an equal partner within a year of the war ending; the right of Indians to frame their own constitution provided that they agreed upon machinery for doing so; a treaty for handling Britain's obligations during a transitional period; the addition of representative Indians to the Viceroy's executive and the creation of an advisory war council. Only Attlee gave Amery strong support. The main critics were Churchill, Lord Lloyd and Simon. No objection was taken to the short-term changes. However, Churchill abhorred such a 'far reaching departure' in policy for the future, while the Cabinet generally wished to emphasize Britain's continuing obligations rather than India's rights. Amery was asked to redraft the declaration, while Churchill individually questioned the Viceroy direct about the wisdom of making any declaration at all. Linlithgow's response was to retrace his steps, claiming, somewhat unfairly, that he would not have gone so far had not Amery's entreaties led him to assume Cabinet support for a declaration going beyond past statements. He modified his recommendation, now playing down the freshness of the proposed declaration's policy, suppressing the suggested treaty, emphasizing Britain's obligations, and leaving Britain's hands free in the future.

Amery feared the collapse of the initiative. He called upon Attlee and Halifax to help with the Cabinet, and struggled to defend himself against Churchill's unjust accusation that he had gone behind the Cabinet's back, misleading the Viceroy in order to inspire a novel policy departure. It had always been customary for the Secretary of State to develop his personal views in correspondence with the Viceroy prior to placing them before Cabinet. Amery pleaded (in vain) for Churchill to realize that with Britain's acceptance of the principle of self-government, the principle of trusteeship became an anachronism. Britain must now say to India: 'We are prepared to implement immediately after the war any agreement which you may by then have reached among yourselves.'[33]

The declaration survived, but in much weakened form. Linlithgow's modifications were incorporated, while Churchill himself revised the text, excising the one year's time limit and the pledge to accept in advance the decisions of a constituent assembly. Britain merely undertook to assist the creation of a body, 'with the least possible delay' after the war, to devise a constitutional framework, which, though 'primarily the responsibility of Indians themselves', must be 'subject to the due fulfilment of the obligations which Britain's long connection with India has imposed upon her'. Furthermore, the pre-requisite to advance was that Indians must agree on the form of the constituent body and the principles of the constitution that it devised. In other words, there was no provision for Indian dominionhood on any basis other than unity.

When Linlithgow announced the offer on 8 August all parties rejected it without hesitation. At once Churchill counselled Linlithgow against further change: 'Declaration represented the farthest Cabinet was prepared to go.'[34] It was agreed not to proceed with the short-term reforms.

The first year of war-time negotiations to bridge the constitutional impasse had ended in stalemate. A new individual satyagraha was soon launched and soon crushed. By September 1941 some 23,000 Indians had been convicted in connection with it. During the second year of war no further constitutional initiative was taken. In May

1941, in response to pressure from a gathering of Indian moderates, reinforced by Amery's reading of sentiment in the House of Commons, Linlithgow proposed and the Cabinet approved the addition of three non-official Indians to the Viceroy's executive and the creation of a war advisory committee. The enlarged executive's first action in November was to secure the release of the satyagraha prisoners whose sentences had not expired. This was a necessary but by no means sufficient condition of further negotiations. On both the short-term reforms and the gaol delivery Amery had to overcome Churchillian hostility. Moreover, in September Churchill had denied the applicability of the Atlantic Charter to India.

IV

Towards the end of 1941 opinion in London was becoming favourable to a new initiative. In September, Ernest Bevin (Minister of Labour and National Service in the War Cabinet) wrote to Amery:

I must confess that leaving the settlement of the Indian problem until after the war fills me with alarm.... We made certain definite promises in the last war and practically a quarter of a century has gone, and, though there has been an extension of self-government, we have not, in my view, 'delivered the goods' in a broad and generous way. It is quite understandable that neither Muslim nor Hindu places much confidence in our 'after war promises'. It seems to me that the time to take action to establish Dominion Status is now—to develop or improvise the form of Government to carry us through the war but to remove from all doubt the question of Indian freedom at the end of the war. I firmly believe that a bold step now would rally Indian opinion behind us.[35]

Bevin had previously expressed interest in India in conversation with Amery, and earlier in the year had pressed him to have an Indian Labour member added to the Viceroy's executive in order to win over the American Labour press. In October Schuster began to inform Amery that among all parties in the Commons there were members who favoured an initiative, perhaps by an all-parties' delegation visiting India to discuss the details of a new constitution with the leaders. At the same time American opposition to aid to Britain was making much of the persecution of Indian patriots and the insincerity of British 'intentions of applying to her the democratic principles for which she professed to be fighting'.[36]

On 19 December, thirteen days after Pearl Harbour, at a Cabinet meeting presided over by Attlee, Bevin questioned whether present policy was 'calculated to get the fullest war effort from India'.[37] As Churchill was then in Washington he was well placed to relate the Pacific war situation to India, but, as usual, he was hostile to 'raising constitutional issue'.[38] Attlee replied that it was bound to be raised in Parliament soon. Early in 1942 a group of Indian moderate elder statesmen appealed to Churchill for 'some bold stroke [of] far-sighted statesmanship'. Labour and American pressures upon him soon became irresistible. In January Attlee argued for 'someone' to be sent out to bring the Indian leaders together.[39] He was echoed by a Labour peer, Lord Faringdon, early in February. At this time, Cripps, returning from a successful ambassadorship in Moscow and about to become Lord Privy Seal and leader of the Commons, told the press that he might visit India 'later on'.[40] Meanwhile he became a member of an India Committee of the War Cabinet charged with drafting a new constitutional statement. Churchill set it up on 26 February, the same day that Mr W. A. Harriman, the President's Special Representative on Lend-Lease to the British Empire, raised the Indian question with him.[41]

The 'draft declaration' that eventually issued from the India Committee, and Cripps's exposition of it in India from 22 March to 12 April, mark an historic departure in British policy on the problem of freedom with unity.

The draft declaration defined Britain's object as 'the creation of a new Indian Union which shall constitute a Dominion, associated with the United Kingdom and other Dominions by a common allegiance to the Crown, but equal to them in every respect, in no way subordinate in any aspect of its domestic or external affairs'. It laid down in precise and clear terms the steps by which self-government was to be achieved. Immediately after the war an assembly of British Indians would be elected by the provincial assemblies on the basis of proportional representation, and charged with making a new constitution. The states would be asked to send delegates on the same proportionate basis as British India. Alternatively, Britain would accept any other constituent body that Indians themselves agreed upon. Britain undertook to accept and implement the new constitution forthwith, subject to two conditions: first, the conclusion of a treaty covering all matters arising from a complete transfer of power (including the protection of minorities) but imposing no 'restriction on the power of the Indian Union to decide in the future its relationship to the other Member States of the British Commonwealth'; secondly, the right of any province to stand out of the Union and become a separate Dominion. In the immediate future, that is during the war and the post-war period of constitution making, Britain would retain control of the defence of India but the organization of India's resources would be the responsibility of 'the Government of India with the cooperation of the peoples of India'. The declaration ended with an invitation to the leaders of the principal sections of Indian opinion to participate 'in the counsels of their country', and so help with 'a task which is vital and essential for the future freedom of India'.

The declaration contained the essential aspects of Cripps's scheme of November 1939, but with one vital difference for which Amery was responsible.

First, complete independence was conceded. While the language of the Balfour declaration was used, once the treaty between the Dominion of India and Britain was signed India was free to stay in or leave the Commonwealth. Cripps expounded the point at press conferences. When a questioner put it to him that 'what is required is one word, "freedom" ', Cripps replied: 'There is no conceivable doubt that [the declaration] allows complete and absolute self-determination and self-government for India.'[42] Sir Reginald Coupland, the eminent constitutional historian who joined the Cripps Mission, dates the 'Declaration of Indian Independence' to the publication of Cripps's offer on 29 March 1942.[43]

Secondly, Indians secured the right to frame their own constitution immediately after the war, subject to the treaty provision. The treaty method of handling transitional arrangements underlined India's equality. Further, with Cabinet approval Cripps stated that Britain would not attempt to protect its commercial interests in the treaty.

Thirdly, representative Indians were invited to participate in wartime government, which meant the provinces and the Viceroy's executive.

The vital difference between the 1939 and 1942 schemes was the departure from constitution-making by a three-fifths majority vote of delegates drawn from all of the provinces. In 1939 Cripps was prepared to impose a democratically devised constitution upon the Muslims. In 1942 Muslim majority provinces might opt out of the new Union once the constitution was formed. Indeed, as the declaration provided for an alternative assembly on any agreed basis, it was possible for the redistribution of provincial boundaries, or partition, to precede the transfer of power. Probably Cripps accepted this new departure, for which Amery was responsible, because of his first-hand acquaintance with the views of Jinnah and Liaqat Ali, together with their success since 1939 in making the Muslim League the mouthpiece of Muslim nationalism.

The contrast between the declaration and the August offer is strong. Independence, not only Dominion status, was now conceded, while the time and method of its achievement were defined. Indians would no longer be merely 'primarily' responsible for making the constitution, subject to Britain fulfilling its obligations. They would be solely responsible, and Britain's obligations would be handled in a separate treaty. However, the really decisive policy advance was Amery's answer to the problem of freedom with unity. For the first time Britain conceded India's right to freedom without imposing the condition of unity. No longer was the accession of the states or the agreement of all of the provinces made a prerequisite to dominionhood. The declaration cut the ground from beneath the feet of critics who accused Britain of pursuing *divide et impera*.[44] The answer to the problem of freedom with unity was to admit that it might be insoluble, and to accept the possible consequence: plural dominionhood.

Three caveats may be entered against the argument that the Cripps offer marks the culminating stage in the evolution of London policies for freedom and unity.

First, it may be argued that the offer was contingent upon its acceptance as a whole, and that its rejection by the Indian parties in April 1942 rendered it null and void. But there could be no back step in imperial policy. Once enunciated, the doctrine of independence for one or more Indian nations could not be retracted. In July 1942 Churchill told the King that all British parties were reconciled to giving up India after the war. That month the Cabinet considered the Viceroy's suggestion for the need to affirm that a policy no less liberal than the draft declaration would apply to India after the war. Amery drafted a suitable parliamentary question and the following reply:

His Majesty's Government stand firmly by the broad intention of their offer, which is that on the conclusion of hostilities India shall have it within her power to attain complete self-government through such method of arriving at a constitutional solution and under such form of government as may be agreed among themselves by the principal elements in India's national life.[45]

Churchill was defeated when he sought to retract the draft declaration and return to the language of the Balfour declaration, expunging the former's reference to secession. On 30 July Amery reaffirmed in Parliament that 'the broad intentions of the Government [i.e. 'complete self-government'] remained the same, irrespective of the immediate conduct of the Congress Party'. Pledged now to post-war independence, Britain's problem would be to secure agreement among successor authorities upon the form that it should take.

Secondly, it has been argued that whatever the declaration said about the future, its limited application to the present betrayed a persistent unwillingness to transfer responsibility to Indians. It has been suggested that the Cabinet intended the offer of participation in war-time government to be rejected by Congress, that there was no will to enlist Congress as an ally, and that the Mission was a clever propaganda exercise: 'a "plant" merely devised so as to range world opinion against India'; 'just "bluff" to influence American opinion'.[46]

The truth is that London opinion was divided on the key question of reconstituting the Viceroy's executive, with Churchill and Cripps at opposite poles, and that Linlithgow's opposition to Cripps's negotiations was sufficient to secure Cripps's repudiation.[47] Cripps's position on the reconstruction of the Viceroy's executive had not changed in substance since October 1939: the constitution could not be changed in war-time but party representatives could be empanelled and treated as if they were Cabinet ministers. The Viceroy would normally accept their advice, as the Crown accepted that of His Majesty's Government, but he could not, of course, divest himself of his statutory responsibility to veto measures affecting 'the safety, tranquillity or interest of British India'.

Cripps left London with a brief, written by himself and approved by the Cabinet, which required him 'to negotiate some scheme' for the Indian leaders' participation 'in an advisory or consultative manner in the counsels of their country'.[48] He could offer Indians seats on the executive to any extent consistent with 'defence and good government', while the 'advisory or consultative manner' in which the Viceroy might employ them was not circumscribed. He was required to consult the Viceroy and the Commander-in-Chief. Cripps negotiated with the leaders chosen by the Congress, Azad and Nehru, in terms of a fully Indianized executive (save for the Viceroy and the Commander-in-Chief) that would normally operate as a Cabinet. They welcomed the proposal. It was broadly consistent with the July 1940 plea for a 'provisional National Government', while in December 1941–January 1942 the Congress Working Committee and the All-India Congress Committee had agreed on a resolution that removed defence from the operation of Gandhi's policy of non-violence, thus paving the way for Congress co-operation in the war effort if suitable opportunity arose. Linlithgow, who believed any reorganization of the executive to be his own affair, was opposed to offering full Indianization as part of a political deal and hostile to the application of Cabinet conventions to his Government. Cripps's Mission was doomed from 6 April, when Linlithgow won the support of Amery and Churchill on the latter point. Cripps's freedom to negotiate on the executive was withdrawn. On 9 April, at his last meeting with Azad and Nehru, Cripps could only say that they must discuss the reconstruction of the executive with the Viceroy. Linlithgow's reputation among Congressmen now became the decisive point in the rejection of the Cripps offer. Nehru's view was that 'with a more accessible person with whom the Congress leaders could have talked around the table and discussed actually how the Executive worked, they might possibly have accepted'.[49]

The truth of London's tergiversation has been masked by Cripps's loyal denials that there was any change to his brief, or even that he had offered a quasi-Cabinet to Azad and Nehru. However, it was known at the time by Roosevelt's circle (for the President's representative Louis Johnson had become involved in the defence aspect of the negotiations), by a member of the Mission's staff (F. F. Turnbull, Amery's secretary) and by Amery's acting secretary (Miles Clauson).[50]

The change to Cripps's brief was effected in London despite the presence of such strong supporters as Attlee and Bevin in the War Cabinet. The progress of negotiations was reviewed by the India Committee, normally chaired by Attlee. Its members were the wavering and uncertain Amery, the essentially illiberal Simon, Sir James Grigg, a recent Finance Member of the Viceroy's executive who had found Linlithgow too conciliatory towards Congress, and Sir John Anderson, a former Governor of Bengal and an opponent of centralization in India. What enabled Churchill to destroy the Mission after 6 April, and to deliver the *coup de grace* from the chair of the India Committee four days later, was Linlithgow's antagonism, together with Cripps's injudicious failure to keep the Viceroy informed of the detail of negotiations on the defence question in which he, Louis Johnson and Nehru were involved. Attlee found it difficult to stand his ground once the Viceroy's hostility to Cripps became apparent, and impossible to do so when it seemed that Cripps was negotiating behind the Viceroy's back.

On 10 April 1942 the Congress, aggrieved at Cripps's retraction of his earlier offer, raised its demand to government by a Cabinet with full power. Later in the year it again resorted to civil disobedience, indeed to the less than civil Quit India movement. Cripps's plan for a provisional National Government ceased to be practical politics. The India Committee consistently rejected the proposals of Linlithgow's successor, Lord Wavell (October 1943–March 1947) to revive the plan.[51] Only at the end of the war was the Viceroy permitted to arrange a conference at Simla in an ill-fated attempt to set up an interim Indian government.

The third objection to accepting Cripps's offer as the final breakthrough to Indian freedom is the argument that the offer implied a new imperialist policy, empire by treaty.[52] It is suggested that Cripps's provision for the opting out of provinces, and for the abstention under British protection of states unwilling to accede to the Union, would make a parody of freedom, leaving imperial forces to hold the ring. With regard to the princes, Cripps did undertake that Britain would honour its treaties to protect them, even if that meant maintaining forces in Ceylon. However, as the Resident to Hyderabad, the largest of the states, realized as early as 1930, it would scarcely be practicable for Britain to defend a prince against aggression by a self-governing India, which in many cases would encircle his state. Cripps acknowledged that the states' defence would require the concurrence of the Indian Union, and he never envisaged that the treaty whereby Britain discharged its obligations should be more than transitional. In 1939 he had made it clear that the treaty was, in effect, a means of serving the princes with fifteen years' notice. Certainly in 1942 Cripps denied Britain's intention to confer dominionhood upon a state or group of states. As for the provinces, the opting out provision was intended to make Congress face the necessity for conciliation, while Cripps (like Wavell after him) hoped that the creation of a National Government would countervail the drift to disunity. But even if some of the Cabinet looked forward to a plurality of Indian Dominions, could they realistically have expected Britain to help bear the burden of their defence? Such an arrangement must depend upon the Dominions' agreement to meet heavy costs, for already by 1942 India's sterling balances had grown alarmingly. The empire was indeed, as Gandhi perceived, a failing bank. Yet Amery doodled with plans for a continuing imperial presence in a federal Indian enclave; and even after the war Churchill wistfully told Wavell to 'keep a bit of India....'[53]

V

The relationships between events in India and British policies are, of course, complex. As long as Britain remained in India, tactics and strategies for winning and holding collaborators were necessary. Together with the preservation of interests and the influence of moral and political principles they explain the timing and the form of the stages in the devolution of empire.

The 1917 and 1929 declarations were undoubtedly attempts to 'rally the moderates' behind the Raj. On the former occasion Britain needed war-time allies at a stage when the 'extremist' home rulers had gained control of the Congress. On the latter occasion Irwin and the Labour Government wanted to break the solid unity of the Hindu nationalists who were boycotting the Statutory Commission. At both stages Britain needed to win enough support to make the coming reforms work. But neither declaration was merely tactical. In 1917 the principle of responsibility exceeded the Congress demand for self-government. The war-time and early post-war shibboleth of self-determination was certainly influential in the general reorientation of policy from 1917 to 1922. Again, Irwin, Baldwin and the Labour Cabinet believed sincerely in the principle of India's equality within the Commonwealth, behind which lay their acceptance of the moral right of a new brown Dominion to the status of the old white ones. It was a tenet of the Montford reforms that India should enjoy fiscal autonomy, while Irwin and the Labour Secretary of State, Wedgwood Benn, resisted attempts to manipulate tariffs to Britain's advantage during the slump. The 1939, 1940 and 1942 declarations were clearly intended to win Indian support for the war, and were prompted or influenced by Labour pressures and world, especially American, opinion.

What is remarkable is that Britain was not responsive to the Congress satyagrahas in protest against the inadequacies of declarations or reforms. The 1920–2 non-cooperation movement evoked no London offer to advance beyond the 1919 Act. Though in December 1921 the Viceroy contemplated moving at once from provincial dyarchy to full responsibility a Committee of Cabinet refused him power to negotiate. The 1930–1 Civil Disobedience movement gave rise to the Gandhi-Irwin Pact, but that won Gandhi no modification to the all-India federation scheme that had emerged at the first Round Table Conference. The revival of the movement in 1932–4 was suppressed ruthlessly, leaving Willingdon feeling like an imperial Mussolini and disposed to make concessions. Whitehall overruled him firmly when he pressed for a British Indian federation to be granted central responsibility if the princes became a ball-and-chain, and again when he proposed to appoint an Indian to the traditionally British Commerce membership of his executive. The muted satyagraha that followed the rejection of the August 1940 offer was crushed in 1932 style. When, a few months later, Linlithgow proposed a more limited expansion of his executive than the offer had allowed, some members of the Cabinet now demurred. The Quit India movement was a major reason for the India Committee's disallowance of Wavell's proposals for the reconstruction of his executive.

Once a declaration was made, or reforms were in progress, satyagraha simply led Britain to rely upon the non-Congress parties and the princes. As the Congress protest movements were largely an attempt to win a national mandate by direct action, it is scarcely surprising that Indians who could not subscribe to Congress policies sought British protection under the constitution. Separate electorates after 1909; Muslim ministries in the Punjab and Bengal under dyarchy; provincial autonomy, the separation of Sind, and weightage in all-India federation, under the 1935 Act; the recognition of Jinnah as a nationalist leader in 1939; all were the natural consequence of Congress tactics and Britain's need for collaborators. All worked towards separatism, until the possiblity of Pakistan was officially conceded in 1942, and three years later at Simla Jinnah was able to reject the countervailing machinery of a National Government. Similarly, Congress frightened the princes into the welcoming arms of the Raj, until the princes' exercise of their veto on British Indian progress wrecked the possibility of central responsibility in the 1930s.

This is not to argue that satyagraha was responsible for disunity. The periods of constitutional activity by Congress parties saw a diminution of Congress unity and national coherence. In the 1920s the proliferation of essentially Hindu parties (Liberals, no-changers, Swarajists, responsive co-operators, Mahasabhites) was a function of participation in the parliamentary game. In the 1930s proliferation followed the end of civil disobedience, as the Swarajists, Malaviya's Nationalists and the Congress Socialists emerged. The exercise of office by provincial Congress ministries weakened the central control of the Working Committee and helps to explain the apparently cavalier resignations of November 1939. As Gandhi knew, participation in government reduced an organization that claimed to speak for all India to one among many competing parties. The process of devolving power by stages in a politically and socially disparate country was inherently divisive.

Devolution by stages seemed appropriate when political and social development was so uneven that the transfer of power at a stroke would contravene the cardinal doctrine of trusteeship. Effete princes with loyal subjects, the historically important but often backward Muslim minority, the scheduled castes, these and others required special protection under the constitution, which the more precocious, more westernized and primarily high caste Hindu Congress was not trusted to provide. Devolution by stages would enable the elements of modern politics, in particular parties based upon principles and interests, to supplant the divisions of caste and creed.[54] The difficulty with such a policy was the time-scale that it assumed. Before India secured self-government it must pass through the stages of evolution that Britain had experienced since the Middle Ages. Lord Curzon, the draftsman of the term 'responsible government' in the Montagu declaration, noted: 'When the Cabinet used the expression "ultimate self-government" they probably contemplated an intervening period of 500 years.'[55] Birkenhead thought it 'frankly inconceivable that India will ever be fit for Dominion self-government'.[56] Simon anticipated that the emergence of Indian nationhood would involve a 'prolonged evolution'.[57] In an article on 'The Evolution of Political Life in India', Irwin followed Stubbs's account of 'the gradual unfolding of the primitive institutions of our forefathers who made the England which William conquered, into the parliamentary government which our country knew on the eve of the modern age', as if to suggest that India must pass through a similar succession of stages under British tutelage.[58] Churchill charged the National Government that introduced the 1935 Act with running 'counter to nature', with 'trying to put the clock forward without regard to the true march of solar events'.[59]

The main flaw in Britain's inter-war India policy is that it was cast in the evolutionary mould characteristic of late-Victorian thought, of the stable era in which the statesmen of the 1920s and 1930s were reading Stubbs and Maine at Oxford and Cambridge. Policy was essentially unconstructive. As Zetland realized in 1939 the follies of the princes were Britain's reward for thirty years of *laissez-faire*. They had not been pressed to introduce parliamentary government, which Britain might have made a condition of continued protection. Again, programmes for social and economic reform were insufficient to the task of modernization, the normal concomitant of democracy. It was not until December 1942 that the India Office had before it a comprehensive plan for the mobilization of India's resources (the work of Cripps and Bevin).

This is not to deny that the advantages of empire acted as a powerful brake on British initiative. As long as India was a major area of trade and investment, a large contributor to the costs of imperial defence, and a fair field for the employment of British civil and military officers, the policy of gradual devolution must seem a rationalization of self-interest. In the early 1930s, at a time of economic crisis, a National Government could still manipulate Indian tariffs and the exchange rate to Britain's advantage. Yet between the wars the relative importance of the India trade declined sharply. In the year preceding the First World War India took £83.5m worth of British goods, in the year before the Second, £35m worth. The corresponding years' Indian exports to Britain were £39m and £41.25m. By 1939 India had a favourable balance of trade with Britain. At the time of the Joint Parliamentary Committee on Indian reform (1933–4), Lancashire interests, their cotton trade with India largely lost, refused to join with Churchill in his attack upon central responsibility. Certainly, the Indian Army remained vital to imperial defence between the wars, but increasingly at Britain's own expense. The process of Indianization made the civil services less of a haven for Britain's youth, and indeed, the decimation wrought by the First World War opened up so many opportunities at home that an Indian career was often no longer the necessity that it had once been. It has been suggested that the transfer of power in India was largely the result of a manpower shortage.[60]

On the eve of the Second World War, while some tendencies in imperial relations pointed towards a transfer of power, Britain's policy of constitutional gradualism, together with the deepening of divisions in India, made early self-government seem unlikely. The most likely policy after the princes' rejection of the federal offer in September 1939 was that favoured by Linlithgow and Hoare: the application of further pressure upon the princes to secure their accession.[61] But that would scarcely have solved the problem of freedom with unity. The Congress Working Committee, already concerned at the provincialization of politics under the Act, would scarcely co-operate in a central government that it could not hope to control. Neither the princes nor the Muslims were likely to participate in a central government that it *could* hope to control.

The war created the necessity for a change in British policy. By 1942 the underpinning of the empire was gone. Special arrangements for trade no longer seemed necessary. India's sterling debt was fast being obliterated by its sterling balances (credits earned by contributions to the war effort). Lend-Lease had given America a voice in imperial affairs. Labour leaders demanded an equal place for India in the new order for which the free world was fighting. It was in these circumstances that, twenty-five years after Montagu's declaration and in the third year of a second war, Britain cut the Gordian knot of the problem of freedom with unity. The departure was so inconsistent with inter-war policy that it would scarcely have been made so early in peace time.

2
The Making of India's Paper Federation, 1927–35

> As a matter of historical record, when one looks back over the last few years it is surprising how late in the story it was that partition emerged as a practical and pressing political proposition, and the fact that it was never seriously put forward in the Round Table Conference debates, ... or indeed in any of the discussions between 1930 and 1940, suggests that Federation, if only it could have been quickly implemented, might have saved the situation.
>
> Lord Halifax, *Fulness of Days*, 1957

The 'ifs' of history tantalize retired statesmen no less than scholars. Conservative British statesmen who helped to make the Government of India Act of 1935 have aired an 'if' of central importance to students of Indian history: if the Act's federal provisions had become effective before the war then partition could have been avioded. Attempting to explain the failure to set up a federation they have found fault with diehard colleagues and the executors of policy in India.

In their memoirs Lord Templewood and Lord Halifax have emphasized that Churchill's sustained attacks delayed by crucial years the preparation and passing of the India Bill. They also argued that more might have been done by the viceroys to secure the number of princely accessions required to bring the federation into being. In a private correspondence of 1953, when Templewood was preparing *Nine Troubled Years* (1954), they exchanged views frankly, freed from the restraints of loyalty to former colleagues. Templewood wrote:

> My general conclusion is that we were within reach of starting the All-India Federation, and that if it had not been first, for Winston, and secondly, for the slow-moving machine, we should have had it in operation by the time that the war started.... My view in London was that most of the officials [in India], who were working quite loyally, did not believe in All-India Federation. If there was to be any federation they wished it to be a federation of British India.... The Princes were given very little help in making up their minds.... When Willingdon succeeded you and I became Secretary of State, I

came to the conclusion that it was we in London who were pressing the reforms, and that the brake came not from Whitehall but from Delhi.[1]

Halifax agreed that Churchill's opposition 'was undoubtedly one of the blocks in the road of Federation' and expressed the 'broad thought . . . that the brake was generally in India':

I have often thought, though this was after my time and I may have been wrong about it. that a good part of the trouble and delay came from the fact that Freeman [Willingdon] liked the Princes and really disliked the British Indian leaders, and Hopie [Linlithgow] had not much use for the Princes and did not really get on human terms with anybody. The machine of course, moved slowly as all machines do, but I suspect the principal cause of obstruction lay in India rather than in Whitehall; i.e. Freeman and Hopie! If they had really been willing to push the Federation idea and had not been inhibited by one cause or another, either in approach to Princes or Congress, you would have been able to get the Cabinet and the Party to move more quickly.[2]

That Churchill delayed the Act of 1935 and aroused hostility among Indian nationalists is clear. He also encouraged princely truculence after 1935 by insisting that the princes should not be bullied into acceding to the federation. There were sufficient diehard respecters of treaty rights among the Tories to make Prime Minister Neville Chamberlain (1937–40) fearful for party unity. In consequence, Linlithgow was held tightly in leading-strings from home and cannot be adjudged primarily responsible for the failure to hustle the princes.[3] Again, it is difficult to see to how Willingdon could have acted more expeditiously. During his viceroyalty the tempo of constitutional change was determined in Whitehall. However, the major weakness of the Templewood-Halifax interpretation of the failure to set up a federation lies not in its assertion of viceregal dilatoriness but in its assumption that the Act embodied a workable solution to the Indian problem. The valid criticism of the viceroys concerns not their speed but their insight into the political situation in British India. It is also the fundamental charge against the Conservative policy-makers of 1930–5: they failed to take sufficient account of the fact that the paper federation met the minimum demands of neither the Congress nor the Muslims. The story of the making of the federation, told against the background of those demands, suggests that the idea of an all-India federation was a chimera.

I

The process of constitution-making began inauspiciously with the appointment of the 'all-white' Statutory Commission in November 1927. Irwin must be held chiefly responsible for this blunder, which alienated the Congress, the Indian Liberals and a section of the Muslim League. While Sir John Simon and his colleagues tackled their task in the face of hostile public opinion an Indian All-Parties Conference met under Motilal Nehru's chairmanship to prepare constitutional demands. The Nehru Report, published in 1928, and more moderate than a significant section of the Congress would have wished, called for Dominion status for India under an essentially unitary system of government. The provincial governments would remain but a strong responsible centre would be created and residuary powers would devolve upon it. Separate communal electorates would be abandoned.

A minority of the Muslim League, under Jinnah's leadership, boycotted the Simon Commission, attended for a time the All-Parties Conference and sought accommodation with the Congress on the heads of a constitution. However, the majority of prominent Muslims refused to join in the boycott and in December 1928 met under the Aga Khan's chairmanship as the All-Parties Muslim Conference, to formulate their answer to the Nehru Report. In letters to *The Times* the Aga Khan had already fulminated against the Nehru Report's unitary system. He favoured the recasting of provincial boundaries on racial, cultural and linguistic lines and an eventual federation of free states. These sovereign units, among which there would be Muslim and Hindu states, formerly in British India, and princely states, would even possess their own armies.[4] The Muslim League had, as early as 1924, resolved that in any future constitutional reforms India should be reorganized on a federal basis, with the provinces enjoying full autonomy and the authority exercised at the centre being confined to the minimum. It had resolved that separate electorates and the Muslim majorities in the Punjab, Bengal and the North-West Frontier Province must be retained. Again, no Bill affecting inter-communal matters should be discussed or passed in any legislature if three-quarters of the Muslim representatives opposed it. The Conference of 1928 reaffirmed these demands and added others to them. Sind should be separated from Bombay, and the N.W.F.P. and Baluchistan should be given the status of governors' provinces. Muslims must have their share of the seats in central and provincial cabinets. In any central legislature one-third of the members should be Muslims. In essence, the Muslims demanded a belt of autonomous Muslim provinces extending across eastern and north western India, together with statutory safeguards of Muslim interests in other provinces and a balance of authorities that implied the negation of majority rule and collective ministerial responsibility. Jinnah's fourteen points were more conciliatory than the Conference demands only in as much as Jinnah was prepared to open separate electorates to negotiation.

In December 1928 the Congress resolved that if Dominion status were not conceded within a year then they would demand complete independence and resort to civil disobedience. The Simon Commission was proceeding deliberately and Britain intended that in due course its Report should be considered by a Joint Committee of Parliament and Indian assessors. In January 1929 Irwin was seriously worried by the unanimity of Hindu opposition. Sir Chimanlal Setalvad made him aware that the Hindu Liberals were disturbed at the growing influence of extremism in the Congress and that they were anxious for him to make a conciliatory gesture. Irwin came to feel that whilst he could offer nothing by way of immediate reform he might win some Hindu friends by clarifying Britain's ultimate objective and by promising a liberal procedure for the review of whatever proposals Simon made. By June, when he returned to England on leave, he had drafted proposals for a declaration that Britain's intention was eventually to confer Dominion status upon India and that after the completion of the Simon Report a Round Table Conference of Indian leaders and representative Britons should assemble in London to consider the reform of the constitution.

Irwin distinguished between 'purpose' and 'policy'. He held that the Simon Commission's concern was 'policy', or the proposal of reforms, and that to declare Britain's ultimate 'purpose' would not trench on its work. He recognized that a declaration of purpose might precipitate Indian demands for its early accomplishment. He argued, however, that Congress demands were already so strong that to ignore them was to invite separatist agitation.[5] He believed that many Indians sought an assurance of the right to full partnership in the Empire rather than the immediate enjoyment of that right. Moderate Indians would rest content with the assurance of eventual parity, just as a minor looked forward happily to enjoying full rights within a family, or a junior member of a firm was satisfied with the knowledge that he would in time become a full partner.[6] He put his case before Simon, Wedgwood Benn, the Labour Secretary of State (1929–31), and Ramsay MacDonald, the Prime Minister (1929–35). Simon was at first disposed to accept it but after discussing it with his colleagues and Lord Reading (Viceroy, 1921–6) he came to feel that such an avowal of purpose would prejudice the Commission's enquiry. The minority Labour Government recognized the advantage of obtaining Conservative and Liberal support for a declaration and Baldwin and Reading were sounded. Both agreed to endorse the declaration if the Commission concurred. Knowing of the Commission's opposition but impressed with Irwin's case MacDonald and Benn authorized Irwin to make his Dominion Status announcement on 31 October 1929.

The promise of a Round Table Conference that Irwin's declaration contained had implications for the scope of the Simon enquiry. The Commission's original terms of reference were confined to framing recommendations for the revision of the Act of 1919. They thereby excluded consideration of the Indian states. Immediately prior to his departure from India on leave Irwin met the Standing Committee of the Chamber of Princes at Poona. The princes had been shaken by two recent documents. First, the Nehru Report had called for the transfer to an Indian Dominion of the Government of India's role in relation to the states. Then the Indian States Committee Report, whilst it assured the princes that paramountcy would not be transferred without their consent, proclaimed the paramount power's virtually unlimited right to interfere in the administration of the states. By June 1929 the Chamber of Princes was pondering the consequences for the states of constitutional reforms in British India. It behoved their highnesses to look ahead. They declared themselves 'in sympathy with the legitimate aspirations of British India... and willing to open avenues of negotiation with a view to the closer association of the two Indias in the future'.[7] The appearance of this 'new element in the Indian situation' required, as *The Times* of 1 July 1929 observed, a revision of the procedure for constitutional review. Clearly, the Simon Commission must 'make recommendations as to the future relations between the States and British India' and the states should 'have their place in the subsequent discussions in London'. The editor of *The Times*, Geoffrey Dawson, was Irwin's Yorkshire neighbour and earlier in the year he had been a house guest at Viceregal Lodge in Delhi. Whether he was privy to the Viceroy's plans at this time is uncertain. But there is no doubt that Irwin 'ghosted' the letter of 16 October in which Simon proposed the extension of his terms of reference to embrace British India's relations with the states and the summoning in due course of a Round Table Conference. He also drafted MacDonald's acquiescent reply of 25 October.

Irwin's declaration of purpose and procedure was a qualified success in winning Hindu support. Whilst the Liberals agreed to co-operate the Congress refused to recognize Irwin's distinction between purpose and policy or to attend a Round Table Conference, unless the function of the conference was stated to be the formation of a Dominion status constitution. Despite Irwin's earnest statement of Britain's intentions, in December 1929 Congress chose to explore the wilderness of civil disobedience. For this Irwin blamed 'the clatter created in England by my Declaration, which... did so much to undermine the confidence of Indian leaders in our purpose, or at least in our capacity to give our purpose effective shape'.[8] For whilst Baldwin and Simon, though they disliked the disingenuous manner of Labour's authorization of the declaration, accepted the *fait accompli* with grace, such eminent Tory and Liberal authorities as Birkenhead (Secretary of State, 1924–8), Churchill, Reading and Sir Austen Chamberlain (Secretary of State, 1915–17), condemned it as foolish and dangerous.

The Simon Commission reported in June 1930. It recommended the early replacement of dyarchy by full responsible government in the provinces, though the governors should have large reserve and emergency powers. It also proposed far-reaching changes in the central government. The only constitution capable of combining 'elements of diverse internal constitution and of communities at very different stages of development and culture', the only constitution into which the states could be fitted, and therefore the only constitution that could provide for a central legislature 'capable of expansion into a body representative of All-India in the wider sense', was a federal constitution.[9] It is true that Montagu and Chelmsford had expressed a shadowy notion that the only form of government suitable to British India and the states was some sort of federation.[10] However, the 'Montford' central legislature, consisting of a Council of State and a Legislative Assembly, included majorities elected directly by territorial, communal or special interest constituencies. The system was essentially unitary. The Simon Commission denied the possibility of a unitary government of a democratic kind in India. A democracy of 250 million people was 'unprecedented'. 'If self-government is to be a reality, it must be applied to political units of a suitable size....'[11] The Commission would change the name of the Legislative Assembly to 'Federal Assembly' and have it elected by the provincial assemblies through a proportional representation system. The Council of State would be partly nominated and partly elected by the provincial legislatures. The central legislature was, in short, to be fundamentally reconstituted, on a federal basis.[12]

The Commission shrank from proposing any measure of responsibility in the central executive. Responsible government must be tried first in the provinces, and for the trial to be fair a stable central executive was essential. It was argued, however, that the reconstruction of the legislature on federal lines would make the executive more 'responsive' to the legislature. Furthermore, it was proposed that the Governor-General should himself appoint the cabinet, some of whom should be drawn from the legislature. This would leave open the possibility of an advance towards responsible government.

Whilst an all-India federation was the Commission's ultimate objective, immediate federation was thought impossible. The most that seemed feasible was that British India and states' representatives should meet to discuss 'matters of common concern', in preparation for an 'eventual Federal Union'.[13]

It has become common to say that the Simon Report fell stillborn from the press. Irwin condemned its failure to mention Dominion status as exposing a lack of imaginative insight into the Indian situation. However, Irwin had played the Dominion status card already, and Britain could scarcely accept that the purpose was capable of achievement at that time, as Congress had claimed. The constitutional historian, Sir William Holdsworth, commended this 'report of statesmen used to dealing with affairs' and its concentration on 'the actual operation of the Indian constitution in practice' rather than on 'constitutional theory'. Those who were obliged to consider its proposals should clear their minds of 'the tyranny of catchwords' such as 'Dominion Status'.[14] Irwin's declaration had indeed won the Liberals' co-operation. However, that it was the cause of some worry to Benn on the eve of the first Round Table Conference is evidenced by a Cabinet memorandum (dated 14 November) that he circulated on the alternative line to be taken if Dominion status were demanded by Indian delegates.

Irwin, in fact, was prepared to offer little more than Simon was by way of immediate reforms. The Government of India's despatch on the Commission's Report endorsed the ultimate object of all-India federation and agreed that it was a 'distant ideal'.[15] It questioned the wisdom of reconstructing the central legislature on federal lines by substituting indirect for direct election, chiefly because public opinion would be hostile to the change. It concurred in extending provincial autonomy, and denied the wisdom of central responsibility.

Irwin's only significant advance on Simon was to propose the extension of the principle of 'responsiveness'. The Government of India favoured the definition of the portfolios of continuing interest to Parliament and their retention by offcial ministers. The remaining departments should be handed over to elected Indian members of the legislature, who were to be selected by the Governor-General. Parliament's continuing interests would be defence, foreign relations, internal security, financial obligations and stability, the protection of minorities, the rights of the services, and the prevention of discrimination against British trade. Irwin denied that he was proposing dyarchy at the centre. He expressly opposed any formal departure from a unitary central executive. Transferred departments should be capable of resumption.

Assuredly, the Round Table Conference was not to be limited to the consideration of the Simon Report. It was to be a free discussion of India's constitutional future. Nevertheless, as the British delegates prepared themselves it was clear that the non-governmental teams, the Liberals under Reading and the Tories under Hoare, the latter of whom were to be the chief makers of the new constitution, were basing their position on the leading principles of the Simon Report: provincial autonomy, reconstruction of the central legislature on federal lines, no central responsibility, and the eventual creation of an all-India federation.

II

Delegates invited from the Indian subcontinent to London to confer freely with representatives of the major British parties about their country's future polity naturally prepared themselves well. Princes and ministers of princes, Hindu Liberals and Muslims of all camps (save only the Congress) gathered together for preliminary discussions, on the ship that brought them, the *Viceroy of India*, at the Aga Khan's Ritz suite, with the Maharaja of Bikaner at the Carlton. Speeches and schemes were rehearsed and attempts were made to concert a common plan.

The Muslims had long favoured a loose federation and provincial autonomy. As early as May 1928 a conference of princes at Bombay had resolved to seek a union council of the states and the Viceroy's executive. Within two days of Irwin's October 1929 declaration Bikaner stated that 'the ultimate solution of the Indian problem and the ultimate goal' was 'Federation, a word which had no terrors for the princes and governments of the States'[16] When he and the ministers of the greatest Indian states, Akbar Hydari of Hyderabad and Mirza Ismail of Mysore, arrived in London each had a different scheme, drafted in some detail, for an all-India federation. Long dormant potentates were now aware of the dangers to their sovereignty if the Viceroy, enjoying undefined paramountcy, were to become responsive to a progressive British Indian executive. Negotiated entry to an all-India federation promised internal autonomy and a voice in affairs of common interest.

There was one group of delegates to whom an all-India federation had never appealed—the Hindu Liberals. Tej Bahadur Sapru, their leader, had joined with Motilal to draft the Nehru recommendations for a responsible, unitary central government. Now, however, to win Muslim and princely support for a measure of immediate responsibility at the centre he was prepared to back the idea of all-India federation. At that stage he could not assess the cost of central responsibility in terms of the powers to be retained by Muslim provinces and princely states, of Muslim and princely representation at the centre and of safeguards for communal interests. His colleague, Srinivasa Sastri, with characteristic pessimism and prescience, wrote on 24 October 1930: '...if there is agreement, it will be by surrendering to the Princes and the Muhammadans.'[17] Among Hindus of British India Sapru was outstanding for his readiness to avow the federal objective and leave the definition of terms for a later stage of horse-trading. He was prepared to give more to the Muslims for the sake of central responsibility than were his colleagues, and by the end of the year he had resigned from the National Liberal Federation over the issue. It was chiefly because of him that when the Conference opened the Indian delegates were able to present a united appearance. At the first plenary discussion on 17 November, he called for an all-India federation and central responsibility. He was followed by princely and Muslim delegates who avowed the ideal with a show of enthusiasm.

Like the Indian delegates the British met to concert a common approach. MacDonald accepted Hoare's argument on the need to avoid 'a divided British front and a repetition of the Irish precedent'.[18] The Conservative and Liberal delegates were supplied with information by the India Office and with appropriate Cabinet papers. The greatest Indian Civil Servant of the century, Sir Malcolm Hailey, had advised Hoare that the Government of India's despatch, with its opposition to the reconstruction of the central legislature and its advocacy of 'responsiveness', was 'unreal and very transitory'.[19] He suggested that Hoare should seek an undertaking from the Government that they would yield central responsibility for certain portfolios only if the legislature were reconstituted on the federal basis proposed by Simon. When Hoare and Reading met the Government delegates at Downing Street on the eve of the first plenary session, Reading pressed in vain for MacDonald 'to define the limits beyond which they were not prepared to go'.[20] However, the Prime Minister did say that the Government 'certainly could not go less far than the Viceroy, but there must obviously be reserved subjects, e.g. defence, foreign affairs, Indian Princes, and, probably, finance'. A Cabinet memorandum of two days previously suggests that the government was disposed to yield to the British Indian central executive the largest degree of self-government consistent with Parliament's retention of responsibility over certain essential matters. The Government seems to have done no detailed work on the reconstitution of the centre on federal lines and MacDonald seemed loth to press federalism if Indian delegates proved averse to it, though he did regard it as 'the most favourable line of advance'.

On 19 November a Cabinet memorandum recommended the encouragement of the all-India federation idea. Such a federation was 'right for India' and could be 'used to establish, with Indian support, a "safer" form of Government, thus making a transfer of power easier'. Under an all-India federation, the portfolios for all departments except defence and external affairs, and perhaps law and order and finance, would be transferred to responsible Indian ministers.[21] A week later Hoare spoke with Simon, who shrewdly pointed out the 'danger of our agreeing to an all-India framework with [the] Princes in it, and then a withdrawal of the Princes and a claim that our acceptance applies also to a Federal British India alone'.[22] From this conversation came an idea that was to be of cardinal importance in the making of India's paper federation. Simon advised Hoare: 'Try to get out of the Conference general resolutions in favour of federation of all-India and provided that all-India is federated, then a cautious acceptance of Government corresponding to responsible government.' Here was the origin of the princes' 'veto' on British India's constitutional development, the central provision of the federal section of the Act of 1935.

On 12 December Hoare sought the Conservative Party business committee's endorsement of the principle that Simon had enunciated: a measure of central responsibility on condition that an all-India federation was established. He stressed that the princes' declared willingness to enter a federation had merely shortened the time scale of the main principle of the Simon Report. He reported that the federal structure subcommittee of the Conference had agreed 'that there should be only one executive and one system of legislative Chambers for India and that the executive and the Chambers should be federal'.[23] This prospective elimination of the Legislative Assembly of British India was, he claimed, 'a very remarkable step to have taken.... And by taking it we have made it possible to rescue British India from the morass into which the doctrinaire Liberalism of Montagu had plunged it.' A fundamental shift in the polity of India, from a unitary to a federal structure, had been negotiated. Hoare urged that a federal government would be more stable than a unitary one, for it would operate under a written constitution and a supreme court, the system of representation would have a less popular foundation, and the constituent governments would exercise a steadying influence on the centre. He regretted that the 'Montagu-Chelmsford reforms and the policies and promises of the last thirteen years' rendered impossible the creation of an irremovable executive separated from the legislature. It would be necessary to concede some responsibility. However, it was possible to transfer certain portfolios and yet retain the 'threads that really direct the system of government'. Britain could insist upon a broad definition of the Viceroy's overriding powers. She could keep the army, 'the ultimate instrument of control, completely in our hands'. She could 'tie up' finance, with a statutory currency board to control the exchange and a reserve bank to manage the reserves. She could make the army, service salaries and pensions, and the interest on loans permanent prior charges on the federal revenues. Thus could financial responsibility be circumscribed so that some eighty per cent of the federal revenues would be kept out of the hands of an Indian minister. Commerce could be safeguarded through a trade agreement. Again, the central legislature would be so constructed that the executive need be only technically removable: 'In actual practice an executive composed of such divergent elements as British India and the Indian States, the one dependent on election, the other upon nomination, could never be responsible or removable in the British sense of the word.' Hoare was advocating the mere semblance of central responsibility. Even that was to be 'entirely dependent upon an effective federation being in actual existence in India', a condition which would, he believed, take a period of years to fulfil.

Such was the spirit of the Tory agreement to the Indian demand for an all-India federation and central responsibility and MacDonald's high-sounding declaration at the close of the Conference must be seen against it. 'With a Legislature constituted on a federal basis', he announced on 19 January 1931, 'His Majesty's Government will be prepared to recognize the principle of the responsibility of the Executive to the Legislature.'[24] In an official statement of Conservative policy on 5 February Hoare could justly claim: 'During ten weeks of almost incessant discussion, basing ourselves upon the Simon Report, we steadily maintained our position.'[25]

Britain had indeed yielded little. She had diverted the Indian demand for Dominion status by nodding assent to the nebulous formula: central responsibility with reservations and safeguards, upon the creation of an all-India federation. This was closer to Simon's recommendations than to the Nehru Report. It was clearly very different from what Congress had demanded. For the Hindu Liberals it was a slim basis on which to attempt to persuade their Congress brethren that Britain was prepared to concede the substance of Dominion status. In the month following the appearance of the Simon report Sastri had read to the East India Association in London a paper in which he insisted that the 'essential aspect' of Dominion status, 'the very bond and cement of the Commonwealth', was 'the right of secession'.[26] Sapru's claim now to have won Dominion status subject to safeguards was unjustifiable, though it is explicable in terms of the mission that he had in prospect.

III

However nebulous the terms of the formula agreed at the Round Table it seemed at the time that a reservoir of goodwill had been built. The Indian parties had concerted a goal which the British had accepted. It had been agreed that there should be provincial autonomy and that the Governor-General must retain, for some time, reserve powers over the army, law and order, external affairs and the rights of the minorities and the services, and hold safeguards over certain aspects of finance. A subcommittee had been set up to consider the knotty problem of defining the federal structure, including such difficulties as the size of chambers, the electorates, the powers of the centre over the provinces and finance. Another was to decide upon statutory safeguards for the minorities in the provinces and at the centre, which raised in particular the vexed question of separate electorates. The subcommittees' work had been inconclusive. Before the reassembly of the Conference the Indian parties would need to determine their views on the matters that had not been resolved. 1930 had ended with euphoria at apparent accord. During 1931, as each of the Indian parties defined the Round Table formula in its own way, a gulf of discordance could be seen yawning between them.

The Hindu Liberals' reports to Gandhi of the atmosphere favourable to a constitutional settlement at the Round Table, their effectiveness as peacemakers between him and Irwin, and the latter's sympathetic disposition, brought the hopes of the Round Table to their apogee at Delhi in March 1931. Gandhi agreed to suspend civil disobedience and to consider 'the scheme for the constitutional Government of India discussed at the Round Table Conference'.[27] He acknowledged that federation was 'an essential part' of the scheme, as were 'Indian responsibility and reservations or safeguards in the interests of India, for such matters as, for instance, defence; external affairs; the position of Minorities; the financial credit of India, and the discharge of obligations'. Having reached this working agreement with the Government, Gandhi had now to achieve accommodation with the Muslims.

The hopes of March faded in April, when Delhi saw a sign of the intractability of the communal problem. The All-India Muslim Conference indicated the terms on which it would accept a constitution of the type proposed by the federal structure subcommittee. It demanded the 'autonomy of the constituent units and . . . complete residuary powers to be vested in them'.[28] In fact, 'all transfer of power should be made from Parliament to the Provinces, and . . . no subject should be made Federal without the previous mutual consent of the autonomous units of the Federation.' Further, 'there should be no difference between the powers of the various units', which meant that internal sovereignty should be as strong in the provinces as in the princely states, that the Muslims would cede to the centre only such powers as the princes would relinquish. The Muslims must have one-third of the seats in the central legislature. This demand was not new, but before the Round Table proposal for an all-India federation it had concerned British India only. Now, with the predominantly Hindu princely states involved, the demand was for a third of the seats in an all-India centre. The old demand for a belt of Muslim majority provinces across eastern and north-western India was reiterated. There were to be separate Muslim electorates. Executive councils were to be so composed as to recognize Muslim interests. No legislature was to discuss any inter-communal matter if three-quarters of the Muslim members opposed the discussion.

In May Gandhi launched an initiative to open to negotiation the fundamental Muslim demand, separate electorates. Jinnah had long been prepared to negotiate the issue and in this he had not been alone among the Muslims at the Round Table. However, such delegates had been excoriated in private letters from the Muslim member of the Viceroy's Council, Mian Fazl-i-Husain, and in the Muslim press. Gandhi was now dealing through the Nawab of Bhopal with Sir Muhammad Iqbal and other representatives of the Muslim Conference, together with Congress Muslims. The proposals that emerged would have opened the way for the gradual withering of separate electorates; but again Fazl-i-Husain exerted himself to ensure their rejection. In consequence the problem of separate electorates remained. In September Muslim delegates returned to the Round Table wedded to the system.

Federal structure was less obviously a communal issue than electoral arrangements. The Muslim approach to the question of federation was investigated by a *Manchester Guardian* correspondent, who reported in June 1931:

The Moslems see that the new Federal Government, if and when it comes into existence, will have a large Hindu majority. The entrance of the States has increased the majority, for the States are chiefly Hindu. There is a strong tendency to counteract this permanent majority by trying to form a large northern block of provinces which will be Moslem, and in which the Hindus will be, as it were, hostages for the good behaviour of their co-religionists in the centre and the south.... Many Moslems do not believe in the permanence of a Federal India, and they foresee a Moslem state in the North stretching from Karachi to Northern Bengal. The writer found this 'hostage' theory to be very widely held.[29]

A Cabinet paper of September 1931 similarly probed the communal aspect of the central authority issue. It was, the paper concluded, a 'question whether the Muslim provinces, or the provinces in which the Muslims hope to consolidate their power, should be under any degree of control from a centre which will be predominantly Hindu'.[30] The paper considered the Muslims' 'primary object' to be the creation of 'a Muslim India'; the secondary object was to secure Muslim interests elsewhere by the operation of the hostage theory.

At the second Round Table Conference the Muslim delegates all sat pat on the resolutions passed at Delhi in April. Shafat Ahmad Khan insisted that the centre's power of interference in the provinces in case of emergency should rest with the Governor-General alone, and that neither the federal cabinet nor the federal legislature should have such jurisdiction. The Aga Khan hinted that emergency powers should rest not with the Governor-General but with the Viceroy, as was intended for the paramount power's authority over the states. There was no inclination to allow potentially great powers to fall to the Hindu dominated centre. The Muslims opposed weightage for the states in the central legislature and adhered to their demand for one-third of the seats. The Government was aware that the Muslim delegates were controlled tightly by Fazl-i-Husain and, behind him, orthodox Muslim opinion. Gandhi stood no chance of solving the communal problem. To make agreement even more difficult, the Muslims achieved a common front over safeguards with the delegates of the Depressed Classes, the Anglo-Indians, the Indian Christians, and the European population.

At the second Conference the stark realities of the Indian problem came into sharp focus. Whilst a deadlock occurred over the communal question the breach between Britain and the Congress over India's constitutional status was re-opened. The Congress had commissioned Gandhi to demand acceptance of their conception of the essence of Dominion status: the right to secede from the Empire. This was firmly rejected and the responsibility with safeguards and reservations formula reiterated. Gandhi called in vain for complete Indian control of finance, without which he believed there could be no central responsibility 'worth the name'. In March he may have felt that if the goodwill of the Round Table prevailed then he might achieve a common front with the Muslims as a means of extracting from Britain the substance of Dominion status. By December such hopes were seen to have been delusions.

As communal troubles mounted and the Delhi pact dissolved the princes showed themselves to be no enthusiasts for federation. Before the first session of the Conference, when a British Indian constitutional advance had seemed imminent, they had been careful to avoid being cast as opponents of *Swaraj*. They had appreciated that it would be difficult to do a favourable deal with a self-governing India. They had shrewdly supported the all-India federation scheme and gained a veto on British India's constitutional advance. It was a veto they would scarcely dare use against a united British India for fear of the unrest that would arise among their own subjects. Still, it was not long after the return of the states' delegates from the first Conference that some princes expressed anxieties about acceding to an all-India federation. The Maharaja of Patiala, Chancellor of the Chamber of Princes, launched an alternative scheme, developed by Sir P. Pattani in 1930, for the union of a federated British India with a confederation of Indian states. The princes would then face British India as a body. The all-India authority would have minimal powers and it would consist of equal numbers of British Indian and 'Indian Indian' representatives. The scheme did not command widespread support, though Dholpur, Indore and Bahawalpur adhered to versions of it. However, it was indicative of the tendency of the princes to divide among themselves over federation. The scheme was calculated to appeal to small states, which could not expect to be represented separately in an all-India federation and which would take comfort from unity. On the other hand, states of a moderate size were probably attracted more by a scheme of Bikaner's for the separate representation of the states that enjoyed individual representation in the Chamber of Princes. The major Indian states, which did not belong to the Chamber, wanted representation commensurate with their importance. The states also differed over the arrangements to be adopted for federal finance, and some began to show alarm at the financial implications of federation.

On the eve of the second Conference, Sir Reginald Glancy, expert adviser to the Hyderabad delegation, wrote an illuminating account of the states' attitudes. He believed that sufficient states were committed to federation to make any general withdrawal impossible provided that British India agreed to reasonable terms. Yet just two months later, in a rueful supplementary paper, he observed that the cleavage in the British Indian delegation had caused a 'marked change' in the princes' attitudes:

Now that the outlook is so gloomy and the chance of agreement between the British Indian parties so remote, the Princes have begun to hope that nothing will come of the Conference, and that they will be able to continue their sheltered existence while Hindus and Muhammadans wage communal war in British India.

When the Conference began there was not enough accommodation for the princes but by the end of October many of their chairs were empty. Some had gone home and others stayed in London only to see that they were not blamed for the failure of the conference. Glancy felt compelled to write that there was 'not one genuine friend of Federation left amongst the Princes'. The key to the situation was British

Indian unity: 'If only agreement can be reached in that quarter, the States will very quickly fall into line.' The assessment was ominous.[31]

IV

Amid communal deadlock, the Congress challenged British policy and with the princes resiling the Government had to determine a course of action. The political climate in Britain was not conducive to bold or enlightened statesmanship. Britain was licking her wounds. Prolonged economic depression had forced her off the gold standard in September. To many it seemed that an age in English history had ended. Ramsay MacDonald now headed a National (essentially Conservative) Government, and from October operated with a 'doctor's mandate' accorded by a desperate electorate. To the Cabinet it seemed that imperial resources—of prestige no less than of finance—were incapable of supporting a liberal policy in India. In September the Cabinet had complained to the Viceroy that an increase of the Indian duties on piece goods was driving 'the final nail into the Lancashire coffin' in order to pour 'money into the pockets of Congress'.[32] On this issue the Viceroy stood his ground; but when, to balance the budget, he supported the reduction of civil service salaries the cabinet overruled him. He vainly resisted to a point just short of resignation the Cabinet's decision to keep the rupee tied to the pound, regardless of the price of gold. If in the circumstances of late 1931 the British Government had little concern for the economic interests of India, she had no patience for the dissent of the Congress from the agreed formula for the reformed constitution. Imperial malaise must be added to communal antipathies as a reason for the evaporation of the Round Table's reservoir of goodwill.

It is known that in 1886, when Gladstone seemed to threaten the Empire by his announcement of a scheme for Irish home rule, Lord Randolph Churchill, remembering Ulster, observed that 'the Orange card would be the one to play'.[33] In 1931, when Gandhi's repudiation of the Conference formula was added to the economic crisis ('the greatest Imperial emergency since the war', were Baldwin's words to Willingdon),[34] 'the Crescent card' became a trump in the hand of the Conservative and Unionist Party.

Hoare, now Secretary of State, considered future policy in a memorandum of 9 November. He reasoned that Britain could not afford to withhold all constitutional advance until the communities composed their differences, for fear of losing her friends, 'the 120 million Indians who have hitherto refused to take part in civil disobedience'.³⁵ The Government should therefore determine the communal issue and proceed immediately with a Bill to confer provincial autonomy. The difficulties inherent in the federation question should be resolved subsequently. He thought that the Hindus could not 'afford to stay out' if Britain proceeded at once to 'the provincial autonomy stage'. He denied that he wanted to abandon the federal scheme, insisting merely upon the need to recognize that a Bill to implement it would take some time. Indeed, he would announce immediately the appointment of subcommittees to prepare for federation with investigations in India of the outstanding problems of finance and franchise. However, the following passage suggests his private thoughts:

Few delegates would concede what history and logic suggest—that it is premature to consider federation till parties are in being in the shape of autonomous provinces, with experience and power to decide the form of the centre. To concede this would be to postpone federation for five, or, probably, ten years.

If the circumstances proved favourable to it, Hoare would not, apparently, regret a return to the Simon Report's leisurely approach to federation.

The Viceroy could see no difficulty in a two-phase approach provided that provincial autonomy was clearly presented as only the first part of an integrated scheme; for there could be no going back on the undertaking to establish a federation as soon as possible. Neither Hoare nor Willingdon expected the determined opposition that the two-phase plan aroused, especially in Gandhi and the Hindu Liberals. Gandhi questioned the possibility of the provinces functioning effectively as autonomous units as long as an alien despotism persisted at the centre. Sastri was deeply suspicious of the Tories' motives. He feared that once central responsibility was relegated to a second phase Britain would find excuses for withholding it. The provinces would be required to prove their fitness for federation. Congress would boycott the first phase and Britain would call up the Muslims to govern the provinces. Provincial autonomy would raise leaders who would refuse to cede newly won powers to a central authority. Faced with such arguments the Government abandoned for the moment the two-phase scheme, agreeing to embody provincial autonomy and federal provisions in a single Bill.

The two-phase plan was symptomatic of a British concern for Muslim support that grew as the possibility of reaching agreement with Gandhi receded. Early in November, Hoare had been responsive to the Muslim delegates' apprehension that in India Congress was trying to do a deal with the Muslims of Sind and the N.W.F.P. that would destroy Muslim solidarity. In his memorandum of 9 November he proposed the separation of Sind and the conferment upon the N.W.F.P. of the status of a Governor's province. Ten days later he cabled to Willingdon that he was 'most nervous lest we should send them [the Muslim delegates] back discontented'.[36] Assurances were given to the Muslims that Sind and the N.W.F.P. would become full provinces.

On 1 December 1931 Ramsay MacDonald closed the second Round Table Conference with a reaffirmation of His Majesty's Government's 'belief in an all-India Federation as offering the only hopeful solution of India's constitutional problem'.[37] To prepare the way for provincial autonomy the Government would, if necessary, issue an award on the communal problem. Committees would be sent to India to report on the major practical problems involved in federation.

An old-fashioned Liberal like Willingdon found some difficulty in following the logic of this policy. Many of the obstacles to federation arose from the attempt to draw in the princes. Certainly the communal question was awkward but if an award would settle it in the provinces then surely its federal aspect could be decided similarly. In short, at the close of 1931 and early in 1932 he contended that a British Indian federation was the logical first step towards an all-India structure. He and his Council were critical of MacDonald's pronouncement that an all-India federation was the 'only hopeful solution of India's constitutional problem': 'We think such a declaration unnecessary and dangerous, particularly as it leaves [the] fate of India at the discretion of the states.'[38] But of course the Tories had accepted central responsibility only on condition that the princes came into the centre as a stabilizing element. The all-India nature of federation was simply not negotiable. Even if Hoare's own inclinations had been liberal he was faced with a strong and growing diehard faction, drawing support from Lancashire, which disliked central responsibility on any terms, but more particularly in a British Indian form.

It was Willingdon, however, who determined British policy towards the political situation that arose in India after the second

Round Table Conference; and he was not altogether without influence on the development of the new constitution. When Gandhi returned to India he requested an interview with Willingdon to discuss the repressive measures that had been introduced to combat terrorism in Bengal and civil disobedience in the U.P. and the N.W.F.P. Willingdon required that Gandhi repudiate the local Congress manifestations of civil disobedience as the condition of an interview. When Gandhi rejected this demand Willingdon, unopposed from home, arrested him and declared war on civil disobedience. Now Willingdon too became solicitous of Muslim interests. In March 1932, fearing Muslim non-cooperation, he obtained permission to state categorically that the Government would issue an award to settle the communal problem. And he was certainly effective in helping to ensure that the terms of the award were such as to retain Muslim goodwill.

Willingdon's strategy was to keep such Indian friends as Britain had whilst refusing adamantly to parley with the architect of civil disobedience. Doubtless his attitude towards Gandhi was inspired partly by personal animosity. But he did believe that Irwin's conciliatory policy had increased Gandhi's influence by conceding him apparent equality of status. Again, any weakening before civil disobedience would discourage the loyal elements in India, the services and the Muslims, and the agents of law and order, the army and the police. If Congress were given no quarter they would eventually come to heel. This policy the home Government questioned occasionally but never with conviction. At the same time, Willingdon was always anxious to give evidence of Britain's good faith and liberal intentions in order to win the support of moderate men. In January 1932, soon after incarcerating Gandhi and bringing full-scale civil disobedience down upon his head, he cabled home: '...it is essential at this juncture to show our *bona fides* by strengthening Indian representation on my Council.'[39] Hoare placed before the Cabinet the Viceroy's proposals on the matter. They were rejected, as he recommended, for they would have weakened the Government of India without appeasing the Congress demand for central responsibility. Willingdon took the rebuff with doubtful good grace.

Willingdon's Government enjoyed a notable success in constitutional controversy when, in April–May 1932, Hoare, with Cabinet support, tried to revive the two phase plan. Hoare stressed that the India Committee of the Cabinet was concerned at the delay that would fall between the issue of the communal award to prepare for provincial autonomy and the completion of the India Bill. However, Willingdon emphasized that reversion to a two phase approach was bound to arouse suspicion of Britain's motives. Only the Muslims would be satisfied; and the newly autonomous provinces would insist upon a further round of consultations before a federation was established. Sastri heard of the Cabinet's proposal and protested pleadingly to MacDonald. He wrote to a friend: 'Imagine what will happen if provincial autonomy is granted and four provinces under Muslim rule oppose central responsibility (or stipulate impossible conditions) while seven Hindu provinces wish to go ahead.'[40] In the face of Willingdon's appreciation of the situation, and shaken perhaps by Sastri's representation, the Cabinet backed down. Willingdon welcomed this development and pressed for an announcement on the programme for preparing the reforms. He was certainly anxious to hasten the India Bill. Indeed he caused consternation at home when, on one occasion, he publicly expressed a hope to leave India a constitutional Viceroy.

V

Gandhi's departure in disappointment from the Round Table marked the failure to concert reforms by a consensus among the major British and Indian parties. So little had come of the second Conference that Hoare was disposed to proceed unilaterally. Early in 1932 the promised committees visited India and reported on the franchise, federal finance, and financial relations between the centre and the states, whilst a consultative committee containing nominated representatives of the Conference was set up in India. On 27 June, partly no doubt in response to Willingdon's plea for a policy declaration, Hoare announced the Government's programme to the House of Commons. The first step would be the issue of a communal award. Next, whilst he did not close the door to further consultation with Indians, Hoare indicated that the Government would itself proceed to frame proposals in the form of a White Paper, which would be placed before a Joint Committee of Parliament with Indian assessors. The Hindu Liberals accepted the need for a communal award but regarded the further programme as offensively authoritarian. Sastri saw it as evidence of Tory reaction and Sapru resigned from the consultative committee. Willingdon became anxious that abandoning the Conference method would alienate the Liberals utterly. Sapru, Sastri, Jayakar, Setalvad, Joshi, Sethna, Chintamani, and others condemned Hoare's procedure for doing 'away with ideas of equality during discussions between British and Indian delegates and agreement between them on [the] basis of proposals to be laid before Parliament'.[41] The Liberals demanded a further Conference session in London as the condition of their co-operation. Willingdon cabled of the gravity of losing the vital support of the Liberals and intimated that if British India's Hindus denounced the new constitution then there was 'reason to fear that the Princes will not do business'.[42]

Quite apart from tactical factors, Willingdon considered it essential to bring British India and the states together to resolve the outstanding problems in federation. The reports of the federal finance and states finance committees had seemed to favour the states and had widened the cleavage between the two Indias. Agreed solutions to questions of finance and central representation and powers must be found:

Without such a Conference it does not seem possible to make progress in determining a workable Federal scheme to be placed before Parliament, and without such a Conference the responsibility for failure to evolve a workable scheme . . . will fall solely on His Majesty's Government.[43]

Hoare yielded. The Round Table was assembled for a third session in November 1932. It was a depleted gathering for none of their highnesses appeared. In their absence no firm decisions could be taken on federal finance or the states' representation, though the proportions of princely and Muslim seats at the centre were agreed. The states would have two-fifths of the seats in the Council of State and one-third of those in the Assembly. The Muslims would have a third of the British Indian seats at the centre and Britain would use her best endeavours to secure a fair representation of Muslims among the princes' nominees. Agreement was also reached on two other important matters. The Assembly would be elected directly by all-India constituencies; and where doubt arose whether a subject was central or provincial the power of decision should lie with the Viceroy. Hoare adjourned the Conference after five weeks.

From the end of 1932 the Hindu Liberals, now the only firm friends of federation, became increasingly anxious about the reception of the proposed White Paper.[44] Sapru and Jayakar pressed Hoare for the release of Gandhi and the civil disobedience prisoners in advance of the publication of the White Paper. Failure to make this gesture would seriously impair the prospect of the White Paper's acceptance.

Hoare sounded Willingdon, who had his answer ready. In November, at his request, Sastri had in vain pleaded with Gandhi to suspend civil disobedience, which must, Willingdon insisted, remain the condition of releasing prisoners. At home the diehards would have quickly condemned any tendency to truckle to sedition.

At the close of the third Conference the Liberals were also anxious 'lest through indecision and inaction of [the] Princes [the] launching of [the] Federal Constitution might be indefinitely delayed'.[45] Hoare saw that such fears arose because of the princes' failure to attend the Conference, their disagreements among themselves over representation at the centre, and the lukewarm resolutions of the Chamber of Princes. From the beginning of 1933 Hoare began to prod Willingdon to obtain assurances from the princes of their intentions to accede.

Independently of Liberal anxieties, Hoare had good reason for concern about the princes. He was uneasy about the Joint Committee's reception of the federation scheme should members feel that princely accession was unlikely. There was a strong group of Conservatives, including the esteemed and influential Marquess of Salisbury, that was hostile to central responsiblity and would seize evidence of princely apathy in order to destroy the federal proposals. Hoare toyed with federal chambers of various sizes and with the minutiae of princely representation, seeking the formula most likely to ensure the accession of rulers who accounted for half of the seats and half of the population of princely India. Large chambers would give individual representation to more states and were therefore more attractive to smaller states but less so to the more substantial ones. On this problem Willingdon failed to give the firm, judicious lead that only the Viceroy could. In 1932 he had put the merits of a scheme that would attract the large princes. The case might have been argued convincingly, for the eight largest princes represented almost half the population and area of the states. However, early in 1933, when Hoare proposed a small centre, Willingdon seemed to see safety in numbers. A small centre would deny individual representation to seventy-two per cent of the members of the Chamber of Princes. He dismissed almost lightheartedly the difficulty of obtaining firm assurances of princely intent: 'They have always said they would decide when the picture was filled in, and their ideas of a picture are pre-Raphaelite rather than futurist.'[46] Carried away by his optimism, he asserted that if Hoare could pass a Bill 'without more definite assurances of adhesion but also without definite resolutions condemning [the] federation scheme as set out in the White Paper, I hope and believe that the passage of the Bill will make entry of most of the important States practically inevitable'.[47]

Hoare was not to be put off with generalities. He asked that Political officers commend the federal scheme, with a large centre (as drafted in the White Paper), to the princes and that they secure wherever possible 'provisional assurances of... intentions to federate'.[48] Willingdon did come to appreciate Hoare's apprehension of difficulty with the Joint Committee in view of the 'somewhat nebulous attitude of [the] Princes'.[49] After further investigation he sent home some reassuring calculations. Of the White Paper's 104 princes' seats in the Council of State, 65 would, he computed, be taken up, and by princes who accounted for 33 million of the 70 million states' peoples. He cabled: '...there seems definitely assured prospect that [the necessary] majority, measured in terms of population, will be attained.'[50] Ominously, however, he reported that some of the larger states—Hyderabad, Mysore, Travancore, Udaipur, Bhopal—were still standing out. Once Willingdon had obtained these intimations of the princes' intentions regarding the White Paper scheme he felt committed to a large centre. He thought, too, that the temporary abstention of the big southern states would be less inconvenient administratively than that of the smaller but more numerous northern ones.

Willingdon was doubtless over sanguine that the princes would eventually toe the line. He did see the force of the argument that if British India repudiated the India Bill then the princes would recoil. But he seems to have thought that provided the Liberals and the Muslims stood by the Government the Congress would eventually see the advantage of co-operation. Since January 1932 his policy had been to suppress civil disobedience and wait for moderate counsels to prevail. In 1934, when the Swaraj Party decided to contest the Central Assembly elections under the 1919 constitution, he looked forward to the return of moderate Congressmen with whom he could open the constitutional dialogue. Despite occasional misgivings Hoare proposed no alternative to this policy of waiting hopefully.

It is unlikely that a more conciliatory Viceroy could have influenced in essentials the form of the constitution, in a bid for Congress goodwill. Nor could he have pressed the princes harder. For in England a Tory backlash menaced even the modest White Paper scheme for federation and central responsibility. During the years 1933–4 occasions were frequent when Hoare felt that the federal provisions would be lost. He, the Prime Minister and the Cabinet were so nervous that they became obsessively concerned about minor Indian questions that might affect reactions to the federal scheme at home.

The attitude of the Lancashire interest seemed of critical importance. In 1933 Hoare delayed the presentation of Lancashire evidence before the Joint Committee pending the outcome of a Lancashire trade delegation's visit to India. Concern for Lancashire opinion affected the selection of an Acting-Viceroy during Willingdon's home leave. The Secretary of State and the Viceroy agreed that Hailey was the very best choice. However, the Governor of Madras was then Sir George Stanley, brother of Lord Derby, whose support for the White Paper was vitally important. Besides being influential in the Party Derby was paterfamilias in Lancashire. Hoare discussed the matter with MacDonald and a secret telegram was sent to Willingdon confiding the decision to appoint Stanley. Again, towards the end of 1933 Japan pressed India for arrangements more favourable to her cotton textiles, under threat of cancelling orders for Indian cotton, of which she was the largest buyer. Hoare cabled Willingdon that acceptance of Japan's demand 'would evoke the relentless opposition of [the] Lancashire members on an issue in which they command wide support here, and there would be a risk, the gravity of which can not be exaggerated, that the Government's proposals for constitutional reform could not be carried'.[51] Willingdon was incredulous of the Cabinet attaching such significance to a minor tariff adjustment. But so seriously did the Cabinet take the matter that they demanded the rejection of Japan's terms and undertook to indemnify India against loss from any cancellation of the orders for raw cotton. In the event Japan backed down and settled for a face-saving concession. Hoare's problem was to steer a course that would enable the moderate majority of the Manchester Chamber of Commerce to remain ascendant. Extreme members of the Chamber were prepared to go to almost any lengths to defeat central responsibility in India. In February 1934. Hoare acquainted Willingdon that a textile magnate had solicited Patiala's support against the federation scheme.

In April 1934 Hoare and his colleagues were apprehensive of the effect that an election campaign for the Legislative Assembly would have upon the reception of the India Bill. Extreme speeches would furnish the diehards with ammunition. 'We all felt', cabled Hoare, 'that this would almost certainly be fatal to the Bill.'[52] At this stage he was apt to jump at shadows. A few days earlier Churchill had accused him of a breach of parliamentary privilege. He stood charged with having exerted undue influence upon the Lancashire witnesses to the Joint Committee, causing them to alter the evidence that they had intended to submit. He defeated the motion but only after months of distracting toil and anxiety. It seemed to Willingdon that consternation in the face of difficulties at home led Hoare and the Cabinet to an unrealistically gloomy appreciation of the Indian situation. He strove to overcome the Cabinet's aversion to holding elections, arguing that to postpone them would prejudice Indian opinion against the Bill. In reply, the Cabinet asked him whether he would not prefer to face hostile public opinion at that stage rather than hold elections and risk a campaign that would rouse British opinion and force the Government to withdraw the federal provisions of the Bill. Willingdon claimed that the danger of a violent election campaign was being exaggerated, and he carried his point.

When the White Paper came before the Joint Committee Hoare was forced to make significant amendments to its federal section. Salisbury proposed the abandonment of central responsibility whilst such non-diehards as Derby, Zetland, and Austen Chamberlain sought a centre that would be more certainly stable, i.e. conservative. The White Paper proposed a Council of State with 260 members, up to ten nominated by the Governor-General, 100 appointed by the princes, and the remainder elected by the provincial legislatures; and a federal assembly with 375 members, 125 appointed by the princes and the remainder elected directly by all-India constituencies, arranged territorially, communally, and by special interests. Direct election was a sop to the democratic pretensions of British India. The large houses reflected an attempt to satisfy a substantial number of princes. There was a strong body of opinion on the Joint Committee which believed that small houses and a system of indirect election would be more stable. Hoare had to compromise in order to save the federal scheme. Whilst Willingdon set his face effectively against any modification that would give the princes an excuse to resile, he counselled that the sacrifice of direct election, while it would cause disappointment, was not crucial. In consequence, Hoare accepted that the Assembly should be elected by the provincial lower houses and that the Council of State should be elected by the upper houses or, where these did not exist, by *ad hoc* electoral colleges. These changes brought the centre closer to the Simon model; and, of course, they made the scheme less palatable to the

Congress. Considering the balance of power in the Conservative party at this time, the passing of a Bill more liberal than that which was enacted in 1935 is inconceivable.[53]

VI

The Templewood-Halifax interpretation of the failure of the paper federation makes much of the weakness of British approaches to the princes. Before the passing of the Bill Hoare was already stressing the priority of the states problem. He pressed it on Willingdon frequently, for example in November 1934:

> The problem is in one sense more difficult and important than any connected with the views that may be expressed in British India, since if there were anything in the Act as passed to which most of the Princes were irreconcilably opposed we might find it impossible to bring the Federation into being.[54]

Willingdon was misleadingly optimistic, even after the Chamber of Princes' resolution of February 1935, which attacked the draft instrument of accession's failure to limit paramountcy sufficiently and the statutory power of the Viceroy to interfere in the states in the event of a threat to India's peace and tranquillity. In September 1935 he cheerily told Lord Zetland, the new Secretary of State (1935–40): 'My own opinion at present with regard to the Princes is that they will come in and not try and delay the proceedings.'[55] He might himself have cajoled the princes to accede. However, his similarly sanguine but misguided appraisal of Congress attitudes—he assured Zetland in June 1935 that he had 'every reason to think that when the Bill is through even Congress will work it, and work it properly'[56]— gives little ground for confidence in his judgment. He favoured approaching the princes through the Political officers, on a regional basis, and in October 1935 wanted to appoint a political adviser to begin preparations. Zetland, however, insisted upon leaving the incoming Viceroy, Linlithgow, free to determine his own approach. This was commendably liberal but of doubtful wisdom in view of Linlithgow's lack of experience in Indian administration and the acknowledged complexities of the case. Then Zetland certainly applied a brake from home for fear of a diehard revolt, and he viewed the inauguration of a federation as a process requiring some years to complete. Linlithgow was permitted neither the carrot nor the stick to bring the princes into a federation, and he was denied expert assistance.[57] Templewood and Halifax were right to stress that negotiations with the princes were not handled expeditiously, but the Viceroys were less culpable than they suggest.

Furthermore, it is difficult to escape the conclusion that the task of recruiting the princes could not be isolated from the British India problem. The princes' attitudes to federation were conditioned by events in British India. In 1929 and 1930 the princes espoused the federal idea chiefly because they feared the exercise of paramountcy, large and undefined, by a Viceroy subject to the influence of a strong, reformed British Indian centre. After the first Round Table Conference, when their right of free accession was recognized and their accession was made a condition of central responsibility, they had less to fear from British India, though they at once began to seek substantial safeguards of their sovereignty under a federal polity. In early negotiations they obtained weightage at the centre and a strict limitation of the central legislature's powers. To some extent they traded assurances of their accession for a restricted definition of paramountcy. But their fears for their sovereignty could never be assuaged. When the second Round Table Conference revealed a deep communal cleavage in British India their enthusiasm for federation cooled rapidly. Glancy's analysis of their change in attitude was perceptive. The princes could only be brought into a federation if British India were first seen to be united and if public opinion were felt to be irresistibly favourable to federation. In the long term they paid dearly for their assumption that they could remain in splendid isolation as long as the communities were estranged in British India.

In retrospect, the agreement of the first Round Table Conference to proceed by way of an all-India federation can be recognized as condemning India to a constitutional dead end. The scheme came from the princes, who did not really want federation. It was accepted by the Muslims, who were not, for the most part, enthusiasts for central responsibility but who would support it if their interests were fully protected. Nothing would have come of the scheme had Sapru not backed it. Without his support Britain could never have proceeded with the princes and the Muslims to devise a constitution which was such anathema to the spirit of the Nehru Report that it had no real chance of being accepted by the largest party in British India. But given his enthusiasm and authority a well-meaning Labour Government could draft an apparently historic formula. Clever Tory strategy made any central advance dependent on princely accession and made the central responsibility to be ceded the semblance not the substance of power. Hoare saw the formula for what it was: the diversion of the demand for Dominion status; the retreat from Montagu's liberal goal of a democratic, unitary polity.

The steady recoil of the princes from an all-India federation suggests that Britain would have done better to address herself to the British India problem. The enlightened MacDonald-Benn-Irwin triumvirate did attempt to draw Congress into the constitution-making process. However, when Gandhi withdrew from the Round Table, the essentially Tory Government proceeded with a scheme to retain Muslim support, conciliate the princes and ignore Hindu British India. Willingdon's counsel avoided the alienation of the Hindu Liberals. However, from late 1931 until the passing of the Act nothing was done to bring together the major parties of British India. Indeed the tendency of policy was to alienate rather than reconcile the communities.

Whilst the Congress went to gaol the non-Congress Muslims fared well. They obtained full provincial status for the N.W.F.P., the separation of Sind, a virtual statutory majority of seats in the Punjab, and an assured 48.6 per cent of the seats in Bengal; in short, they achieved power in four autonomous provinces. They also obtained separate electorates. However, there was little in the federation scheme to attract autonomous Muslim provinces, though Muslims would have one-third of the British Indian seats at the centre. Residuary powers were not left with the provinces. Through a system of lists powers were distributed as far as possible, but the central powers would be substantial and the federation would be strong rather than loose. Fears of a Hindu raj would still seem justified and communally inclined Muslims would reject the federation.

In 1936 the Congress condemned the federal scheme as giving too little responsibility to India. Indian democrats could scarcely accept a constitution that yoked the future of the Indian people to the princes. In the interests of the minorities and of stability the constitution imposed stern checks on majority rule and collective ministerial responsibility. If Congress were true to its principles it could only seek to destroy the scheme.

Between 1930 and 1935 Britain pursued a chimerical federation. In so doing she brought into being a powerful block of autonomous Muslim provinces in eastern and north-western India, a strong base for Muslim bargaining when the question of central government emerged in more real terms after the federal scheme collapsed. It made Pakistan plausible. Britain's truckling to the princes left them in their medieval dreamlands. This invited the Congress attacks that began in 1937 and sealed all hopes of princely accession. Powerful forces had been created and confirmed to thwart the growth of Indian unity.

The paper federation failed not because of the weaknesses in the Viceroy's execution of the Act, nor because diehard opposition delayed its passing by a year or so, but because it was flawed in essential respects. It was not the viable alternative to partition that Templewood and Halifax suggest. Perhaps there was no alternative approach for Britain to have pursued with profit from the early 1930s. There are indications that the cards were stacked against a communal settlement that would preserve Indian unity. The Muslims already wanted a block of autonomous eastern and north-western provinces, and a loose federation of sovereign states. However, it would be rash to knock down the 'if' of federation only to set up the myth of the inevitability of partition. If Britain wanted Indian unity her main problem in the early 1930s was to achieve accord between the communities. This may not have been impossible. Amity might have been encouraged. Jinnah, who was prepared in 1934 to bargain separate electorates for a common nationalist front, was not treated with the same cordiality as, say, the Aga Khan. Tory policy recalls the playing of 'the Orange card' in Ireland. One can only speculate upon what might have happened if, after the failure of the second Round Table Conference to solve the communal problem, Britain had declined to proceed unilaterally. The alternative was the Congress proposal to call together a constituent assembly to draft a constitution that provided acceptable safeguards for the minorities and for British interests. Such a procedure would never have been adopted by the Conservatives of the 1930s. Even in the perilous summer of 1940 the Cabinet condoned Churchill's mutilation of a promise of India's right to frame her own constitution that a cautious Conservative Viceroy proposed to give.

3
British Policy and the Indian Problem, 1936–40

> I only wish that between us we might have been able to make a greater contribution towards the solution of the problem with which we have been grappling, but the dice have been heavily loaded against us....
>
> Zetland to Linlithgow, 14 May 1940

The lumbering machinery of parliamentary democracy strained and laboured to produce the Government of India Act of 1935. A commission of enquiry, sent to India pursuant to the statute of 1919, was succeeded by Round Table Conferences with Indian leaders in London, and they in turn were followed by a Joint Committee of Parliament. The dimensions of the Indian problem were at last circumscribed by the longest statute in British history. Probably the Act satisfied nobody completely, which reflects the complexity of the constitutional issues. Two future Prime Ministers attacked it for opposed reasons. For Churchill, leading the diehards, its federal clauses represented a precipitate rush towards self-government. For Attlee, it gave insufficient scope for the operation of 'the living forces of India'.[1] To the policy-makers it seemed that both objections ignored the realities of Indian politics—the need to conciliate the Congress, which demanded self-government, without alarming or alienating the minorities and the princes. They hoped, subject to providing safeguards for the interests of the Muslims, to give the Congress a fair field of action in autonomous provincial governments. They planned to create a central government in which the Congress would be counterbalanced by the representatives of the Muslims and the nominees of princes who ruled over a majority of the peoples of the states.

The Act followed the drift of British policy. Consistent with the declarations of Montagu and Irwin, Hoare introduced the Bill with a reaffirmation that Britain's aim in India was self-government within the Commonwealth. The Act approached constitutional progress by devolving responsibility upon the provinces, a policy which, as Curzon observed in 1911 and Attlee in 1935, naturally fostered separatism. It aimed at the representation of interests, not of numbers, and as some of the most vocal interests in India were communal it encouraged communalism. The separate electorates of Minto, introduced at least in part out of a respect for minority interests that would have delighted John Stuart Mill, had been perpetuated, though criticized, by Montagu and Chelmsford. The communal award, embodied in the Act of 1935, wove together the strands of communalism and separatism by giving to the Muslims virtually perpetual majorities in the legislatures of the Punjab, Sind, the North West Frontier Province and Bengal. The Act also pandered to the princes, whose absolute authority resting upon treaties had remained uninfringed by the paramount power since the Curzon era. Now they had it in their power to veto Britain's plan for a federated India. If the federal sections of the Act were ever to be brought into operation, British diplomatists would need, between 1936 and 1940, to inspire political India with a new spirit of goodwill and compromise. Consummate care would be required if the infant federal constitution were not to die of neglect whilst the *enfants terribles* developed by policy in the past—communalism, separatism and princely petulance—received further nurture.

I

From Willingdon's departure in April 1936 until the fall of Chamberlain four years later British policy was essentially the policy of the Conservative Viceroy, Lord Linlithgow, though he was frustrated by the home Government's leisurely response to his attempts to open negotiations with the princes. Linlithgow's chairmanship of the Royal Commission on Indian Agriculture and of the Joint Committee on Constitutional Reform had given him a certain standing in Indian affairs. Nonetheless, the extent of his authority during this crucial period is arresting. The Secretary of State, Lord Zetland, had been Governor of Bengal during the similarly critical years from 1917 to 1922 and had remained keenly interested in India. The Cabinet contained Lord Halifax, whose stock had risen high during a distinguished viceroyalty, Sir Samuel Hoare, Zetland's predecessor at the India Office, and Sir John Simon, who had been chairman of the Statutory Commission. Linlithgow was competent, conservative, confident and industrious. Given an established constitution he would have ruled an empire creditably. Later when Japan overran Burma and Gandhi launched his 'Quit India' movement he did govern with great courage. However, from 1936 until 1940 it was his misfortune to be confronted with a constitutional conundrum, and his want of political insight and constructive imagination gave his somewhat Victorian virtues the appearance of complacency, pomposity and insensitiveness. He was loth to hasten democratic change and he was sobered by the complexity of the Indian situation. He esteemed the advantage to Britain of her Indian Empire and he stressed Britain's responsibility to the minorities and the princes. To Zetland he was 'wise, catutious Hopie'.[2]

It was the Viceroy who stood firm when after the elections of 1937 the Congress refused to take office in the provinces unless Britain agreed to waive the governors' reserve powers to safeguard the rights of the Muslims and the services and to impose law and order. He remained averse from truckling to the Congress although Halifax criticized his 'stonewalling' as showing a 'lack of imagination'.[3] Zetland became overawed by the situation as British relations with the Congress seemed to approach 'a turning point'.[4] He warned Linlithgow that if the Congress did not take office Halifax would probably persuade the Cabinet to insist upon a peace offer being made to the Congress before it authorized the Government of India to assume authority in the provinces under the emergency powers conferred by section ninety-three of the 1935 Act. The Congress decision to take office was a personal triumph for Linlithgow. This early success of a policy of immobility no doubt encouraged Linlithgow to attempt to call the bluff of Congress at an even more critical stage of his viceroyalty, when the Congress stated steep conditions for their co-operation in the war.

It was Linlithgow, too, who determined the tenor of British negotiations with the princes and drove forward the attempt to bring the federal scheme into operation. Hoare doubted the possibility of enticing the required number of princes to accede and shrank from hastening the day when the scheme would be pronounced a failure. Zetland was distracted from Indian affairs by the abdication crisis and by his natural interest in events in Palestine and Europe. But towards the princes his leisureliness of approach was studied. He failed to press parliamentary counsel ahead with the preparation of an instrument of accession. The princes were 'shy birds . . . and might easily take fright'.[5] Haste would surely 'frighten them off'.[6] He was also apprehensive that any hustling of the princes would give the Conservative diehards a 'handle to make use of' against the federal scheme.' Linlithgow insisted that the princes would not accede unless they were allowed to retain the excise duties collected in their states. Zetland was reluctant to bribe them by conceding revenues or powers that the Act had proposed to transfer to the federal authorities. The offer of a financial concession to one prince would lead others to raise the price of accession. Any concession would offend the provincial governments of British India. Zetland acquainted the Prime Minister of his dispute with the Viceroy and found him averse from a course that, because it involved legislation, might revitalize the diehards. Eventually, in the summer of 1938, Linlithgow came home on leave and convinced Zetland of the need for concessions over excise, customs and salt duties and the corporation tax. An unwilling Zetland at last obtained Cabinet approval for an Amending Bill that would make the concessions possible.[8]

It was January 1939 before an offer of accession was sent to the princes. They had six months in which to reply. In June a large and representative gathering of princes at Bombay declared the offer inadequate. By the end of July the necessary number of acceptances had not been received. Linlithgow, Zetland and the Cabinet agreed to extend the offer to the beginning of September. To spur the princes Linlithgow suggested that Zetland contrive to have a question asked in Parliament that would enable the Government to announce their policy on the establishment of a federation as soon as possible. But Zetland shunned this device. He remained fearful of pressing the princes lest the certain reaction of the diehards encourage them in their lassitude. Linlithgow continued to search for a line of compromise that would draw the recalcitrant rulers into the federation. Zetland was mildly responsive to a suggestion of Halifax's that federal subjects might, for a time, be administered by states' officials. But Linlithgow doubted the appeal of any merely pro tem accommodation. Zetland was ever mindful of the danger of baiting the hook to draw in the princes. Breaching the spirit of the Act would alienate the provinces. However, neither Linlithgow nor Zetland really expected that enough of the princes would accede within the extended term of the offer, and Zetland did accept that some further concession might then be required. He believed that a change of mind might also be effected in the princes if they could be made to realize the drift of public opinion in modern India. He had in preparation a White Paper on the offer and the princes' replies. The folly of the princes in rejecting such favourable terms would, he hoped, bring widespread condemnation upon them and so make them more tractable. This was how matters stood when, on 11 September, Linlithgow announced to the central legislature that the outbreak of war gave Britain 'no choice but to hold in suspense the work in connection with preparations for federation'.[9]

Certainly, then, negotiations over the accession of the princes were prolonged by disputation over the surrender of revenues and powers to a federal authority, until the war brought them to a close. However, the states' accession was not simply a matter at issue between the Government of India and the princes. It came to acquire a communal dimension. The activities of the Congress and the Muslim League were largely responsible for the failure of the princes to accede. The federal clauses of the Act provided for a central government in which the influence of the princes and the Muslims would outweigh that of the Congress. So would the autocrats' fears of democracy and the minority community's apprehension of Hindu domination be assuaged. So too would the Tory diehards be appeased. But the Congress set out democratize the constitution by a *tour de force*. No sooner had they agreed to take office in the provinces than they opened a campaign against the princes. Their object was to ensure that the states' representatives at the centre should be elected by the states' peoples and not simply nominated by the rulers.

Britain could not forbear from clarifying her policy towards reforms in the states. The Congress attached importance to a statement by Lord Winterton, a member of the Cabinet, that 'the Paramount Power would certainly not obstruct proposals for constitutional advance initiated by the Ruler of a State'.[10] That was in February 1938. Ten months later, the Cabinet decided that Britain was bound by the spirit of her treaties to support her princely allies if their position were clearly threatened by agitation for reforms. At the same time, it was thought necessary to impress upon them the wisdom of introducing administrative reforms. Zetland and Linlithgow tried to steer a middle course by encouraging administrative improvement and the creation of advisory bodies whilst retarding constitutional changes. They sought 'a holding position'.[11] The states should neither gallop under the Congress spur nor remain absolutely stationary. Perhaps on paper this seemed a nice compromise, but in practice it was no answer to the question of how to reconcile the new India and the old. In the late 1930s no solution was in fact possible. The contradictory policies of the past had produced an intractable problem. Britain was, in Zetland's phrase, 'on the horns of a painful dilemma'.[12] As a democratic nation she could scarcely oppose the Congress programme for reform in the states. Yet the activities of the Congress were bound to drive the princes to reject the federal offer.

The prospect of a Hindu dominated centre was also bound to alarm the Muslims. The Muslim League could, and did, play on the reluctance of princes such as the Nizam to help impose a Hindu raj upon their co-religionists. Early in 1940, the Aga Khan, who had supported the federal scheme in 1935, admitted to Linlithgow that 'the sugar had all come off the pill the moment the States' representatives were to be elected by the States' peoples rather than nominated by the Rulers, for under such an arrangement the Muslims would not get from the States in the Central Legislature the support they required to balance the Congress votes'.[13] The Muslim League was offended by the Congress refusal to form coalitions in the provinces that the Congress could govern alone, and it was alarmed by the 'mass contact' movement. In the tenor of Congress provincial rule the League found, exaggerated, or imagined incidents sufficient to confirm the Muslims' aversion from a Hindu raj. The growing probability of a Congress dominated central legislature generated a corresponding increase in Muslim opposition to the federation.

From 1937 until the suspension of negotiations with the princes, the states question became an ever larger part of that wider Indian problem which ultimately proved to be soluble only by partition: how could the Congress demand for a self-governing democracy be reconciled with the Muslim League's insistence upon safeguards for Muslim interests? For the perceptive observer the transmutation of the states question brought this problem into ever sharper focus. Zetland was such an observer, and it was unfortunate that the more prescient member of the governing partnership during this period was able to exercise so little influence upon policy. Towards the end of 1937 he began to perceive that 'the strongest opposition' to the federal scheme would come from the Muslims.[14] In his memoirs he claimed that during 1938 'my mind travelled back to my experiences in Bengal twenty years earlier, of the almost irresistible centripetal force of Islam as such; from this time onwards I could not resist a steadily growing conviction that the dominant factor in determining the future form of the Government of India would prove to be the All-India Muslim League'.[15] The assertion is well-supported by his correspondence.

In December 1938 Zetland wrote to Linlithgow: '... if one thing is certain it is that the Muslims are uniting in their determination not to be dominated by the Hindus in any form of Central Government which may come into being.'[16] He remarked then and during 1939 that eminent Muslims were sketching plans for grouping provinces into communal blocs, which might federate under a weak central authority. Separatist tendencies that were encouraged by the Act of 1935 were being expressed in schemes for 'Pakistan'.

By April–May 1939 Zetland was 'almost certain' that the Muslims would refuse to work the federal scheme of 1935.[17] He was considering what should be done next and sounded Linlithgow about the wisdom of conferring with representatives of the Congress, the League, and the princes. The Viceroy, an incorrigible optimist, chose to 'let the situation develop'.[18] In July he had 'little doubt' that the Muslims would accept the federation if it were 'imposed upon them'. He did 'not expect serious trouble' from that quarter. A private letter of 16 October contains an admission that he had failed to discern the gradual sharpening of the outlines of the Indian problem during the preceding two years of provincial self-government:

I had not, possibly, fully realized till now how greatly the gap between Hindu and Muslim has widened since April 1937, or the extent to which experiences... since then have undermined altogether belief in the possibility of common and united action on which the Act of 1935 was so essentially based.[19]

What made Linlithgow belatedly aware of the true nature of the Indian problem was the crystallization of the demands of the Congress and the League soon after the outbreak of the war, and his subsequent interviews with the party leaders. Even then he was lamentably slow to take effective action, despite the promptings of Zetland. It seems possible that during the early stages of the war an outstanding diplomatist might have developed a formula to solve the Indian problem. It is true that as early as 5 September 1939 Jinnah expressed to Linlithgow his concern over the prospect of Hindu domination and advanced partition as an alternative objective to democracy in a united India. However the Muslim League was not committed to Pakistan until March 1940. Britain should have been planning for a free united India and negotiating safeguards that would accommodate the Muslims within it. Certain initiatives were indeed taken during the first year of the war and it is worth recounting in some detail the story of their failure. As that most dedicated of British ministers for India, Edwin Montagu, remarked at a psychological moment during the first world war, 'opportunities lost in India cannot be recovered except at great cost'.[20] In the absence of effective diplomacy during the first year of war, the gap between British policy and Congress demands became a gulf, the communal rift became a chasm, and party resolutions hardened into ultimata.

II

Within a fortnight of the outbreak of war, the working committees of the Congress and the League had framed resolutions on the crisis, and Linlithgow had decided that it would be desirable to associate representative Indians with the conduct of the war. On 14 September the Congress determined not to support a war for the perpetuation of imperialism and called for a declaration of the implications for India of Britain's claim to be fighting for democracy and freedom. What, asked the Congress, are Britain's 'war aims in regard to democracy and imperialism and the new order that is envisaged', and how are 'these aims going to apply to India and so be given effect to in the present'?[21] The Congress wanted an undertaking that Britain would concede to Indians 'the right of self-determination by framing their own Constitution through a Constituent Assembly without external interference'. In the short term, they wanted to participate in the conduct of the war through representation in the Viceroy's executive. On 17–18 September the League condemned the federal scheme of the 1935 Act as giving the majority community power to trample on the rights of the minorities, requested the revision of the entire problem of India's constitution *de novo*, required that Britain make no declaration nor adopt any constitution without its approval, and claimed to be the only organization that could speak for Muslim India. Linlithgow recommended to Zetland that he should consult the leaders of the Congress and the League and offer them membership of a consultative war committee. Britain should then issue a statement reiterating her intention to establish Dominion status in India, and declaring that after the war she would be 'very willing to enter into consultation with representatives of the several communities . . . with a view to securing their aid and co-operation in the framing of such modifications [to the Act of 1935] as may seem desirable'.[22] After some hesitation, chiefly owing to the fear of any consultative committee's trenching on the proper authority of the Viceroy, the War Cabinet approved of Linlithgow's proposed approach.

It seems probable that, even after meeting Gandhi and Rajendra Prasad, the President of the Congress, Linlithgow was sanguine of his approach enlisting the support of the Congress. He was overconfident, perhaps because of his victory over the Congress in 1937. He may also have overestimated the influence that Gandhi, who had initially and emotionally pledged his personal and unconditional support for the war effort, exercised in the Congress of 1939. He led Zetland to conclude that the Congress would be satisfied if their statement of 14 September were 'taken at a good deal less than its face value'. On the other hand, the British Labour Party tried to impress upon Zetland that the Congress were in earnest. Cripps, who was in touch with Nehru, told Zetland that the situation was 'grave' and argued for the direct association of Indian representatives with the central government.[23] Attlee pressed the need for 'imaginative insight' into the situation and saw slipping past the last chance of holding India freely within the British Commonwealth.[24] Linlithgow eventually made his proposed declaration on 18 October. It failed to satisfy the Congress. Linlithgow seemed unrepentant and explained to Zetland: '. . . I do not think that either you or I, or for that matter the Cabinet, can feel that there is anything which we have left undone which we ought to have done . . . . The fact is that the price has been put up a good deal by the other side.'[25]

Yet Linlithgow's conscience was not clear. When his declaration provoked the Congress to reaffirm their demands of 14 September and to call for the resignation of their ministries in the provinces, he soon had Zetland obtain the Cabinet's permission for a fresh approach. He now intended to enlarge his executive to accommodate representative Indians, and early in November he asked Gandhi, Prasad and Jinnah to discuss with him, and among themselves, the means of doing so. He threw upon the Congress and the League the onus of reaching agreement about the reconstruction of the provincial governments as a preliminary to their framing proposals for representatives of their parties to join the central executive. This approach was unacceptable to the Congress, for their demand that Britain concede India's right to devise her own constitution at the end of the war had still not been met.

Britain's ostensible main reason for rejecting the Congress demand was that it ran counter to the League's insistence that no declaration be made or constitution imposed without its approval. Linlithgow had found Jinnah adamant that the League be recognized as the sole representative of the Muslims, and antagonistic to the Congress scheme for a constituent assembly. However, the Congress was deeply suspicious of Britain's motives. Gandhi and Prasad contended that all communities would be represented, on a basis to be agreed, in the proposed constituent assembly. The Congress, they argued, appreciated that to be satisfactory any constitution had to provide safeguards sufficient to commend themselves to the minorities. In consequence of Linlithgow's determination not to be 'bounced' by Congress into making arrangements that would be disliked by the Muslims or the princes, British policy approached an impasse.[26] But it was not long before the Viceroy was jolted into activity.

About the middle of November, Zetland began to ponder ways and means of launching a new initiative. Raghavendra Rao suggested to him that Britain send a parliamentary mission to India to investigate the nature of the proposed constituent assembly and of the safeguards that the Congress were prepared to concede. Halifax and Lord Snell, the Labour leader in the House of Lords, also suggested sending out a non-government mission at this time. Zetland was attracted by the idea of accepting the Congress proposal for a constituent assembly. Was it, he asked Linlithgow, a 'practicable proposition' to agree to ratify any constitution that such an assembly produced, provided that the minorities and the princes accepted it?[27] Whilst he procrastinated, Cripps acted. On 28 November Cripps acquainted Zetland of the purpose of a visit that he was about to make to India. He intended to explore the possibility of creating a constituent assembly. If the scheme seemed feasible then he believed that Britain should allow such a body to frame a constitution, and that she should deal with her outstanding obligations and interests in India by way of a treaty with a term of some fifteen years. Zetland was much taken with Cripps's proposals and sounded the Prime Minister on them in general terms at the beginning of December. He then elaborated upon them in a letter to Linlithgow and enclosed a draft of a restatement of policy. Britain, he argued, should call upon the major parties in India to agree the composition of an all-Indian body to determine a constitution for a self-governing

India. She should announce her willingness to legislate along the lines suggested by the body at the end of the war. He thought that Chamberlain seemed 'quite ready to consider favourably what not so long ago would have been regarded as a revolutionary proposal', and he went on to speculate about attitudes in the Cabinet.[28] Halifax, and probably Hoare, would be 'favourably disposed', but Simon might be 'rather sticky'. Churchill would 'clearly have to be approached with very great caution'.

Linlithgow's reaction to Zetland's proposal was decidedly hostile. Linlithgow was not convinced that the Indian situation warranted any 'radical' move.[29] He felt that the Congress were overbidding their hand. They had been unresponsive to his earlier overtures and unprepared to adjust their differences with the Muslims. Linlithgow believed that he held the trump card. For, as long as the Congress failed to secure the amity of the Muslims it remained impossible to meet their demand for self-government. The existing discords between the communities could strengthen Britain's control in India 'for many years'.[30] If, on the other hand, Britain conceded the Congress demand for a constituent assembly, then the Congress would be confirmed in their recalcitrance and would drive an impossibly hard bargain over the minorities question and over such matters as Britain's commercial interests in a self-governing India. Linlithgow counselled allowing the Congress time to sober, believing that they would then welcome a Government move to settle the communal difficulty in the provinces.

Zetland's initiative did, however, elicit an alternative plan from the Viceroy. He suggested that, in due course, he should extract from Jinnah minimum terms for the accommodation of the Muslims, and then appeal to Gandhi to agree to them. Thereupon, he would call together a dozen or so Indian leaders to ratify proposals for safeguarding the minorities in the provinces, and to accept a temporary expansion of the Viceroy's executive. He would, finally, announce Britain's intention to introduce a scheme of federation as soon as possible, 'with a view to proceeding with the minimum delay ... into the Dominion Status stage, and if possible before the conclusion of the war'.[31]

On 10 January 1940, Linlithgow delivered at the Orient Club, Bombay, a speech so conciliatory in tone that Gandhi at once seized upon it as presenting a better prospect of agreement between the Congress and the Government than the offers of 18 October and early

November. Gandhi sought an interview with the Viceroy. At the beginning of February, the Cabinet approved Linlithgow's proposal to meet Gandhi and to offer: a reassertion of Britain's intention to introduce Dominion status as soon as possible; the expansion of the Viceroy's executive to include Hindu and Muslim politicians; the inauguration of the federation as soon as the states agreed to it; the revision of the federal constitution in consultation with Indians. On 13 January Linlithgow had met Jinnah and obtained his conditions for an agreement with the Congress. Apart from demanding that *Bande Mataram* be abandoned as the national anthem, that the Congress flag should not be flown from public buildings and that the Congress should stop trying to 'wreck' the League, Jinnah required the formation of coalition ministries in the Congress provinces and a provision that no measure should be passed by the provincial legislatures if two-thirds of the Muslim members opposed it. Jinnah would not accept a democratic central government based on a popular vote, or the collective responsibility of ministers to a legislature. Surprisingly, Linlithgow felt that if Gandhi were 'prepared to be reasonable then there is ... some chance of a settlement'.[32] Not surprisingly, his meeting with Gandhi lasted only two fruitless hours. Gandhi would not accept Jinnah's suggested provincial coalitions and he reiterated the Congress demand for a constituent assembly.

Linlithgow concluded that the Congress reckoned that 'if they can but hold out for a little longer ... we shall be prepared to offer them a better bargain'.[33] 'As for the future', he advised Zetland, 'there is nothing for it now but to lie back for the present.' He continued to proffer this advice until the end of June. His letters during this period reiterate that Britain should 'refrain from action', 'wait upon events', 'avoid running after the Congress', 'lie back and not move'.[34] She had, he considered, offered all that she should. At the end of February, he observed that the 'opposition to the Congress' among the minorities and the princes was 'hardening rapidly'.[35] He anticipated 'a situation in which the Muslims are prepared to accept Dominion Status or Self-Government only on terms which cannot be accepted by Congress'. He wrote: '... the more I watch the reaction of people here to developments since the breakdown of my conversations with Gandhi, the longer, I judge, is likely to be the process of advance towards self-government in India.' The chances of agreement among Indians seemed 'negligible'. As agreement was a prerequisite of constitutional advance there seemed no possibility of Britain's withdrawing from India in the 'foreseeable future'. Linlithgow saw clearly enough the steady deterioration of Congress-League relations. But he refused to take a step that would alienate the Muslims, who had not resigned from the provincial governments, and he regarded a Congress retreat as the essential preliminary to a constitutional advance.

Zetland had never abandoned the line of approach that he had begun to pursue in November 1939. Just before Linlithgow's February meeting with Gandhi, he told the Cabinet of his conviction that there was no chance of Linlithgow's proposed plan proving the basis of fruitful discussion. Gandhi, he explained, would simply see it as a further British rejection of the Congress demand. The federal scheme would prove impossible to revive because the Muslims would insist upon amendments that the Congress would find unacceptable. If the talks with Gandhi were not to break down almost as soon as they began, the Viceroy must be prepared to offer a closer accommodation to the Congress point of view. Zetland argued that Britain should be prepared to accept a constitution framed by Indians themselves, provided that the states and the major parties in India agreed to the composition of the constitution-making body. He believed that until discussion amongst Indians of their communal problem and the possible solutions for it was undertaken in the clear knowledge that they and they alone were responsible for finding and maintaining a solution, communal agreement would never be forthcoming. Zetland had wanted the Cabinet to consider his views, and, if it accepted them, to advise Linlithgow of the fact before he met Gandhi. He hoped to induce Linlithgow to convene a small conference of Congress and League leaders, as a first step towards the framing of a constitution by the Indians themselves. However, the Cabinet was divided on the matter and there was some criticism of Zetland's attempting to urge Linlithgow to go further than he considered wise. Linlithgow was left to his own devices. After his unsuccessful approach to Gandhi, Zetland returned to the charge, pressing him to bring the party leaders together.

Whilst Linlithgow 'lay back', Zetland laboured to bring the Cabinet to a realization of the need for action to prevent the Indian situation from reaching a stage of utter intractability. On 11 March he told the Cabinet of his anxiety to have some constructive plan of action. He presented a draft announcement which he hoped that the Cabinet would allow him to send to the Viceroy with the comment that His Majesty's Government was disposed to give favourable consideration to it. The draft envisaged the creation of an all-Indian body to prepare a constitution for India as a member of the Commonwealth. The body would include representatives of the states and the minorities who were acceptable to the states and the minorities. After the war it would appoint delegates to meet representatives of the United Kingdom for the purpose of agreeing the constitution, which it and Parliament would then ratify. The draft announcement stated that the British representatives would be concerned only with ensuring that the constitution would be stable and enduring. Those matters in which Britain had an abiding interest—defence, the sterling debt, commerce, the services and the states that elected not to join the Dominion of India—should be settled either in the constitution or by a treaty. On this occasion, the Cabinet postponed taking a decision until it received Linlithgow's appreciation of the political situation after the meeting of the Congress at Ramgarh. When, on 20 March, the Congress demanded 'complete independence' (the catchcry that had swept India into the non-cooperation movement in 1930), and, four days later at Lahore, the League adopted the Pakistan resolution, Zetland was forced to admit that further time for reflection was required. Accordingly, he let his initiative lapse for the moment. Chamberlain's government fell before he could revive it, and L. S. Amery replaced him at the India Office.

On 1 July Amery wrote to Zetland that he had been 'working in substance along the lines which you suggested to the War Cabinet some months ago and which were not acceptable to that body at that time'.[36] He conveyed the news that Linlithgow had now 'come round very markedly to our point of view'. The gravity of the war situation in Europe had led Linlithgow to appeal for unity in India. At the end of June he sounded Jinnah and Gandhi on the probable reactions of the League and the Congress to a further statement clarifying Britain's intentions in India and to an offer to participate in the Viceroy's executive. He found Jinnah anxious to join the Government and 'indifferent' as to any statement, 'so long as it did not compromise him over Pakistan'.[37] Gandhi remained unprepared to modify the Congress demand for 'complete independence'.

Linlithgow suggested that Amery seek the Cabinet's approval for a declaration to the following effect: (1) that Britain's aim in India was Dominion status; (2) that the 1935 Act would be opened to discussion at the end of the war; (3) that the fullest consideration would be given to the views of all interests; (4) that Britain's continuing interests in India would be dealt with apart from the main constitutional scheme; (5) that, subject to Britain's continuing interests being suitably protected, 'His Majesty's Government would be perfectly content to abide by [the] conclusions of any representative body of Indians on which [the] various political parties could agree'; (6) that His Majesty's Government 'would spare no effort to bring about Dominion Status within a year after the conclusion of the war, and to set up whatever machinery those concerned agreed on as appropriate to work out [a] new constitution immediately on [the] conclusion of the war'. Linlithgow telegraphed that he recognized these ideas to be 'somewhat revolutionary' but that he felt it desirable to implement them with all possible speed.[38]

Amery placed Linlithgow's recommendations before the Cabinet early in July and advocated their adoption. Britain had announced previously that her aim was to establish Dominion status. However, as long as she indicated neither date nor method, she remained open to the charge that she was insincere and was merely playing for time; until she did so her exhortations to Indians to agree amongst themselves would meet with no response and only add to the suspicion that she was deliberately procrastinating. Amery speculated that Gandhi must at once have realized the danger to the Congress, both in the eyes of the public and from the viewpoint of Congress unity, of refusing an offer so reasonable as that which Linlithgow had adumbrated. He anticipated that the proposed declaration would take the sting out of the Congress opposition, and he even believed that a split might appear in the Congress ranks. Amery's draft statement followed the lines of Linlithgow's proposal: at the earliest practicable moment after the war India should become an equal partner in the Commonwealth; immediately after the war the Indian constitution should be examined anew by whatever constituent body Indians might agree upon; given agreement among Indians themselves, Britain would accept any constitution adopted by the constituent body; Britain's continuing obligations and interests would be arranged through a treaty; Indians would forthwith be invited to join the Viceroy's executive and an advisory war council.

Unfortunately, Amery had 'a lot of trouble' with his draft, 'mainly owing to the Prime Minister's strong dislike of any move in connection with India'.[39] In Churchill's hands Amery's 'clear-cut draft' became 'a much more long-winded and imprecise document', and he told Zetland that 'for the style of it' he wished, 'in private at any rate, to disclaim any responsibility'.

Amery's draft finally appeared as Linlithgow's offer of 8 August. The statement surveyed, by way of self-justification, the various unsuccessful attempts of the Viceroy, since the outbreak of war, to reach agreement with the major Indian parties. It offered places in the executive council and in a war advisory council to representative Indians. It stressed that in any revision of the 1935 Act full weight would be given to the minorities, and that 'the fullest practical expression' would be given to the wish of Indians to frame any new constitutional scheme.[40] 'With the least possible delay' after the war, Britain would agree to the setting up of a body of representative Indians to devise the framework of the new constitution, and would 'lend every aid . . . to hasten decisions on all relevant matters'. Clearly, the statement did not go as far as Zetland, Linlithgow and Amery had wished towards placing on a constituent assembly set up by Indians themselves the onus of making a constitution acceptable to Indians at large. Britain's responsibilities in India were emphasized and the time within which they were to be discharged was expressed evasively. The offer was presented not as a fresh approach to the Indian problem but as a continuation of past efforts to secure India's cooperation. As neither the date nor the method of introducing Dominion status was specified, Britain remained exposed to the charges of insincerity and procrastination. The Congress observed that the British Government had 'left no doubt that they had no intention to recognize India's independence, and would, if they could, continue to hold this country indefinitely in bondage for British exploitation'.[41] The August offer, in the words of Tej Bahadur Sapru,

> . . . far from easing the tension in India . . . has given rise to grave misgivings and has caused a great deal of resentment. . . . Hedged in by so many conditions, [it] is so incomplete in the enunciation of the aim [of British rule] and so non-committal in regard to its being implemented within any reasonable distance of time that it can afford no satisfaction whatever to the people of this country.[42]

The offer was rejected by all parties. It was ironical that when Linlithgow, who had himself frustrated Zetland's liberal attempts to solve the Indian problem, at last took an enlightened initiative it should have been practically defeated from home.[43]

III

By 1 July 1940 Linlithgow was prepared to offer what for six months after the outbreak of war the Congress had asked as the price of co-operation. But in March the Congress had raised its price, and Linlithgow had forfeited his opportunity. It is difficult to justify his slowness to act. He argued that conceding the Congress demand for a constituent assembly to frame India's post-war constitution would alienate the Muslims and the princes. That objection was certainly no less real in July, yet he then set it aside. He had misjudged the attitude of the Congress in October, and when his offer of a consultative council was rejected he had hastened to suggest the expansion of his executive to include representative Indians. That overture and his approach to Gandhi in February were also rebuffed. His hopes of achieving a compromise were shown to have been based upon a miscalculation of the mood of the Congress. It is true that he sincerely doubted the practicability of the Congress scheme for a constituent assembly. If his doubts were well-founded there was surely advantage in confronting Congress with the shortcomings of their scheme. There was a strain of obstinate pride, a concern for viceregal prestige, in his long refusal to admit the case for a constituent assembly, which was destined to be the machinery to produce a constitution for an independent India. A more skilful diplomatist would have found a means of maintaining imperial prestige that did not inhibit his freedom of manoeuvre. Linlithgow defended his aversion from 'running after the Congress' by pleading that official implacability would make the Congress more tractable. The argument reads as a rationalization of an attitude, rather than as a dispassionate appraisal of political probabilities. It took the end of the 'phoney war' to humble him. Only then would he accept the constructive approach that the Congress, the Labour Party and Zetland had so long advocated. It must be said, too, that he was certainly not eager to hasten the end of the Raj.

Whilst he was slow to make an adequate response to the Congress demand, Linlithgow did little to allay Muslim apprehensions. He had not grasped until October 1939 the extent of the Muslims' discontent in the Congress-ruled provinces and their consequent fears of a Hindu raj. Even then, he failed to investigate the Muslims' alleged grievances, the logical first step towards a serious consideration of the safeguards for which provision would need to be made. The League contended that the governors had refrained from using their reserve powers for fear of offending the Congress. The charge should not have been left unanswered. From late in 1939, Linlithgow seems to have thought that his refusal to concede the demands of the Congress was sufficient to assuage Muslim fears. He looked to the Congress to compose their differences with the League, without having any clear understanding of how that could be done. It is difficult to avoid the conclusion that Linlithgow was more interested in pursuing a policy to retain the support of the League than in solving the problem of devising safeguards to accommodate the Muslims within a united India. In the absence of any British initiative on this problem, the Muslim imagination leapt forward to a future, envisaged by the Congress, when the Raj would be no more. The communal dialectic that had become the dynamic force of Indian politics between 1937 and 1939 meant that each major Congress resolution provoked a Muslim reply.

The Ramgarh demand for 'complete independence', the result of Britain's failure to treat with the Congress, was quickly followed by the Lahore resolution. Linlithgow refused to take the claim for Pakistan seriously:

I do not attach much importance to Jinnah's demands for the carving out of India into an indefinite number of religious areas.... And I would judge myself that his attitude at the moment is that, as the Congress are putting forward a preposterous claim which they know is incapable of acceptance, he equally will put forward just as extreme a claim.[44]

It was, he judged, 'merely put forward... for bargaining purposes'.[45] He may have been right. But the important point is that once the Congress and the League had taken up their extreme positions of March 1940 they could not recede without loss of face. Furthermore, the longer these positions were held the greater the number of their firm adherents.

The war acted as a catalyst in Indian politics. The Congress were encouraged by Britain's difficulties to set their claims high, and in the absence of an effective British response to take up an extreme position. The League raised its bids correspondingly. Perhaps in the early months of war a great Viceroy could have brought the parties into effective communication as the condition of a large constitutional advance. Perhaps, on the other hand, the Indian problem was an inextricable muddle and not a soluble riddle. But certainly Linlithgow failed to test the situation with imaginative statecraft. He was unable to refute the logic of events that Britain's past policies had set in train, incapable of mastering the communal and separatist forces that were shaping India's destiny. Though not an ineffective man in ordinary circumstances, he was too wedded to the ways of the imperial past to fashion a nation of the future. The situation ran away from him. In February 1940 he recognized that 'things [had] . . . advanced at a far more rapid pace than anyone had imagined' six months previously.[46] 'War', he reflected sadly, 'has imposed upon Indians and upon our plans . . . a stern and searching test, and . . . neither has emerged . . . as we would have wished that they might.' In June he realized that the Pakistan demand was sinking into the minds of 'rank and file Moslems'.[47] There is no doubt that he failed to arrest a serious deterioration in the situation. Within two years Britain, by accepting in principle the right of provinces to secede, granted the need for a Muslim escape route from a united India. Perhaps the Lahore resolution marked the beginning of the end of Indian unity. Or perhaps the end should be dated from Churchill's frustration of Linlithgow's belated initiative. Though consonant with poetic justice, it would be fanciful to cast the arch-diehard as an unwitting architect of Pakistan. But by his intervention in July 1940 the bricklayer of Chartwell did help to build the foundations for the wall of partition.

4
The Mystery of the Cripps Mission

> Cripps was stabbed in the back by Englishmen who differed from him.
>
> Louis Fischer, 1942.

On 22 March 1942 Sir Stafford Cripps, Lord Privy Seal and Leader of the House of Commons, arrived in India with a British Cabinet Declaration that invited participation by Indian political leaders in the government of their country during the war. It also indicated the terms on which India would secure freedom after the war. Cripps's discussions in India were mainly concerned with the proposed war-time changes (paragraph (e) of the Declaration), though the Indian National Congress was opposed to the provisions that enabled the Muslim majority provinces and the princely states to stand out of the post-war union of India. On 10 April the failure of the Mission was signalled when Congress rejected the Declaration. The failure was the prelude to the 'Quit India' rebellion, and for the remainder of the war neither the Congress nor the Muslim League was associated with the Government of India.

Comment on Cripps's conduct of his Mission has generally been adverse and sometimes defamatory. The main line of criticism, from the Viceroy and his circle, is that Cripps was devious and deceitful. The Viceroy, Lord Linlithgow, complained that Cripps was 'crooked when up against it' and 'did not play straight' with him over the reform of the Viceroy's Executive.[1] His son, Lord Glendevon, seeks to substantiate such claims and adds that Cripps went 'well beyond his brief' with regard to the Executive.[2] The Reforms Commissioner, H. V. Hodson, agrees that Cripps exceeded his brief and argues that he was foolish not to clear his radical plans with Linlithgow.[3]

In the published British documents on the Mission Eric Stokes finds evidence to support the viceregal circle's arguments. He concludes that 'Cripps' actions still require a great deal of explaining'.[4] On the other hand, Anthony Low regards the viceregal circle's accusations as 'quite unwarranted': the documents show that Cripps had 'no will to break the bounds of the brief he brought from London'.[5]

From the Congress side the charges against Cripps are tergiversation and betrayal. The President, Abul Kalam Azad, and Jawaharlal Nehru contend that, whereas Cripps at first construed the proposed war-time changes as a firm offer of a fully Indianized Cabinet (save for the Viceroy and the Commander-in-Chief), subsequent discussions revealed that they amounted only to the concession of some seats, at the Viceroy's discretion, on the Executive Council. Cripps had gulled Congress into negotiations by promises that he later broke.[6] At the time, Cripps denied such charges vigorously.

The mystery of the Cripps Mission awaits solution. With the opening of the British and Indian archives for the period, it is time to reopen the case. The evidence on the origins of the Mission, Cripps's brief, his relations with the Viceroy, his communication with the Secretary of State and the Prime Minister, and his negotiations with the Congress, will all be examined. It reveals that the verdicts of Cripps's critics represent a serious miscarriage of justice.

I

The Cripps Mission grew out of an initiative by Labour members of the War Cabinet.[7] On 19 December 1941, thirteen days after Japan attacked Pearl Harbour, Clement Attlee presided over a War Cabinet meeting at which Ernest Bevin questioned whether British policy was 'calculated to get the fullest war effort from India' and proposed an early discussion of the position.[8] When Churchill, who was in Washington, read this he cabled to Attlee of 'the danger of raising constitutional issue'.[9] Attlee replied that it was sure to be raised in Parliament soon. He also warned Churchill that if a recent appeal of Sir Tej Sapru were rebuffed then his Labour colleagues would find themselves in great difficulty. On 2 January 1942 Sapru had called for 'some bold stroke [of] far-sighted statesmanship', and, in particular, for the complete Indianization of the Executive and its conversion into a 'truly National Government' responsible to the Crown.[10]

Linlithgow was consulted. He advised that Britain should 'stand firm and make no further move'.[11] Since 1940 his policy had been to 'lie back and not move'.[12] He believed that the Hindu-Muslim problem clinched the case for imperial rule and that its solution by Indians themselves was the necessary prerequisite to a British initiative to end the constitutional deadlock. The Secretary of State, L. S. Amery, was in broad agreement with a policy of inactivity and he commended it to the War Cabinet. However, with the Japanese fast overrunning the Burma annex to the Indian Empire, Labour and American pressures ensured that a fresh attempt would be launched to bring the Indian parties together and into full co-operation with the war effort. While Roosevelt tackled Churchill Labour ministers prepared for battle in the War Cabinet.

On 2 February Attlee prepared an impressive memorandum that attacked the Viceroy's 'crude imperialism'. Britain must unite the leaders of the Indian political parties. As Linlithgow was 'not the man to do this . . . , a representative with power to negotiate within wide limits should be sent to India now, either as a special envoy or in replacement of the present Viceroy, and . . . a Cabinet Committee should be appointed to draw up terms of reference and powers'.[13]

For the moment the War Cabinet shelved this proposal. It concentrated on two other approaches to change: the drafting of a fresh constitutional statement that would serve as a reply to Sapru and a scheme of Churchill's for the creation of an advisory Indian council of defence. The Viceroy scotched the Churchill plan but proceeded to suggest limits to which the proposed statement might safely go.

On 26 February an India Committee of the War Cabinet was set up to prepare the statement. Its chairman was Attlee and its members were Churchill (who became a regular non-attender), Amery, Cripps (who had joined the War Cabinet on 19 February), Sir John Anderson, Lord Simon and Sir James Grigg.

On 1 March a Draft Declaration, which was essentially the document that Cripps took to India, was sent to Linlithgow for comment. The paragraph concerning the immediate changes was then as follows:

While during the critical period which now faces India and until the new constitution can be framed, His Majesty's Government must inevitably bear the full responsibility for India's defence, they desire and invite the immediate and effective participation of the leaders of the principal sections of the Indian people in the counsels of their nation to give their active and vital help in the discharge of that task.[14]

On 3 March the War Cabinet asked the India Committee whether the paragraph 'should be made more explicit, and, if not, what answer should be given when we were asked in what way we hoped that the leaders . . . would participate . . .'.[15]

It was common ground within the Committee that major constitutional changes were impossible during the war and that the supremacy of His Majesty's Government over the Government of India through the Viceroy was not in question. However, there was no agreement over the exact limits to the participation that the paragraph envisaged. Cripps later claimed that the matter was 'purposely left vague'.[16] Amery felt that the prospective changes were nearer to earlier British offers of portfolios to Indians in an enlarged but otherwise unchanged Executive than to Sapru's conception of a National Government.[17] It is certain only that the Committee replied to the War Cabinet that the point raised should be met by instructions to the Viceroy, and that the Committee approved the following draft that Cripps prepared:

You are authorised to negotiate with the leaders of the principal sections of Indian opinion, upon the basis of paragraph (e) of the declaration, for the purpose of obtaining their immediate support for some scheme by which they can partake in an advisory or consultative manner in the counsels of their country.
This does not preclude your offering them—if you consider it wise or necessary—positions in your executive council, provided this does not embarrass you in the defence and good government of the country during the present critical time.[18]

Churchill was not party to the Committee's discussion on this point. It is clear that he disliked the Draft Declaration. On 5 March he expressed a strong bias against it when he presented it to the non-War Cabinet ministers.[19] For some days its fate hung in the balance. There were rumours that Cripps would resign if it were shelved. On the 7th the initiative was menaced by a statement of Nehru's that nothing short of a National Government would satisfy Congress.

Amery was coming to the view that the Declaration was not sufficiently self-explanatory. On the 5th he revived Attlee's idea of despatching an emissary to India, 'charged with the task of getting Indians to agree to co-operate now on the basis of a general understanding as to the future'.[20] He thought of going himself, for sending anyone else 'would be a slap in the face for Linlithgow'.

However, on 9 March, amid widespread feeling that without a preliminary sounding of Indian opinion the Congress at least would reject the Declaration, the War Cabinet accepted an offer that Cripps had made the previous day to visit India and 'discuss matters' with the political leaders.[21] The War Cabinet noted that Cripps was taking out a specific scheme: 'Otherwise, it would be said that he was going out to negotiate'. He was to discuss the scheme with Indian leaders 'with a view to seeing whether it met with the measure of acceptance vital to its success'.

Now the India Committee was asked to consider the draft instructions for implementing paragraph (e) that Cripps had prepared. It agreed that they should become 'an essential part of the instructions to the Lord Privy Seal', and the following sentence was added: 'In relation to this matter you will, no doubt, consult with the Viceroy and Commander-in-Chief, and will bear in mind the supreme importance of the military situation'.[22] On 10 March Amery cabled to Linlithgow that Cripps would be 'going out not on a roving mission but with the plan embodied in the draft declaration as his general instructions. His further general instructions as to the interpretation to be put on paragraph (e) of the draft declaration will be sent in a separate telegram and will of course have to be discussed with you in detail.'[23] Two days later Amery cabled that 'apart from this he has no specific instructions'.[24] In fact, the 'further general instructions' were not sent to Linlithgow until 28 March.

Attlee's scheme for an envoy had prospered. Cripps departed with an agreed War Cabinet Declaration but with a brief, which he had written himself, to '*negotiate* ... some scheme' for the Indian leaders' participation 'in an advisory or consultative manner in the counsels of their country'. The brief allowed the offer of seats on the Executive to any extent consistent with 'defence and good government' and did not circumscribe the 'advisory or consultative manner' in which the Viceroy might employ Indian ministers.

Cripps was quite deliberately sent out to 'negotiate'. From the time of the first draft of the Declaration it was intended to leave the invitation of participation 'open for negotiation'.[25] On 9 March Amery explained to Churchill the 'serious objections to referring to [Cripps's] instructions as if they were an absolutely cut and dried plan (even though from our point of view they are something fairly near that)'.[26] The same day he wrote to Cripps that his Mission amounted to 'squaring the circle ... by negotiation'.[27] Of course Cripps knew that the Cabinet must approve any scheme of participation that he might negotiate, and that in deciding the issue it would weigh with care the advice of the man on the spot. Common sense as well as the India Committee's injunction demanded that Cripps consult the Viceroy.

II

A month before the announcement of the Mission Linlithgow read with dismay a Reuter report that Cripps had said that 'he might visit India later on'. He cabled to Amery that the effect of the visit would be 'disastrous'.[28] When Cripps visited India privately in December 1939 Linlithgow had not welcomed him. He was critical of Cripps's advocacy of the Congress demand for a constituent assembly as the means of breaking the deadlock that had followed the suspension of the scheme for an all-India federation. He regarded with hauteur Cripps's entreaty that he take an initiative to bring the Hindus and the Muslims together. He thought Cripps an unpractical radical. Cripps found him sphinx-like. The encounter augured ill for their relations in 1942.

Cripps spent his first two days in New Delhi at Viceroy's House but then moved to a house of his own. At the outset he showed Linlithgow a list of a new Executive, wholly Indian except for the Commander-in-Chief. 'That's my affair', snapped Linlithgow, who held that 'the implementation of paragraph (e) should be done by him as Governor-General'.[29] Cripps noted that 'the ultimate responsibility lay with the War Cabinet but if it was merely a question of collecting the right personnel in India that was obviously a matter for him'.

On 24 March Cripps told the existing Executive that the participation of Indians in the Council would, save Defence, 'be welcome to any extent that His Excellency desired'.[30] Linlithgow cabled to check the point with Amery, who replied: 'War Cabinet are uncommitted on this issue though it was clear from discussions that they would be prepared for positions on Executive Council to be offered to political leaders provided this would not embarrass the defence and good government of the war . . .'.[31] He could not say that the War Cabinet 'would not be prepared to reduce or abolish official members'. It is worth noting that on 6 March the Advisers to the Secretary of State had recommended that 'the Viceroy's Executive Council should be forthwith Indianised'.[32]

On the night of 25 March Linlithgow drew Cripps's attention to telegrams of February and early March in which he had set forth the maximum concessions that he would make in order to secure Indian co-operation. While he was prepared to invite party leaders to join his Executive he would not promise the removal of all official members as 'a pre-requisite of a political truce'.[33] However he would discuss the matter 'as a practical problem of administration with such leaders as may emerge as likely to be those from among whom his future colleagues in a National Government will be drawn'. He had in mind the heavy administrative burden that the Viceroy would incur if he lost official advice in the Home and Finance departments. Still, his cables express a desire 'to recognize without delay the *de facto* status of India under a National Government'.[34] He now said that if Cripps secured the Indian parties' assent to the Declaration then he 'was prepared to take big risks. . . . If Sir Stafford could do the big thing he would not find His Excellency falling short.'[35] Linlithgow imposed two conditions: first, both the Congress and the Muslim League must agree to co-operate; secondly, Cripps must not 'steal His Excellency's cheese to bait his own trap'.

Cripps accepted the reasonableness of Linlithgow's conditions, though the obscurity of Linlithgow's language gives cause to doubt whether he made his meaning clear. Cripps certainly granted the Viceroy's wish to allot the various portfolios to particular party leaders, and the need to involve both of the main parties. With regard to the extent of Indianization, Linlithgow's somewhat magnanimous language gave Cripps cause for confidence in the Viceroy's support.

As for the manner of Indian participation in the counsels of government, the question seems not to have been discussed. However, Linlithgow mentioned the cables in which he had expressed a wish 'to recognize without delay the *de facto* status of India under a National Government'. Two days previously Cripps had listened to B. Shiva Rao's exposition of the term 'National Government': '. . . even within the framework of the existing constitution, a great deal could be done to convert in practice the executive council into a cabinet . . . and to make the viceroy the *normal* constitutional head of the government'.[36] Cripps's mind was 'working on the same lines'. It would be reasonable for Cripps to assume that the Viceroy's desire for a National Government would carry him in the same direction.

Certainly, after the nocturnal meeting on 25 March Cripps did assume Linlithgow's broad agreement with the lines on which he was negotiating. On 27 March he told a group of Europeans 'that the form of the Government under clause (e) was a matter for the Governor-

General but assented to their proposal that the Executive Council would be substantially Indianized. He explained to them that until the new constitution became operative, the Government would have to be carried on on the basis of the existing Act subject only to some possible minor alteration which might be necessitated after a new Executive Council were constituted'.[37] On 28 March he told Jinnah that if the League and the Congress accepted the Declaration he would 'ask the Viceroy to get into touch with them as regards the questions of formation of a Government under clause (e)'.[38] Next day, at a press conference, he told the whole world:

The object of the scheme is to give the fullest measure of government to the Indian people at the present time consistent with the possibilities of a constitution which cannot be changed until the end of the war ... All you can do is to change the conventions of the constitution. You can turn the Executive Council into a Cabinet.[39]

There is no evidence that Linlithgow demurred at the tenor of this open diplomacy.

From 2 April, when Cripps saw the draft of the Congress rejection of the Declaration, he concentrated upon their main objection: the reservation of Defence. In February Linlithgow had written that 'it may well be found possible to associate a non-official member much more closely with the problems of co-ordination of the Defence'.[40] Cripps, together with Linlithgow and Sir Archibald Wavell, the Commander-in-Chief, now sought to define the functions of such a member in terms acceptable to Congress.

On 4 April Cripps cabled a progress report to Churchill via the Viceroy. He suggested various approaches to the Defence member problem but the most remarkable passages in the cable concern the general reconstitution of the Executive:

18. ... Under the new arrangement whereby the Executive Council will approximate to a Cabinet presumably any question coming within the competence of the Government of India ... will be for decision by the Government of India as a whole and not by any particular Minister ....
27. ... In the event of [the Indian parties'] acceptance, there will of course be difficulties as to apportionment of seats when the Viceroy comes to form his new Government and I would propose in that event to stay till the new Government is formed.[41]

Next day, in a cable to Amery, Linlithgow demurred at paragraph 27 if it meant Cripps assuming for a time 'the functions of the Governor-General'.[42] However, in relation to paragraph 18 he merely observed that such an arrangement would preclude the Muslim League's co-operation unless it was assured of a majority in the Cabinet or a substantial proportion of members reinforced by the clear maintenance of the Governor-General's control. In short, Linlithgow foreshadowed a League objection to introducing the conventions of Cabinet government but he expressed no objection of his own.[43] Neither did Churchill's reply to Cripps's cable object to 'the new arrangement'.

By 5 April Cripps had been in India for a fortnight, negotiating on the clear assumption that if the Declaration were accepted by both parties then a National Government would be set up, essentially Indian in composition and approximating to a Cabinet in its operation. He had worked within his brief and neither Linlithgow nor Amery nor Churchill had challenged him. Then, on 6 April, everything changed.

III

After a conversation with Wavell about the implications of Cripps's cable for the Defence question, Linlithgow now took a more literal view of his relationship with his Executive. On 6 April he cabled to Amery and Churchill that there could be 'no question of majority decisions of the Council being effective against the requirements of His Majesty's Government'.[44] The 'vital test of Cabinet Government, namely, responsibility to an Indian legislature, does not and cannot exist in the interim period': '. . . it is essential that the position of the Executive Council should not be glozed over in any clarification of the offer. This is the more necessary because of popular references to an Indian Cabinet or National Government.' Later that day, he saw a cable from Churchill to Cripps[45] which revealed that Churchill was ignorant of Cripps's assumed changes in the Executive.

Linlithgow now tackled Cripps. He said that he 'had been apprehensive of the course of negotiations, but was not aware of what H.M.G.'s instructions were'.[46] (Yet the instructions, in full detail, had been sent to him on 28 March.) Next day (7 April) Cripps was due to send a memorandum to Azad, responding to Congress questions about the Defence portfolio. Linlithgow pressed Cripps to alter the draft of the memorandum where it referred to Indianization and Cabinet government. Cripps insisted that H.M.G. were prepared to eliminate the official members if necessary. After being revised in consultation with Linlithgow and Wavell, the memorandum as sent envisaged full Indianization and a 'National Government'. Cripps might well remain confident of the Viceroy's co-operation.

But now Amery, too, was taking a hand in proceedings. Cripps's negotiations had developed in a direction that he had never favoured. Linlithgow's cable of 6 April revealed that Cripps was proceeding on the false assumption of viceregal support, or rather in spite of viceregal apprehension. On 6 April Amery prepared a memorandum for the India Committee, arguing that paragraph (e) 'did not envisage any fundamental change in the relations between the Viceroy and his Executive.... Nor was it understood that the special reference to His Majesty's Government's control of Defence was to involve a clean sweep of the whole of the existing Executive and their replacement by Indian political leaders.'[47] Amery carried the Committee with him on the former point. In a cable from Amery that he received on 7 April Cripps was told that the constitutional position 'must remain that the Viceroy in Council acts as a collective body responsible to the Secretary of State and subject to the Viceroy's special powers and duties.... There should be no misunderstanding between you and Indian political leaders on this point'.[48] However, though Amery wanted to challenge Cripps on the question of Indianization, the Committee expunged his reference to it from the draft of his cable.[49]

On 8 April Linlithgow received assurance that Churchill and Amery were opposed to any 'obscuring of the constitutional position' and to Cripps's remaining in India to help reconstitute the Executive in the event of the Declaration being accepted.[50]

On the night of the 8th Linlithgow felt compromised and insulted when he learnt that a draft of the proposed functions of an Indian Defence Member had been concocted by Colonel Louis Johnson, Roosevelt's personal envoy, and shown to Nehru with Cripps's blessing. It seems probable that Cripps's somewhat impulsive handling of the matter strengthened Linlithgow's resolve to undermine Cripps's negotiations. Late that night Linlithgow complained to Cripps 'about the manner in which I and the Commander-in-Chief had been passed over'.[51] He then cabled to Amery, expressing a 'strong feeling of grievance' and warning that 'the latest Congress manoeuvres might well be designed to drive wedge between His Majesty's Government and U.S.A.'[52]

Next morning (the 9th) Linlithgow wrote to Cripps of the meeting that Cripps was to have with Azad and Nehru in the afternoon. Consistently with the Amery-Churchill policy, he advised Cripps to make the constitutional position of the Executive clear. That evening he asked Cripps whether he had done so. Cripps replied that he had talked to the Congress leaders of National, not Cabinet, government, and had told them that 'the Viceroy would doubtless do all he could by means of appropriate conventions'. Linlithgow objected.[53] On the 10th he cabled:

> ... I must know with precision what are the instructions of His Majesty's Government to which I am to work. It is really no use trying to shuffle round this difficulty. Either the Governor-General must continue to have the right to differ from his colleagues ... or he must promise that in no circumstances will he refuse to act on their advice .... I need not emphasize the difficulty of operating a system of conventions when we are dealing with a written constitution ....[54]

Linlithgow and Amery were taking an excessively literal view of the situation. Cripps had never suggested that the constitutional rights of the Viceroy should be modified. Indeed he had denied the possibility publicly. His cable of 4 April had merely referred to 'the new arrangement whereby the Executive Council will approximate to a Cabinet'. When Churchill asked him to explain the point he had promptly cabled his agreement with Linlithgow that there was no question of a majority of the Executive overriding the responsibility of the Viceroy to H.M.G.[55] As a negotiator Cripps was seeking a middle position between the letter of an imperialist constitution and the spirit of a national government.

On 9 April the War Cabinet displayed disquiet at Cripps's memorandum to Azad (7 April), in which the transfer of all portfolios to Indians and a 'National Government' were foreshadowed. It was also ruffled by Colonel Johnson's intervention over Defence. It felt that discussion on paragraph (e) had gone beyond its original intentions. Cripps was asked to explain exactly what he envisaged.

On 10 April Churchill himself took the chair of the India Committee. He declared that a convention limiting the Viceroy's authority had never been contemplated in the discussions prior to Cripps's departure. He delivered the *coup de grace* in a cable that reached Cripps on 11 April:

> ... you speak of carrying on negotiations. It was certainly agreed between us all that there were not to be negotiations but that you were to gain acceptance with possibly minor variations or elaborations of our great offer which has made so powerful an impression here and throughout the United States.[56]

Since 6 April Churchill and Amery had disavowed the possibility of introducing a Cabinet convention. They had reacted against the term 'National Government', even though Linlithgow had employed it with approval in February and early March, and though he and Wavell were privy to the memorandum to Azad in which Cripps had used it. They recoiled from the full Indianization of the Executive, though Amery had revealed that the War Cabinet would accept it if necessary. Finally, they denied Cripps the status of a negotiator, though his instructions explicity required him to negotiate some scheme whereby Indian political leaders might be brought into full co-operation with the war effort.

The cable from Amery that Cripps received on the 7th had, in effect, changed his brief. The cable from Churchill that he received on the 11th had cancelled it. But by then Congress had rejected the 'great offer'.

IV

Like many British observers of Indian politics Cripps had been convinced of the national status of the Congress by its remarkable victory in the provincial elections of 1937. In 1938 he believed that the long Indian battle against the Empire was at last over, and that the Conservative enemies of freedom were confined to the few insignificant Churchillians. When war was declared he encouraged Nehru in his demand that Britain declare its war aims and recognize India's right to frame a free constitution through a popular assembly. During his December 1939 visit to India he sought the confidence of Azad and Nehru. In 1942 he went back as a friend of the Congress. Indeed this was thought likely to prejudice the Muslim acceptance of the Declaration. Ironically, it seems certain that the Muslim League was prepared to accept the offer; whereas the Congress not only rejected it but mistrusted Cripps for evermore.

When Cripps met Azad on 25 March he held out the prospect of an Indianized Executive that would normally function as a Cabinet. In his memoirs Azad claims that Cripps 'said categorically that [save Defence] the Executive Council would function *exactly* like a cabinet', whose advice would be binding on the Viceroy.[57] However, in his official letter rejecting the Declaration he is less precise:

... you had referred both privately and in the course of public statements to a National Government and a Cabinet consisting of Ministers. These words have a certain significance and we had *imagined* that the new government would function with full powers as a Cabinet with the Viceroy acting as a constitutional head....[58]

In a letter that he wrote to Cripps on 11 April he alleged that at first Cripps had said 'that there would be a National Government which would function as a Cabinet and that the position of the Viceroy would be *analogous to* that of the King in England vis-a-vis his Cabinet'.[59] On 13 April Nehru cabled to Krishna Menon: 'Cripps made clear early stages he envisaged national cabinet with Viceroy as constitutional head *like* King subject reservation Defence....'[60] In his most specific written reference to the question Cripps assumed that the Executive would *approximate* to a Cabinet. In his cables he had denied any intention to bind the Viceroy to his Council's advice, yet expressed confidence that Congress would accept the sort of convention that he envisaged. His early conversation with Shiva Rao suggests a conception of government in which the Viceroy would *normally* act as a constitutional head. Despite Azad's claim, it seems unlikely that Cripps spoke of the Viceroy abdicating his responsibility to H.M.G. except for Defence.

Though Cripps was never explicit about his intended Cabinet convention, his constitutional adviser, Sir Reginald Coupland, may be taken as a guide to his thoughts. Coupland had been in India for some months, preparing his famous analysis of 'the Indian problem', and stayed on as a member of Cripps's staff. He interprets Cripps's assumptions about a National Government in his *Report* and in a pamphlet on the Mission.

Coupland refers to the precedent of the ministries in the provinces, which had operated not as 'Cabinets with full power' but as 'quasi-Cabinets': 'The Governor ... had acted on the advice of his Ministers on all save certain matters on which he retained and occasionally exercised his power to dissent and override'.⁶¹ However, whereas the provincial Governor had normally to accept his ministers' advice, the Viceroy was entitled by statute to dissent from a majority of his Council over any measure 'whereby the safety, tranquillity, or interest of British India ... may be' in his judgement 'essentially affected'. Cripps accepted that a convention whereby the Viceroy set such power aside would be in breach of the law and he did not contemplate it. Yet, in other cases, the Viceroy might still work his Council as if it were a Cabinet. He could normally act on the Council's advice. Coupland argues that since the addition of three Indians to his Council in July 1941 (making its composition eight Indian and four British members) Linlithgow had in fact been working his Council as a Cabinet. In August and September 1942 two members, Sir Firoz Khan Noon and Sir J. P. Srivastava, asserted that Linlithgow had never overruled a majority decision of his enlarged Council. This is not to say that the Viceroy could have worked a reconstituted Council without exercising a veto but merely to conclude that within the existing constitution Cripps might well envisage the Council normally operating as a Cabinet.⁶² Coupland affirms, then, that the convention that Cripps contemplated could confer the realities of power upon the Indian parties. Furthermore, as India and Britain had a common interest in winning the war, the political leaders were unlikely to press advice that was contrary to 'the safety, tranquillity, or interest of British India'.

The rub would come after the war if Britain did not quit India expeditiously. Cripps's contemplated convention applied the acid, test to Britain's post-war promise of freedom. There is reason to question the *bona fides* of Prime Minister, Secretary of State, and Viceroy on the point.

Though Churchill might write to the King in July 1942 that the British parties were reconciled to giving up India to the Indians after the war, in September he revealed to A. R. Mudaliar his own persistent attachment to the doctrine of imperial trusteeship.⁶³ In March 1943 he told R. A. Butler: 'What I really feel about the central government is that we might sit on top of a tripos—Pakistan, Princely India and the Hindus.'⁶⁴ Even in August 1945, when he had lost office, he still urged Wavell to 'keep a bit of India'.⁶⁵

In March 1942 Amery wrote to Linlithgow:

... in some form or other the Viceroy will have to remain, not merely as constitutional Governor-General, but as a representative of broader imperial aspects of government for a good long time to come, and to be equipped with the instruments of power required to carry out his functions.... So whatever else you do or agree to, you had better keep in mind the desirability of retaining Delhi and a considerable area around it as the ultimate federal territory of an eventual united India, and not let it pass into the hands of any one of the 'Dominions' that may temporarily emerge....'[66]

Britain would reserve Defence 'for a good while' after the transfer of power. R. A. Butler wrote critically to Amery that the Draft Declaration did not make clear 'what I am told is implicit in [it], namely that Great Britain still has some role to play in India' after the demission of power upon India's component parts.[67] He thought it impossible for Britain to 'attain in one coup in India what Campbell-Bannerman achieved in South Africa', that is, freedom with unity. The 'powers-that-be' were 'reconciled to the idea of a Moslem Confederation in the North'.[68] Conservatives simply assumed that India would break up after the war and that Britain would remain, with forces, to provide a central link under the Crown.

Linlithgow regarded self-government and unity as incompatible. In January 1942 he argued against any concession in the central government that 'would make it impossible for us after the war to regain any ground given now, and which we thought it desirable to retrace'.[69] In October 1943 he told his successor that 'we shall have to continue responsibility for India for at least another 30 years....'.[70]

The triumvirate justified their anticipation of a post-war imperial presence by denying the representativeness and capacity of the Congress. Churchill told the House of Commons in 1942: 'The Indian Congress Party does not represent all India. It does not represent the majority of the people of India. It does not even represent the Hindu masses.'[71] Linlithgow observed that the Congress Working Committee were, except for Nehru, 'a collection of declining valetudinarians who have no grip on the country'.[72] Churchill regarded the Congress as a 'hostile political element' who would paralyse executive action.[73] Amery wrote of Nehru and Gandhi as 'niggling, unpractical creatures'.[74] Linlithgow saw Congressmen as 'entirely ruthless politicians' who sought only to enhance their own prestige: 'short of acceptance of their full demand no sacrifices however great can be relied on to keep them quiet'.[75] When Amery expressed doubt 'whether people of that type could ever run straight', Linlithgow noted: 'They could never run straight. One will have to plough through the old gang down to better and younger stuff.'[76]

It was such attitudes that lay behind the Churchill-Amery-Linlithgow onslaught on Cripps. None of the trio trusted Congressmen or wanted them in the Executive. None of them wished to concede any authority to Congress. None of them was really sincere about bringing the Congress and the League together in the central government of India.

The Churchill-Amery-Linlithgow axis that developed after 6 April ensured that when Cripps saw the Congress leaders on 9 April he could tell them only 'that nothing could be said . . . even vaguely and generally about the conventions that should govern the new government and the Viceroy. This was a matter in the Viceroy's sole discretion and at a later stage it could be discussed directly with the Viceroy.'[77]

It is not surprising that Azad and Nehru believed that Cripps had betrayed them. Nehru cabled bitterly to Krishna Menon:

Congress . . . emphasised in view great crisis prepared set aside all proposals for future provided responsible national government with defence formed now leaving control armed forces with Commander-in-Chief. . . . Ultimately Cripps stated . . . no national cabinet with joint responsibility possible nor could assurances be given about use Viceroy's powers intervention veto. This entirely Viceroy's discretion may later be discussed with him. Viceroy also functioning as prime minister. Thus no major change only addition popular representatives Executive Council, legal position unaltered, and no assurance even about conventions. Practically repeating August offer with minor variations. This entirely different picture from what Cripps originally suggested. Impossible call this national government or evoke enthusiasm people . . . . Congress went uttermost limit giving up precious objectives in negotiations. Crux of matter organization national defence on popular mass basis but this only possible by free national government. Increasing bitterness here and in future impossible accept anything short complete national freedom . . . .[78]

After the fateful meeting of 9 April Congress scorned compromise. Betrayal bred belligerence. Azad's rejection of the Declaration demanded a 'Cabinet Government with full power'. There must be 'definite assurances and conventions which would indicate that the new government would function as a free government, the members of which act as members of a Cabinet in a constitutional government'.[79] Such terms were so extreme that Congress alienated former sympathizers. It seemed unreasonable to claim the full transfer of power in the midst of a world crisis. Britain was enabled to claim a propaganda victory.

After 10 April Cripps had two courses of action open to him. He could announce that he had offered Congress a substantial concession which the opposition of the Prime Minister, the Secretary of State, and the Viceroy had forced him to retract. He could justify his negotiations by reference to his instructions, reveal that he had consulted the Viceroy, and argue the practicability of the convention that he contemplated. He could condemn the imperialist creed of his adversaries in terms such as Attlee had used in February. The effects of such action would have been to redeem his reputation with the Congress and substantiate the Congress imputation of betrayal by the British. He would be damning his Cabinet colleagues and precipitating his own and probably other Labour resignations. Alternatively he could keep the inside story of the Mission to himself, present a loyal defence of British policy, and grasp the handle that the Congress rejection gave to the propagandist.[80]

Cripps decided promptly upon the latter course. One side to the negotiations was sure to be blamed and he determined that it should not be Britain. His riposte to Congress was bound to be disingenuous. He claimed that 'the proposals of His Majesty's Government went as far as possible, short of a complete change in the Constitution which is generally acknowledged as impracticable in the circumstances of today'. He carried his criticisms even further, raising the communal issue for the first time: Congress wanted a 'nominated cabinet ... responsible to no one but itself', which would 'constitute an absolute dictatorship of the majority' over 'all minorities in India'.[81] Nehru was chagrined that this should come from one whom he had regarded as a friend:

> This plea [against dictatorship of the majority] at last stage after breakdown talks without previous discussion [or] reference most unfair [and] unjustified.... Ever since, Cripps emphasising communal issue in old Amery manner and endeavouring divert attention from real issues .... His whole approach has been wrong and vitiated by communal outlook.[82]

In his publications Coupland maintained the pretence that Congress had rejected an offer that included full Indianization and an Executive normally functioning as a Cabinet. He, too, explains the rejection in terms of Congress determination to exercise a dictatorship of the majority. At times of world crisis even the historian must subordinate truth to propaganda.[83]

Attlee also blamed the communal problem for the mission's failure:

Cripps did all that a man could do to achieve success, but despite his great sympathy with Indian aspirations and his outstanding ability, he failed to get agreement. The old stumbling block of Hindu-Moslem antagonism could not be overcome and Gandhi, at this time, was not helpful.[84]

Indeed Attlee's position in relation to the repudiation of Cripps calls for explanation. The 1942 initiative was largely his handiwork and he was chairman of the India Committee. Yet he seems to have acquiesced in the sabotage of the Mission. He was party to Amery's cable that Cripps received on 7 April, stressing the constitutional supremacy of the Viceroy over his Council and his responsibility to the Secretary of State. On 9 April he accepted joint responsibility for the War Cabinet's demand that Cripps give an account of his proceedings in relation to paragraph (e). He concurred in Churchill's taking the chair at the India Committee on 10 April and in the meeting's endorsement of Churchill's cable rejecting the possibility of a convention limiting the Viceroy's authority and rescinding Cripps's brief to negotiate.

The pace of events between 6 and 10 April, together with the obscurity of Cripps's intentions with regard to the conventions under which the reformed Executive should operate, made it difficult for Attlee to support his Labour colleague. In the circumstances private correspondence between Cripps and Attlee was impracticable. Attlee must have noted that Cripps himself seemed to accept Linlithgow's insistence that the Viceroy could not abrogate his constitutional responsibility to the Secretary of State. He must have failed to realize that the Viceroy might *normally* operate his Council as a Cabinet without yielding his ultimate authority. It is understandable that he should have joined with his Cabinet colleagues in asking Cripps to explain his proceedings under paragraph (e). It is also understandable, in the context of confusion over this point, and in view of the unfortunate incident involving Colonel Johnson, that he should have yielded to Churchill's determination that the Viceroy's final authority must not be negotiated away. Again, in Cripps's absence Attlee was the only Labour member of the India Committee. As chairman he could scarcely resist the combined opinion of his Coalition colleagues without precipitating a dangerous split in the Cabinet. Attlee's staunch loyalty to Churchill during the war is well-known. Between 6 and 10 April Churchill applied the acid test to it. Attlee's knowledge of Cripps's activities in India was, in the end, insufficient to enable him to stand his ground against the imperialists.

V

The solution to the mystery of the Cripps Mission appears when Cripps's actions are counterpointed against, first, the forbearance, and later, the opposition, of 'Englishmen who differed from him'.

The Mission was the product of Labour pressures for an initiative to bring the Indian communities together and thereby to break a constitutional deadlock that dates from September 1939, when Britain had battened down the imperial hatches for the duration. With Churchill away in Washington, Attlee encouraged the pressures. When Churchill, Amery, and Linlithgow resisted he pilloried the imperialists for their ineptitude and proposed that an envoy be sent out 'to do in India what Durham did in Canada'.[85] Jointly with Cripps he guided a Cabinet Committee that forced the hand of his Conservative adversaries. Cripps was despatched with the brief that he had written himself. For the moment, Prime Minister, Secretary of State and Viceroy had been worsted, partly because world opinion was against them.

At first, Linlithgow gave Cripps reason to suppose that he would go to the utmost limits rather than let the Mission fail over the reconstitution of his Council. Until 6 April his opposition was mild. Cripps might well hope to satisfy him by conceding his right to choose his own ministers, and he readily agreed that the Viceroy's power to overrule them must not be abrogated.

However, Linlithgow's cable of 6 April, insisting upon the Viceroy's constitutional supremacy, gave Churchill his cue. The first sign of viceregal opposition to Cripps's negotiations led Churchill not to support but to reduce the emissary who had gone to India with a brief to negotiate. The cables that shuttled between Whitehall and New Delhi on 6 April revealed that Churchill, Amery, and Linlithgow were all opposed to any change in the conventions of the constitution. The position of Churchill and Amery in the War Cabinet was doubtless strengthened by patriotic sensitiveness over the intervention, behind Linlithgow's back but with Cripps's collusion, of an American envoy. It was also reinforced by the Labour ministers' ignorance of the exact nature of Cripps's contemplated changes in the conventions of government. Missives from the powerful triumvirate soon demonstrated to Cripps that even if the Congress accepted his 'National Government' it would be repudiated by his own countrymen. He accepted personal defeat honourably and converted it into a propaganda victory for Britain.

The allegations of the viceregal circle are misguided and unjust. On the other hand those of the Congress are substantially warranted, though if the facts had been known Cripps may have found a place in India's nationalist hagiology.

Once again Churchill had barred the road to Indian freedom. Throughout the 1930s he had fought to prevent the introduction of responsibility in the central government. In 1940 he had so watered the draft of the August offer that Congress were bound to reject it. In 1944–5 he was to obstruct Wavell's scheme for a conference that would set up an interim national government of the type that Cripps had wanted, finally allowing the new initiative only when he felt sure of its failure. His constant interventions gave the Muslim League precious time in which to substantiate its claim to separate nationhood.

The repudiation of Cripps in 1942 was one of many bricks that Churchill placed in the wall of Partition.

5
Jinnah and the Pakistan Demand

In an age sceptical of the historic role of great men there is universal agreement that Mohammad Ali Jinnah was central to the Muslim League's emergence after 1937 as the voice of a Muslim nation; to its articulation in March 1940 of the Pakistan demand for separate statehood for the Muslim majority provinces of north-western and eastern India; and to its achievement in August 1947 of the separate but truncated state of Pakistan by the Partition of India. Subcontinental judgements of Jinnah are bound to be *parti pris* and to exaggerate his individual importance. While Pakistanis generally see him as the Quaid-i-Azam, Great Leader, or father of their nation, Indians often regard him as the Lucifer who tempted his people into the unforgivable sin against their nationalist faith. Among distinguished foreign scholars, unbiased by national commitment, his stature is similarly elevated. Sir Penderel Moon has written:

There is, I believe, no historical parallel for a single individual effecting such a political revolution; and his achievement is a striking refutation of the theory that in the making of history the individual is of little or no significance. It was Mr Jinnah who created Pakistan and undoubtedly made history.[1]

Professor Lawrence Ziring believes that Jinnah's 'personality . . . made Pakistan possible' and that 'it would not have emerged without him'.[2] Sir Cyril Philips has argued that without Jinnah's leadership regionalism would probably have competed seriously with Muslim nationalism as the aim of the Muslim majority provinces.[3] Professor Nicholas Mansergh looks to Jinnah for 'the classic exposition of the two-nation theory' in his March 1940 address prefiguring the Pakistan resolution and revises sharply upwards the determining influence of the concept upon the interplay of men and events that culminated in the Partition of India.[4]

Yet the relation of Jinnah to the rise of the League and its demand and movement for Pakistan is still obscure. Eminent contemporaries were puzzled by the sources of his apparent power. For example, as last Viceroy, Lord Mountbatten thought the idea of Pakistan 'sheer madness' and wrote of Jinnah in bewilderment: 'I regard Jinnah as a psychopathic case; in fact until I had met him I would not have thought it possible that a man with such a complete lack of administrative knowledge or sense of responsibility could achieve or hold down so powerful a position.'[5] Mountbatten saw Jinnah as a leader whose 'megalomania' was so 'chronic' that he pursued his own power to the material detriment of his misguided followers.[6] British statesmen and officials and Congress leaders alike attached immense significance to vanity and pride in Jinnah's quest for Pakistan and their views continue to influence the historiography of the Partition.[7]

In a perceptive analysis Professor Khalid Bin Sayeed seeks the key to the relationship between Jinnah's personality and the Pakistan movement in the 'congruence' between the ambition of Jinnah, a domineering man whom reverses in life had made desperate, and the needs and characteristics of his people, 'a community . . . looking for a great saviour . . . who was prepared to unite the community and bring earthly glory to Islam'.[8] Nevertheless, for Sayeed 'it continues to be an enigma how these people followed a leader who was so austere and so remote from them'.[9] The link, he speculates, was 'that this power-conscious man promised to them the political power which the Qur'an had promised to them and which their forbears had wielded in India'.

Historians have also emphasized the enigmatic nature of Jinnah's 'promise'—the vagueness of the Pakistan demand and the variety of constitutional forms that Jinnah seemed willing to accept in satisfaction of it.[10] Some have sought to resolve the paradox by construing the demand as a bargaining counter, whereby Jinnah sought to enhance the power of the League and himself within a united free India.[11] Others have argued that Jinnah was 'hoist with his own petard': he fell captive to his promise of separate statehood for six provinces and was left by the Partition with the truncated state that was alone consistent with the concept of a nation defined by the religious map of the subcontinent.[12]

The following analysis seeks to clarify the relation between Jinnah and the Pakistan movement during the decade preceding Partition, in terms of both his charisma and his constitutional strategy, but not, it should be stressed, in terms of party organization and political mobilization, on which much more work remains to be done.[13]

I *Sources of Charisma*

Jinnah was born on Christmas day 1876 in a tenement house in Karachi. He was to be the eldest of seven children of a hide merchant, whose means were modest but sufficient to despatch Jinnah at the age of sixteen direct from the Sind Madrasa to London for commercial experience. The precocious youth instead registered at Lincoln's Inn and as an exemplary pupil qualified for the Bar. During his short four-year absence his mother and his child-wife died and his father suffered financial ruin. He chose to make his way at the Bombay Bar. After three briefless and penurious years his powers of application, analysis, and advocacy brought him rapid success and wealth, the springboard to his political career. By the age of forty he had been prominent in the Indian National Congress, toured Europe with Gokhale, represented the Muslims of Bombay in the Imperial Legislative Council, and acted as principal negotiator of the Lucknow Pact for Congress–Muslim League unity. When Edwin Montagu visited India in 1917 he recorded meeting this 'young, perfectly mannered, impressive-looking . . . very clever man', who, 'armed to the teeth with dialectics' tied the Viceroy up in verbal knots.[14]

By the standards of his gilded youth the next twenty years of Jinnah's life were leaden. Poised to scale political heights he fell and suffered disappointment. Gandhi's Congress–Khilafat non-cooperation movement, which was inimical to his constitutionalist style, was partly responsible for his eclipse, but perhaps as important was the shift that the dyarchical provincial councils effected in Muslim politics. Given the realities of office and patronage the Punjab Unionist Party became the powerhouse of Muslim policy.[15] Confronted with Congress initiatives to inherit the central government of India, the All-India Muslim Conference, led from the Punjab by Mian Fazl-i-Husain, espoused schemes for entrenching the Muslims in quasi-sovereign provinces, yielding to a federal centre only such powers as they chose and given effective safeguards for Muslim interests. Jinnah remained a leader of the League and a member of the Central Legislature but the action had moved elsewhere. In 1928 he was worsted by the forces of Hindu orthodoxy when he sought accommodation with Congress on an all-parties constitutional scheme. At the Round Table Conference he was suspected by the dominant Muslim delegates as an unreliable conciliator, and he seemed to speak for no one but himself. For three or four years he turned his back on India and tried to settle in London, living in Hampstead and practising at the Privy Council Bar. When he returned to India in 1936 to set up the League's Parliamentary Board to contest the 1936 elections under the India Act of 1935's provisions for provincial autonomy, he was shunned by the Punjab Unionists. He remained hopeful of achieving an all-India Hindu–Muslim settlement under a Congress–League *rapprochement* until, after its electoral triumph, Congress made it apparent that its terms were the League's capitulation.[16]

Jinnah's personality and experience disposed him to feel bitterly the Congress denial of the Muslims' political identity. Lacking inherited status, from an early age his place in the world had rested wholly upon his own efforts. By observing a regimen of discipline and self-denial he had earned a place of dignity in Indian politics. The single-minded pursuit of professional and political success left him little opportunity to cultivate a private life that might mitigate the sense of public rejection. The exaggerated refinement of the English dress and personal style that he adopted seem more like carapaces than indulgences. The political reverses of middle-age were unrelieved by any of the usual pleasures of personal or domestic life. His marriage at the age of forty-two to the eighteen-year-old daughter of a Parsi friend had, after several unhappy years, finally collapsed in 1928. Her death soon afterwards left him bereaved and with a sense of guilt. For the rest of his life his sole companion was his loyal sister Fatima, who, from living with it daily, came to share his acute sense of persecution.[17]

Like Jinnah's personal standing the status that the Muslims had achieved by 1937 had been hard won. Late-comers to western education, official employment and party politics, they had, as collaborators of the British Raj, advanced rapidly in the twentieth century. In the United Provinces they had consolidated their tenure of land and won weightage well beyond their numbers in councils and government service.[18] Since the first elections to the Montford councils they had succeeded to decades of Congress ascendancy in Bengal and won office in Punjab. The All-India Muslim Conference had defended separate electorates in both majority provinces and applied a strategy of 'provincial balance' to secure the separation of Sind from Bombay and its elevation, together with that of the North-West Frontier Province, to full provincial status. In 1936, the last year of his life, Fazl-i-Husain could reflect that the Muslim position was now 'adequately safeguarded'.[19] The sense of achieved security owed much to checks that the India Act of 1935 seemed to place on the power of the Congress, for in its contemplated all-India federation a third of the seats were reserved to the Muslims and a third to nominees of the Indian princes. The emergence of Congress dominance in 1937 changed all that.

In March 1937, when Nehru remarked that the Congress and the Raj were the only two parties in India, Jinnah replied to the rebuff by claiming the Muslim League as a third, a rightful 'equal partner' of the Congress.[20] It was the Muslims of the Congress provinces who first apprehended the dangers of Hindu ascendancy under a Congress Raj and reacted with a sense of persecution.[21] Muslim grandees in the United Provinces grew anxious when Congress denied them a share in government and threatened their culture, property and prospects of public employment.[22] In Muslim minority provinces it seemed that under responsible government the Congress could withhold their participation in office permanently. In Muslim majority provinces Congress sought power through alignments with Muslim factions. Rajendra Prasad commented:

> The attempt of our party in most [of these] provinces has constantly been to win over members of the government party and thus secure a majority for itself, so that it may form a ministry. In effect its action has been not so much to consider the criticised government measures on their merit and secure the adoption of its own programme by the government, but to try somehow or other to oust the party in power. The result ... has been to create much bitterness against the Congress. ...[23]

At the all-India level the Congress High Command pursued its advantage by pressing the princes to fill their federal seats by election instead of nomination, which would open the prospect of sufficient Congress victories to destroy the statutory check upon its power.[24] Jinnah became convinced that parliamentary government would mean Congress 'totalitarianism' in India.[25] The only safeguard of equal rights to India's Muslims lay in their achievement of equality of power through their solidarity within the All-India Muslim League. Under his organization the League's membership grew from a few thousand to several hundred thousand in 1937–8.

Jinnah harped on the theme of equality. At the League's annual session at Lucknow in October 1937 he insisted that 'an honourable settlement can only be achieved between equals'.[26] He demanded of Nehru that Congress must recognize the League 'on a footing of perfect equality'.[27] He internalized the Muslims' sense of 'suffering and sacrifice' from the 'fire of persecution'. He expressed himself with personal conviction: 'I have got as much right to share in the government of this country as any Hindu'; and 'I must have [an] equal real and effective share in the power'.[28] The appeal was underpinned by an assertion that Islamic society was based on the equality of man.[29]

The essential link between Jinnah's leadership and the emergence of a Muslim national consciousness was that Jinnah personified the sense of persecution felt by Muslims—more precisely, Urdu-speaking Muslims—at the Congress denial of their achieved status. The widespread assumption that vanity, pride, ambition and megalomania were the dominant facets of his personality has masked it. In a similar way, the extension of impressions of his personality to generalizations about his political style has exaggerated the intellectual distance between the leader and his followers, obscuring the doctrinal cut and thrust from which emerged the constitutional strategy that would afford a refuge from persecution.

II *From Karachi to Lahore*

Almost all who observed Jinnah described him as reserved, remote, aloof and, above all, lonely. His remoteness in later life was caused partly by his chronic bronchial infection, which had probably appeared in 1936,[30] and from July 1943 partly by the precautionary measures of up to three official bodyguards who were assigned to him after he was attacked by an assassin. But clearly he did not enjoy physical contact and kept the world at a distance. The famous monocle and frequent changes of clothing seem, like his aversion to shaking hands and travelling by train unless in a first class coupé, expressions of immaculacy. When Sir Stafford Cripps visited him in December 1939 he noted: 'Altogether he gave me the impression of an intensely lonely man in perpetual conflict with himself and with no-one in whom he could confide or who could give him reliable advice, but he put his case with great ability and clarity.'[31] In January 1942 Sir Reginald Coupland visited him at his new house on Malabar Hill and was struck by the 'great forensic ability . . . admirable lucidity . . . and clear conclusions' of this 'very able advocate'.[32] His notes suggest Jinnah's clinical detachment and self-sufficiency, living and working in a mansion with 'beautiful rooms, lavishly furnished, and a most attractive curving marble terrace, with lawn beneath it sloping to a belt of trees with a gap in it through which the sea'. Jinnah plied him with League literature, 'largely reprints of his own speeches'. A few weeks later Coupland described Jinnah as 'virtually dictator' of the League,[33] a judgement that A. V. Alexander echoed at the time of the Cabinet Mission: 'Mr Jinnah, the so-called Man of Destiny of the Muslim League [is] a clever lawyer ... and I should think in his own way pretty near to being a complete dictator'.[34] Mountbatten believed that 'the only adviser that Jinnah listens to is Jinnah'.[35]

Yet in the crucial eighteen months preceding the proclamation of the Pakistan demand at Lahore Jinnah's role in the formation and expression of constitutional thought and strategy was certainly not that of an isolated, lonely and self-sufficient leader.

In October 1938 Jinnah returned to a king's welcome in the city of his birth, Karachi, for a conference of the Sind branch of the All-India Muslim League.[36] He rode from the railway station in an open limousine at the head of a procession three miles long. Some 20,000 delegates were assembled, among them the provincial premiers Sir Sikandar Hayat Khan (Punjab) and Sir Fazlul Haq (Bengal), the U.P. leaders Liaqat Ali Khan (Secretary of the League), the Raja of Mahmudabad and Choudhry Khaliquzzaman, the old Khilafat leader Shaukat Ali, and prominent Sindhis. The main object of the Sindhis in organizing the conference was to bring to bear upon the province's faction-ridden Muslim establishment the unifying influence of the national body. The benefits of the separation from Bombay of this majority province had been squandered by the recourse of its Muslim premiers to Hindus for their survival. In July 1937 M. H. Gazdar (a future mayor of Karachi) had written to Jinnah in disgust at the state of Sind politics and proposed the creation of an independent Muslim state comprising the four north-western provinces.[37] The initiator and reception committee chairman of the conference was Sir Abdoola Haroon, a self-made merchant and industrialist prince of Karachi, campaigner for the separation of Sind, member of the Central Legislature (1926–42), founder of the Sind United Party on the model of the Punjab Unionists, and member of the League's Working Committee.[38] In his opening address he focused attention upon the need for an all-India Hindu–Muslim settlement, failing which Muslims may need 'to seek their salvation in their own way in an independent federation of Muslim states', in the division of Hindu India and Muslim India 'under separate federations'.[39]

Haroon was moving further and faster towards a separatist objective than Jinnah, who emphasized the primary need to consolidate Muslims to resist Congress oppression. Fourteen months later Jinnah was still professing to be as much an Indian nationalist as Nehru, and in January 1940 he could still write of India as the 'common motherland' of Muslims and Hindus.[40] He was disquieted when Haroon incorporated the goal of an independent Muslim state in a resolution:

The Sindh Provincial Muslim League Conference considers it absolutely essential in the interests of an abiding peace of the vast Indian continent and in the interests of unhampered cultural development, the economic and social betterment and political self-determination of the two nations, known as Hindus and Muslims, that India may be divided into federations, namely, the federation of Muslim States and the federation of non-Muslim States. This conference therefore recommends to the All-India Muslim League to devise a scheme of constitution under which Muslim-majority-provinces Muslim Indian States and areas inhabited by a majority of Muslims may attain full independence in the form of a federation of their own . . . .[41]

Jinnah is reported to have entered a caveat: 'The Government is still in the hands of the British. Let us not forget it. You must see ahead and work for the ideal that you think will arise 25 years hence.'[42] Next day, with his tacit consent, Haroon's draft was passed thus modified:

This conference considers it absolutely essential, in the interests of an abiding peace of the vast Indian continent and in the interests of unhampered cultural development, the economic and social betterment and political self-determination of the two nations, known as Hindus and Muslims, to recommend to the All-India Muslim League to review and revise the entire conception of what should be the suitable constitution for India which will secure honourable and legitimate status to them.[43]

While the two nations theory now became the League's creed it was clearly not synonymous with separatism. Even the mover of Haroon's original resolution, Shaikh Abdul Majid, expected that the Hindu and Muslim federations would be linked by a common centre for foreign affairs, defence and the settlement of disputes.[44] Clearly, too, Jinnah was drawn this far by the initiative of the Sindhis and the need to accommodate policy to it in the interests of solidarity.

Jinnah was unwell during the following weeks and made no speeches until 26 December at the League's annual session at Patna, when he spoke impromptu. He then observed the awakening of a 'national consciousness among the Muslims' comparable to that of the Hindus, but warned that a 'national self and national individuality' had yet to be developed.[45] The session authorized him to explore suitable constitutional alternatives to the 1935 Act,[46] and the following March the Working Committee set up a committee to examine those that had already appeared and others that might emerge.[47] Jinnah was to head the committee and eight others, including Haroon, Liaqat, Sikandar, Nazimuddin (Bengal), and Aurangzeb Khan (N.W.F.P.) were empanelled. Next month Jinnah intimated that several schemes were before the committee, including one for dividing the country into Hindu and Muslim India. In fact the committee never met and the initiative remained in Haroon's hands.

During the interim between the Karachi and Patna conferences Haroon took a number of steps to advance the general cause of a separate federation of Muslim provinces and states. His resolve was strengthened by Congress activities in the states towards the end of the year.[48] He failed in an attempt to enlist the support of the Aga Khan.[49] However, the Council of the League now established a Foreign and Inland Deputations subcommittee, and Haroon became its chairman. It was to send deputations abroad, to explain the views of Muslim India and counter Congress allegations that the Muslims were reactionary and unpatriotic, and from the Muslim majority to the minority provinces, to consolidate links between their organizations.[50] The committee performed some of the functions appropriate to offices for foreign affairs and propaganda. Haroon also involved it in planning when he asked Dr Syed Abdul Latif to meet it in Lahore in January 1939 to discuss his ideas for the recognition of the two nations by the redistribution of India into cultural zones.[51] Though Latif's approach was to accommodate the two nations within a 'common motherland' under a single federal authority, rather than to pursue the separate federations that he himself favoured, Haroon advanced Rs 2000 for the publication and foreign distribution of Latif's scheme in expanded booklet form.[52] The circulation of Latif's views in 1938–9, in pamphlets, newspapers and the booklet, stimulated controversy over the constitutional future of Muslim India.

Much of the constitutional planning occurred in the Punjab, where there was already a significant legacy of separatist thought. As president of the League in 1930 the philosopher-poet of Lahore, Sir Muhammad Iqbal, had called for the amalgamation of the four northwestern provinces, less some non-Muslim districts, into 'a Muslim India within India'.[53] As the religious units of India had never been inclined to sacrifice their individualities in a larger whole 'the unity of an Indian nation must be sought, not in negation, but in mutual harmony and co-operation'. The 'effective principle of co-operation' in India was the recognition of 'homelands' in which the Muslim might enjoy 'full and free development on the lines of his own culture and tradition'. In 1933 the Cambridge student Rahmat Ali, the Punjabi coiner of the name 'Pakistan', proposed the separation from India of a Muslim state embracing the four provinces and Kashmir, and soon afterwards launched the Pakistan National Movement.[54] During the year preceding his death in April 1938 Iqbal's opposition to a single Indian federation had hardened and he had urged Jinnah to demand one or more separate Muslim states, though he was silent as to their relations with the rest of India.[55]

In March 1939 the fact that the League Working Committee had Latif's scheme before it provoked Ahmad Bashir, secretary of the youthful and intellectual Pakistan Majlis, Lahore, to petition Jinnah, Liaqat, Haroon, Fazlul Haq and Sikandar.[56] Latif's scheme would prejudice the political and economic integrity of Pakistan by casting the eastern tracts of the Punjab and Kashmir into a Hindu–Sikh zone:

> As the scheme is likely to influence the natural boundaries of Pakistan I feel the interest of Pakistan and the Movement started towards the creation of an independent state in the North-West of India comprising the whole of the Punjab, Kashmir, the North Western Frontier Province, Sind and Baluchistan would materially suffer if the Cultural Zones Scheme is extended towards the North West of India.... The Pakistan mind is slowly believing in its physical whole and any attempt to disintegrate this natural geographical identity will certainly be detrimental to the cause of Muslim India.[57]

The references to the Pakistan Movement and the claim to the full four north-western provinces plus Kashmir reveal the influence of Rahmat Ali on the Pakistan Majlis but they also drew on Iqbal's ideas. The Majlis's full title, 'Majlis-i-Kabir Pakistan, Lahore', reflected its reverence for the saintly poet who was also the prophet of Indian unity. In the spirit of Iqbal, Ahmad Bashir wrote to Jinnah: 'Nobody questions India's unity but how that unity can be achieved is a matter that deserves special attention of all the parties concerned. It is a matter... [that] must be given precedence to everything else.'[58] The recognition of 'separate homelands by dividing India into autonomous homogeneous states' was 'the one and the only way to India's unity'. Ahmad Bashir was to supply Jinnah with ringing passages for his inspiring Lahore presidential address.[59]

In summer 1939 the alternatives open to the League were clarified by Sikandar's formulation of a scheme for a loose all-India federation of zones including provinces and states,[60] and its rejection first by

Ahmad Bashir[61] and then by scholars at Aligarh. The latter favoured the division of British India into 'three wholly independent and sovereign states'.[62] Two Aligarh authors, Professor Syed Zafarul Hasan and Dr M. A. H. Qadri, insisted that the Muslims of India, 'a nation by themselves', must not be 'enslaved into a single all-India federation with an overwhelming Hindu majority in the Centre'. The three sovereign states of British India would be North-West India or Pakistan, Bengal, and Hindustan. The principalities within these states or exclusively on the frontier of one of them would be attached automatically, while those adjoining more than one state might choose their attachment. But Hyderabad must recover Berar and the Karnatic and become a fourth sovereign state, 'the southern wing of Muslim India'. Pakistan would include the four north-western provinces, Kashmir and other adjacent states. Bengal would embrace the existing province less the districts of Howrah, Midnapur and Darjeeling, but plus the districts of Purnea (in Bihar) and Syhlet (in Assam). Both Pakistan and Bengal would be Muslim states. Hindustan would comprise the rest of India but within it two new autonomous provinces—Delhi and Malabar—should be formed, with strong Muslim minorities. The three states would have separate treaties of alliance with Britain and should join together in a defensive and offensive alliance. The Hasan–Qadri scheme was commended warmly by eight Aligarh scholars who, at the same time, deplored Latif's proposals.[63] The scholars claimed to have discussed 'the Aligarh scheme' with its authors in principle and detail and were convinced that it went as far as possible to meet the just claims of the 'two nations'.

By September 1939, when Britain shelved the paper federation of the 1935 Act, Muslim constitutional thought was certainly turning against the federal principle, even as expressed in the zonal schemes of Latif and Sikandar. A year after the adoption at Karachi of the two nations theory its practical application was a live issue. On 18 October, when Lord Linlithgow spoke of India's destiny in terms of unity,[64] Ahmad Bashir protested to Jinnah at his blunt rejection of 'the national demand of the Muslims regarding the recognition of their separate national status'.[65] Next month the Aligarh group was provoked when Gandhi attacked the theory of separate Muslim nationhood.[66] On 15 November Professor Hasan, together with Dr Zaki Uddin and Dr Burhan Ahmad (two of the eight who commended the Aligarh scheme), and Ubaid Ullah Durrani, petitioned Jinnah at length upon the matter. They concluded: 'Neither the fear of British-

bayonets nor the prospects of a bloody civil war can discourage [the Muslims] in their will to achieve free Muslim states in those parts of India where they are in majority.'[67] Soon afterwards the several Muslim authors of constitutional plans met for ten days 'to evolve a consolidated scheme', which they sent to Jinnah confidentially.[68] This 'fresh plan on the basis that Moslems are a separate Nation' so constituted Muslim zones in the north and the east as to include seventy-two per cent of the total Muslim population of India. A Delhi province was added to the northern zone and all of Assam to the eastern. A third of the land mass of India was claimed.

On 1 February 1940 Haroon presided at New Delhi over a joint meeting of his Foreign Committee and the authors of schemes. It resolved to recommend that the Working Committee 'state its mind in unequivocal language with regard to the future of the Indian Moslem Nation'.[69] India's Muslims were a separate nation entitled to self-determination. In order to make that right effective 'the Moslems shall have separate National Home in the shape of an autonomous state'. The meeting's resolutions were sent to Liaqat (as League Secretary) and to Jinnah on 2 February. Two days later the Working Committee adopted the nub of them[70] which was, of course, expressed in the Lahore resolution's call for independent Muslim states in the north-western and eastern zones of India.[71]

The Lahore expression of the two nations theory as a demand for separate Muslim statehood was thus the culmination of eighteen months of controversy. The variety of its analogues goes far to explain the vagueness of the resolution over the delineation of the contiguous Muslim regions of north-western and eastern India and the contemplated relations between them. The notoriously obscure provision for 'territorial readjustments' was clearly a hold-all for additions to, as well as reductions of, existing provinces.[72] Doubts about the desirable relations between the regions are revealed by the authorization of the Working Committee to frame a scheme providing 'for the assumption finally, by the respective regions, of all powers' such as 'defence, external affairs, communications, customs and such other matters as may be necessary'. Again, 'finally' suggests an antithesis to an interim period of co-ordination by a common authority, such, perhaps, as the resolution's seconder, Khaliquzzaman, favoured.[73] However, it is clear that by its separatist emphasis the resolution marked the firm rejection of Sikandar's view that Muslim India's national destiny might be achieved within an all-India federation. He indeed acknowledged that his own preferred resolution was lost.[74] One possibility left open was that of an independent Bengal nation, the destiny most favoured by the resolution's proposer, Fazlul Haq.[75]

No more than the resolution itself was Jinnah's Lahore address the achievement of the Quaid unaided. The most remembered passages in his speech were drawn essentially unchanged from the representations of Ahmad Bashir and the Aligarh group. After roundly condemning the 1935 Act as unsuitable to India he followed Hasan and Qadri in quoting for criticism a London *Times* leader of 1 April 1937 that had consigned the difference between Hindus and Muslims to the realm of transient 'superstition', no real impediment to the emergence of a single nation. He then took his refutation of British views from Ahmad Bashir's condemnation of Linlithgow's statement of 18 October 1939:

Ahmad Bashir
His Excellency the Viceroy thinks that this unity can be achieved with the working of the constitution as envisaged in Government of India Act, 1935. He hopes that the passage of time will harmonise the inconsistent elements in India. May be he holds this view with sincerity, but it is in flagrant disregard to the past history of the sub-continent as well as to the Islamic conception of society. The nationalities which, notwithstanding thousand years of close contact, are as divergent as ever, can never be expected to transform into one nationality merely by being subject to the same constitution. What the *Unitary* Government in India has failed to bring about can not be achieved by the imposition of the *Federal* Government.

It is, however, satisfying to note that His Excellency the Viceroy and the Secretary of State along with the House of Lords are fully alive to the fundamental differences between the peoples of the Indian continent. Yet unfortunately, they are unwilling to recognise their separate national status. It is more than truism to say that the Hindus and Muslims represent two distinct nationalities. Therefore, any attempt to dissolve their present differences which disregards this vital fact is doomed to precipitate. Hindu–Muslim problem is not an intercommunal issue and will never be solved on intercommunal lines. It is manifestly an international problem and therefore it must be treated as such. It will submit itself to a permanent solution on that basis alone. Any constitution be it in the form of Dominion Status or even 'Complete Independence', which disregards this basic truth, while destructive for the Muslims cannot but be harmful to the British and Hindus.

If the British Government is really serious and sincere in bringing about peace in the sub-continent, it should not only appreciate the difference but also allow the two nationalities separate homelands by dividing India into autonomous homogeneous states. These states shall not be antagonistic to each other, they on the other hand, will be friendly and sympathetic to one another; and by an international pact of mutual goodwill and assistance they can be just as united and harmonious as today are France and Great Britain. This is the one and the only way to India's Unity.

We are confident that it shall ensure eternal harmony, calm and friendliness between the Hindus and Muslims and materially accelerate the progress of the sub-continent.

If this method for the salavation of India's problems is not adopted the fate of the Muslims as a nation is sealed in India and no revolution of stars and no rotation of the earth would resuscitate them.

Jinnah
So according to the London Times the only difficulties are superstitions. These fundamental and deep-rooted differences, spiritual, economic, cultural, social and political have been euphemised as mere 'superstitions'. But surely, it is flagrant disregard of the past history of the subcontinent of India as well as the fundamental Islamic conception of society *vis-à-vis* that of Hinduism to characterise them as mere 'superstitions'. Notwithstanding thousand years of close contact, nationalities which are as divergent today as ever, cannot at any time be expected to transform themselves into one nation merely by means of subjecting them to a democratic constitution and holding them forcibly together by unnatural and artificial methods of British Parliamentary Statutes. What the unitary government of India for 150 years had failed to achieve, cannot be realised by the imposition of a central federal government. It is inconceivable that the fiat or the writ of a government so constituted can ever command a willing and loyal obedience throughout the subcontinent by various nationalities except by means of armed force behind it.

The problem in India is not of an intercommunal but manifestly of an international character and it must be treated as such. So long as this basic and fundamental truth is not realised, any constitution that may be built will result in disaster and will prove destructive and harmful not only to the Mussalmans, but also to the British and Hindus. If the British Government are really in earnest and sincere to secure peace and happiness of the people of this subcontinent, the only course open to us all is to allow the major nations separate homelands by dividing India into 'autonomous national states'. There is no reason why these States should be antagonistic to each other. On the other hand the rivalry and the natural desire and efforts on the part of the one to dominate the social order and establish political supremacy over the other in the government of the country, will disappear. It will lead more towards natural good-will by international pacts between them, and they can live in complete harmony with their neighbours. This will lead further to a friendly settlement all the more easily with regard to minorities by reciprocal arrangements and adjustments between the Muslim India and the Hindu India, which will far more adequately and effectively safeguard the rights and interests of Muslims and various other minorities.

The Ahmad Bashir text was thus the source of Jinnah's 'quiet assertion' of the international status of the Indian problem that Mansergh has held to be 'the essence of his case'.[76] Jinnah notably dropped the emphasis (following Iqbal) upon present division as 'the only way to India's Unity' in future.[77] He continued by drawing upon the Aligarh petition of 15 November 1939 to fill out the rhetoric of his 'classic exposition of the two-nation theory'. Again, where the scholars' target was specifically Gandhi, Jinnah's is more generally the Hindus:

Aligarh scholars
It is extremely difficult to explain Mr. Gandhi failing to appreciate and understand the real nature of Islam and Hinduism. Islam as well as Hinduism are not only religions in stricter sense of the word, but are in reality different and distinct social orders governing practically every individual and social aspect of their adherents. It should be clear beyond doubt that Hindus and Muslims cannot evolve a common nationality. A few following arguments must convince Mr. Gandhi on this issue.
1. That the Hindus and Muslims belong to two different cultures. They have totally different religious philosophies, social customs, laws and literature. They neither inter-marry nor inter-dine together and, indeed, belong to two different civilizations which are in many aspects based on conflicting ideas and conceptions....
2. That the Hindus and Muslims drive [*sic*] their inspiration from different sources of history. They have different epics, different heroes and different episodes. Very often a hero of one is a foe of the other and likewise, their victories and defeats overlap....

The above facts must convince every body that all those ties which hold people together as one social unit (Nation) are entirely wanting in the case of Hindus and Muslims of India. Nor there is any possibility of their ever being created here.

Mr. Gandhi and other Congress leaders stress the significance of a common country and cite the examples of Egypt, Turkey and Persia. They only state a half truth in this argument. Egypt, Turkey and Persia are wholly Muslim countries and the Muslims there are naturally free to determine their own future.

A discontent is bound to occur wherever two different people are yoked under a single state one as minority and the other as majority. A number of instances like those of Great Britain and Ireland, Czechoslovakia and Poland can exemplify the above. Further it is also too well known that many Geographical tracts which otherwise should have been called as one country, much smaller than the Indian sub-continent have been divided into as many states as are the nations inhabiting them. The Balkan Peninsula comprises of as many as eight sovereign states. The Iberian Peninsula is also likewise divided between the Portuguese and the Spaniards.

Mr. Gandhi stresses the historical unity of India even during the days of Muslim kings. We cannot accept his contention. No student of history can deny the fact that all along the last 12 hundred years India has always been divided into a Hindu India and a Muslim India. The extent of one or the other might have been varying from time to time, but the fact remains untarnished that Hindu and Muslim Indias have always been co-existing. The present unity of India dates back only to the British conquest....

We want to assure Mr. Gandhi that the ideal of having free sovereign Muslim states in India which now inspires a very large number of Muslims is not actuated by a spirit of hatred or revenge. It is initiated by an earnest desire of solving Hindu Muslim problem on an equitable basis and epitomises the natural desire of Muslims of India to determine their future independently in the light of their own cultures and history.

Jinnah
It is extremely difficult to appreciate why our Hindu friends fail to understand the real nature of Islam and Hinduism. They are not religions in the strict sense of the word, but are, in fact, different and distinct social orders and it is a dream that the Hindus and Muslims can ever evolve a common nationality, and this misconception of one Indian nation has gone far beyond the limits and is the cause of most of our troubles and will lead India to destruction if we fail to revise our notions in time. The Hindus and Muslims belong to two different religious philosophies, social customs, and literature. They neither intermarry, nor interdine together and indeed they belong to two different civilisations which are based mainly on conflicting ideas and conceptions. Their aspects on life and of life are different. It is quite clear that Hindus and Mussalmans drive [sic] their inspiration from different sources of history. They have different epics, their heroes are different, and they have different episodes. Very often the hero of one is a foe of the other and likewise their victories and defeats overlap. To yoke together two such nations under a single state, one as a numerical minority and the other as a majority, must lead to growing discontent and final destruction of any fabric that may be so built up for the government of such a state.

History has presented to us many examples such as the Union of Great Britain and Ireland, of Czechoslovakia and Poland. History has also shown to us many geographical tracts, much smaller than the subcontinent of India, which otherwise might have been called one country but which have been divided into as many states as there are nations inhabiting them. Balkan Peninsula comprises as many as 7 or 8 sovereign states. Likewise, the Portuguese and the Spanish stand divided in the Iberian Peninsula. Whereas under the plea of unity of India and one nation, which does not exist, it is sought to pursue here the line of one Central Government when, we know that the history of the last 12 hundred years, has failed to achieve unity and has witnessed during the ages, India always divided into Hindu India and Muslim India. The present artificial unity of India dates back only to the British conquest and is maintained by the British bayonet, but the termination of the British regime, which is implicit in the recent declaration of His Majesty's Government, will be the herald of the entire break-up with worse disaster than has ever taken place during the last one thousand years under the Muslims.

Jinnah was carried to Karachi on the shoulders of his fellow Sindhis and soared to Lahore on the wings of young intellectuals of the city and scholars of Aligarh. The Great Leader who personified Muslim apprehensions synthesized plans to assuage them in acceptable formulations of Muslim nationalism (the two nations theory) and separatism (the Pakistan demand).

III *The Meaning of 'Two Nations'*

In October 1939, when Lord Linlithgow called Jinnah into discussions with the Congress leaders about participation in government during the war, he was certainly recognizing him as the Muslim leader *par excellence*.[78] But in large measure Jinnah had earned the status by the solidarity that the League had then achieved. In May 1939 Sikandar, the senior Muslim premier, had observed publicly that Jinnah had answered for Muslims the question: 'Are we content to lose our identity and to be relegated to the position of political pariahs?'[79] Jinnah's mobilization of the League in reaction to Congress 'totalitarianism' under the 1935 Act had made it the voice of the putative nation. In December 1939 Liaqat estimated that it had over three million two anna members. In the early war-time negotiations Jinnah could, pursuant to the two nations theory, make acceptance of the League's status as sole Muslim spokesman the precondition of co-operation with government or Congress, thereby outflanking dissidents (be they even premiers) by appeals to the national will. It was another corollary of his theory that as one of the two nations Muslim India must be treated as the co-equal of Hindu or Congress India. In consequence, the League called for the right to consultation prior to any British statement about India's constitutional future and to veto any scheme. By November, Rajendra Prasad (now Congress President) shrewdly perceived that Jinnah's insistence upon the League's equality with Congress would mean not only 'equality in the matter of negotiations' but also 'division of power in equal shares between the Congress and the League or between Hindus and Muslims, irrespective of population or any other consideration'.[80]

The meaning of the two nations theory and its implications for Jinnah's leadership became manifest in League Working Committee resolutions in June 1940. In any war-time reconstruction of the central or provincial governments the League must receive half of the seats (more if the Congress was non-cooperating), Jinnah alone might negotiate with Viceroy or Congress, and without his consent no League member might serve on war committees.[81] The resolutions were a rebuff for Sikandar, who, appalled at the grave implications for India of the allies' defeats in Europe, was negotiating with Congress leaders for a constitutional settlement.[82] In August a British statement, effectively according the Muslims a veto on any constitutional scheme, seemed to remove the danger of a Hindu raj.[83] Here was a major victory for the two nations theory. Another was soon to follow.

Leading Muslim politicians, including the premiers, were now prepared to join war committees on a basis short of parity. By so doing they would, in effect, be compromising the cause of Muslim equality embodied in the two nations theory. In summer 1941 Jinnah brought the theory to bear in order to force their resignations from the Viceroy's Defence Council. That this was no mere exercise of personal power but rather the execution of essential League policy is revealed by Liaqat's advice to Jinnah a month before the Working Committee met to consider the matter. Liaqat advised that Jinnah's condemnation of the collaborators had 'given expression to the feelings of a vast majority of Musalmans on the subject'.[84] The question now was 'whether the disciplinary action . . . should be taken by you or by the Working Committee and the Council' (an elected body of 465 members). Liaqat strongly advised the latter course:

Let us put up an imposing show and I think the people will appreciate [it] if the Council is given an opportunity of expressing its views on the conduct of those who have let down the League. . . . Let it not be said that the decision is of only one individual or a few persons. Let the whole Council which is the most representative body of the League give its verdict and I have no doubt as to what the verdict will be. . . .

On 24 August the Working Committee demanded the collaborators' resignations from the Defence Council and expelled from the League those who resisted the verdict. The Council did not meet to ratify the action for two months but its attitude was not in doubt. Jinnah was, of course, aware of allegations that he was a dictator.[85] The two nations theory enabled him plausibly to brand as 'traitors' Muslims who collaborated with the Raj on a basis short of parity. As national leader he saw it as his duty to identify their 'mistakes', leaving the Working Committee and the Council to determine their punishment.[86]

By applying the theory vigorously Jinnah engineered the nationalization of Muslim politics throughout the war. The theory's meaning was revealed most dramatically at Simla in June 1945, when Jinnah demanded not only Hindu–Muslim parity in the Viceroy's executive but also that all the Muslim members must be League nominees. The demand destroyed Lord Wavell's attempt to reconstruct his government on the basis of party representation.

IV *Defining 'Pakistan'*

In February 1941 Jinnah explained the meaning of 'Pakistan', for the term had not been used at Lahore:

> Some confusion prevails in the minds of some individuals in regard to the use of the word 'Pakistan'. This word has become synonymous with the Lahore resolution owing to the fact that it is a convenient and compendious method of describing [it].... For this reason the British and Indian newspapers generally have adopted the word 'Pakistan' to describe the Moslem demand as embodied in the Lahore resolution. I really see no objection to it....[87]

But the resolution was obscure on the demarcation of the Pakistan regions, their relation to each other, and any interim constitutional rearrangement prior to their 'finally' assuming such powers as defence, foreign affairs, communications and customs. While Jinnah demanded parity as the basis of participation in government, the vagueness of 'Pakistan' was such as to make impracticable its acceptance by the Raj, a precondition of co-operation. He did, however, insist that no constitutional scheme that was inconsistent with its eventual achievement must be imposed. The 'Pakistan' demand meant that Muslim India's right to national self-determination must not be transgressed, not that separate statehood must be embodied in a constitutional settlement. Jinnah drew the distinction explicitly in his speeches.[88] The diversity of the schemes embodying 'Pakistan' that were extant in March 1940 helps to explain the obscurity of the

Lahore resolution. Any precise scheme must surely divide the League. However, the resolution did provide for the Working Committee to prepare a particular scheme. Haroon's Foreign Committee seems to have continued to discharge the primary planning function.

In February 1941 a scheme recommended by the Haroon committee was leaked to the press.[89] Consistently with the direction pursued by the Aligarh scholars and the assemblage of authors during winter 1939–40, it delineated sovereign Muslim states: the four north-western provinces plus a Delhi province; and Bengal (save Bankura and Midnapur districts) plus Assam. The principalities adjoining them might federate with them, and Hyderabad would become a separate sovereign state. For a transitional period the four powers listed at Lahore for assumption finally by the regions would be exercised by a co-ordinating central agency. Jinnah denied that the Working Committee had adopted the scheme and on 22 February it merely reaffirmed the Lahore resolution. The main effect of the leakage was to draw from Sikandar a long, reasoned denunciation of 'Pakistan', if it meant separatism.[90]

In his presidential address to the League's session at Madras in April 1941 Jinnah emphasized the goal of 'completely Independent States in the North-Western and Eastern Zones of India, with full control of Defence, Foreign Affairs, Communications, Customs, Currency, Exchange etc.'[91] The League would 'never agree' to an all-India constitution 'with one Government at the Centre'. As if to suggest that the two nations theory did not restrict future development to the emergence of only two states he explained that in Hindu India there was a Dravidian nation, Dravidistan, to which the Muslims would stretch their 'hands of friendship'. In amplification of this trend in his thinking he told the Governor of Madras that he envisaged four regions—Dravidistan, Hindustan, Bengalistan, and the north-west Muslim provinces.[92] They would be separate self-governing dominions, each with its own governor-general controlling its foreign affairs and defence and responsible to the British parliament through the secretary of state. Here was a scheme for subordinate dominions, with the princely states joining them and remaining apart under a Crown Representative. It bore some resemblance to Haroon's leaked scheme.

In February 1942 Khaliquzzaman explained a similar proposal to Coupland:

The Moslem demand is that Britain, after the war, should by Act of Parliament, establish the zonal system, before considering further Swaraj. British control would be still required at the Centre—apparently for an indefinite period—since Defence and Foreign Policy (which is practically all the Centre would deal with) should still be in British hands. The zones would have fiscal autonomy. If they couldn't agree on tariff policy, the British at the Centre would settle it. Pakistan, moreover, would require British aid and capital for its development before it would be able to stand alone.[93]

Khaliquzzaman seemed to be saying that in the event of a complete British withdrawal the Muslims would accept nothing short of sovereign Pakistan; but that they would welcome a protracted British presence—in effect, Indian unity under the Crown, with the sub-national zones standing as recognition of Muslim nationhood. Unlike Jinnah he was opposed to the cession of the non-Muslim districts of Punjab (Ambala division) and Bengal (Burdwan division).[94]

On the eve of Cripps's arrival in India Coupland analysed Jinnah's position on the Pakistan demand:

(i) While claiming Dominion status for Pakistan, Jinnah has more than once intimated that it need not be full Dominion status and that he would like Foreign Affairs and Defence to remain, at least for the time being, in British hands; and
(ii) he has never asked that H.M.G. should accept Pakistan, but only that it should not be ruled out of discussion nor the chances of its adoption prejudiced by the form of an interim constitutional system. Nevertheless, *Pakistanism might triumph as a counsel of despair*.[95]

The Cripps declaration proposed Dominion status for a Union of India, but though it did not accept Pakistan it did accord provinces the right to secede from the Union and become separate dominions.[96] Jinnah and the League saw it as recognizing the principle of Pakistan.[97] From the notes of Coupland, Cripps and the Intelligence Department there can be no doubt that Jinnah and the League were disposed to accept the offer.[98]

On 28 March 1942 Jinnah 'stated [to Cripps] the League's acceptance of the Declaration'. On 7 April he intimated that 'he must hold back the League's acceptance till after the Congress has accepted'.[99] Coupland foresaw that if Congress rejected the offer the League would follow suit, 'so wording their rejection as to obtain some British and world support without losing face as Indian patriots'. On 9 April, when Congress seemed poised to accept, Jinnah was reported as saying 'that Pakistan could be shelved', given a satisfactory position in the Viceroy's executive and a suitable procedure for the secession of provinces.[100] When Congress rejected the declaration the League did likewise, deprecating H.M.G.'s objective of Union, the provision for a single constituent assembly in the first instance, and the eligibility of non-Muslims to participate in the Muslim provinces' decisions on secession.[101]

In February 1944 Jinnah stated that Britain 'should now frame a new constitution dividing India into two sovereign nations', Pakistan and Hindustan, with 'a transitional period for settlement and adjustment' during which British authority over defence and foreign affairs would remain.[102] The length of the period would depend upon the speed with which the two peoples and Britain adjusted to the new constitution. Though the statement clearly contemplated continued subordination to Britain it is too vague to be read as a shift from the notion of zonal dominions.[103] In September 1944 the Gandhi–Jinnah talks concentrated attention on the precise meaning of the Pakistan demand. The Bengal Provincial League now wanted 'a sovereign state in N.-E. India that will be independent of the rest of India', though it was divided over the cession of the Burdwan districts, with some members arguing that their retention would win Hindu approval.[104] The talks themselves did little to clarify Jinnah's conception of Pakistan but he reiterated that for the regions in which the Muslims predominated it was they alone who must determine their future. Jinnah also spoke now of Pakistan as a single state.[105]

Throughout the war Jinnah contemplated the post-war emergence of one or two Pakistan 'dominions', coexisting with one or two Hindustan 'dominions' and the princely states, and with Britain retaining power over defence and foreign affairs. The separateness and equality of the Pakistan and Hindustan 'dominions' would be a recognition of the validity of the two nations theory and of their right to eventual sovereign independence. The conception resembled that which some British Conservatives formed at the time of the Cripps Mission and espoused until the eve of the transfer of power.[106]

V *Definition by Circumstance*

With Labour's assumption of office in July 1945 it was soon apparent that there was not to be a gradual demission of power by stages but an early and complete withdrawal.[107] Jinnah now became adamant that there must be a single state of Pakistan and the League fought the elections of 1945–6 on that platform.[108] The announcement in February 1946 of the imminent despatch of a Cabinet Mission to settle the basis for independence and Jinnah's first meeting with the Mission on 4 April confirmed that Labour was in a hurry. Fortified by the League's electoral triumph, on 7 April Jinnah led a convention of 470 League members of the central and provincial legislatures to an unequivocal resolution in favour of 'a sovereign independent state comprising Bengal and Assam in the North-East zone and the Punjab, North-West Frontier Province, Sind and Baluchistan in the North-West zone'.[109] Acceptance of this precise demand for Pakistan and its implementation without delay; by the creation of a Pakistan Constituent Assembly, was made the *sine qua non* for the League's participation in an Interim Government. The opening of the imperial endgame had precipitated an immediate and full-blooded definition of the Pakistan demand.

By 10 April Cripps had prepared a draft proposal for discussion with the Indian leaders and a few days later the Mission confronted Jinnah with two alternative approaches that it advocated: either a truncated Pakistan, independent and fully sovereign but limited to the Muslim majority areas, and thus short of far more of the territories of Punjab, Bengal and Assam than the League had contemplated; or the grouping together of the whole of the six claimed provinces, beside a Hindustan group, within a Union exercising power over defence, foreign affairs and communications.[110] When Jinnah refused to choose either alternative Cripps prepared a draft that rejected a fully independent Pakistan. But it proposed a powerful subnational Pakistan, with its own flag, forces to maintain internal order, and enjoying parity with Hindustan in an all-India government. The League would draft its constitution and join with Congress on the basis of parity to draft the Union constitution.[111] The Mission was willing to concede its right to secede from the Union after fifteen years.[112] This remarkable scheme was the furthest that H.M.G. ever went towards accepting the full Pakistan demand.

It is scarcely surprising that Jinnah and the League were drawn into negotiations on the basis of this scheme, though some Leaguers speculated that Jinnah's departure from the Legislators' full-blooded resolution evidenced vacillation among 'weak-kneed' members of the Working Committee.[113] During the subsequent month of negotiations the Mission reduced the concessions to the demand in order to woo Congress, so that when its scheme was published on 16 May it was far less attractive to the League.[114] It split the six 'Pakistan' provinces into two groups, the formation of which was to depend upon the voluntary accession of each province to its assigned group. It abandoned parity in the making of the Union constitution, enlarged the Union's power to include finance, and failed to provide for the secession of groups or provinces from the Union. Though some Leaguers feared that the Union's powers would enable Congress to abort the emergence of Pakistan,[115] the counsels that prevailed were that the Cabinet Mission's scheme met 'the substance of the demand for Pakistan'.[116] First, it provided that the provinces must enter constitution-making 'sections' that were conterminous with the groups. Secondly, the section constitution-making procedure was to precede Union constitution-making. Thirdly, the Working Committee assumed, on the basis of discussions that Jinnah had had with the Viceroy, that the League would enjoy parity with Congress in an Interim Government, which seemed a tacit admission of Pakistan's right to separate nationhood.

Jinnah received written letters of advice from Aurangzeb Khan and Jamil-ud-din Ahmad that emphasized the advantages of accepting the Mission's scheme.[117] Ahmad, then Convenor of the League's Committee of Writers, expressed the 'prudent' strategy vigorously. The League should

work the Plan up to the Group stage and then create a situation to force the hands of the Hindus and the British to concede Pakistan of our conception. . . . [We should] make known in most emphatic terms our objections to the Plan specially with regard to the Centre and declare that we will . . . not be bound to submit to a Union Centre which does not accord us a position of equality. We [should] give a chance to the Hindu majority to accommodate us at the Centre. . . . After we have made the constitutions of Groups B and C according to our wishes our position will be stronger than what it is now if we use our opportunities properly. We will have some foothold. When we reassemble in the Union Constituent Assembly we can create deadlocks on really important issues. . . . If the worst comes to the worst and the Hindu majority shows no willingness to compromise we can withdraw from the Assembly in a body, and refuse to honour its decisions. Ours will be a solid bloc as there won't be more than two or three non-League Muslims in the Assembly. . . . We will be on strong ground morally and politically because firstly we will have previously declared that we can never acquiesce in any Centre which reduces us to a subordinate position and secondly we will be in power in the Groups, and will be better able to resist the imposition of an unwanted Centre.

In the spirit of this advice the League resolved that:

... inasmuch as the basis and the foundation of Pakistan are inherent in the Mission's plan by virtue of the compulsory grouping of the six Muslim Provinces in Sections B and C, [it] is willing to co-operate with the constitution-making machinery proposed in the scheme outlined by the Mission, in the hope that it would ultimately result in the establishment of complete sovereign Pakistan....[118]

Jinnah was authorized to negotiate for the entry of the League to the Interim Government. He wrote to Wavell to emphasize that his assurance of parity therein had been 'the turning point' in the League Council's acceptance.[119]

The League's strategy was destroyed by the Congress's refusal to contemplate parity in the Interim Government or the compulsory grouping of provinces for constitution-making, together with H.M.G.'s conviction that Congress goodwill was vital for a peaceful transfer of power.[120] In August 1946 Jinnah was driven to a course of 'direct action' by his mistrust of the Congress and H.M.G.'s infirmity.[121] Certainly, by December, when he and Nehru were called to London in a desperate attempt to secure agreement on sectional procedure, Jinnah had abandoned his mid-year hopes of realizing Pakistan through the Mission's scheme. He now reverted to the notion of a Pakistan dominion and rehearsed it not only with Attlee and the Cabinet Mission ministers[122] but also with British Opposition leaders.[123] Churchill, for whom a secret telegraphic address was established, assured him that the Pakistan areas could not be turned out of the Commonwealth as part of an Indian republic.[124] Indeed, in parliamentary debate Churchill affirmed that Muslim India and the princes should be accorded Commonwealth membership.[125] That winter Jinnah sought assurances that other Conservatives would support Pakistan's dominionhood. His inquiries converged with intrigues for separate princely dominions, to which he gave his blessing.[126]

Jinnah welcomed the prospects of a transfer of power on a provincial basis that Attlee's time-limit statement of 20 February 1947 foreshadowed.[127] In his first discussions with Mountbatten he sought a Pakistan dominion comprising the full six provinces,[128] but he did not oppose the option of separate sovereign provinces that the 'Dickie-bird' or Ismay plan ('Plan Balkan') offered. His objection to Plan Balkan was that it envisaged the severance from Punjab and Bengal of their non-Muslim areas. When he first saw the Plan he argued 'that power should be transferred to Provinces as they exist today. They can then group together or remain separate as they wish.'¹²⁹ When Mountbatten asked his views on H. S. Suhrawardy's proposal for 'keeping Bengal united at the price of its remaining outside Pakistan' he replied: 'I should be delighted. What is the use of Bengal without Calcutta; they had much better remain united and independent; I am sure that they would be on friendly terms with us.'¹³⁰

Whereas in 1946 Jinnah had been prepared to find the Pakistan demand realized, at least temporarily, by the grouping of the six provinces within the Union of India, in 1947 he was willing to see it satisfied by the separate dominionhood of provinces. Now again he was frustrated by Congress, which was no less opposed to the instant loss to India of non-Muslim areas of provinces than it had been to their distant loss by secession from the Union. The outcome of negotiations in 1947, a dual transfer of power to a single truncated Pakistan dominion and a single Indian dominion (to one of which the states were obliged to accede), flowed from Congress policy and H.M.G.'s acquiescence in it.¹³¹ Given the reversals that he suffered in the three-sided discussions from April 1946 to May 1947 it is scarcely surprising that Jinnah eschewed the prolongation of triangularity implied in proposals for Mountbatten to become Governor-General of both dominions and the retention of a Joint Defence Council.¹³² However, at the end of the Raj he still acknowledged Pakistan's need for British agency. The retention by Pakistan of British governors, chiefs of staff and civil and military officers was consistent with his expectation that the transfer of power would be a phased process.¹³³

VI *Man and Movement*

At the age of sixty Jinnah made the cause of Muslim India his life. An extraordinary match of man and movement followed. Ambition, pride and vanity were less important to it than his refined sense of Muslim injury under Congress rule and his capacity to express the hurt and specify the cure. Like Gandhi he evoked national consciousness in opposition to felt wrongs.¹³⁴ While Gandhi had experienced India's emasculation by British imperialism Jinnah felt the impotence of Muslim India under Congress totalitarianism. Jinnah articulated not the Qur'an's promise of political power nor memories of the Mughals but the Muslim's sense of persecution at the sudden threat to all that he had achieved in the twentieth century. When the Congress governments resigned in November 1939 he rallied Muslims to celebrate their 'deliverance from tyranny, oppression and injustice'.¹³⁵ Jinnah's constitutional remedies were not of his own making. The Pakistan demand was no pet scheme of which he dreamed alone but an ideal to which he was converted by others, colleagues of long-standing like Haroon, thinkers in the line of Iqbal, scholars of the Aligarh school. His very formulation of the two nations theory drew upon their thoughts and words. His amplification of the theory into a demand for parity was a brilliant tactical manoeuvre, but its effectiveness rested on the willing support of the League, most notably when Linlithgow set up his Defence Council and Wavell attempted to reconstruct his executive. The tactic consolidated the League as the microcosm of the Muslim nation and Jinnah as its leader.

It is a paradox that the demand for separate Muslim statehood based on the existing Muslim provinces with territorial adjustments should finally have found recognition in a Pakistan truncated to a degree never envisaged by Jinnah and the League. It is inconceivable that they did not realize that the truncation was a logical corollary of the distribution of the peoples of the two nations. The arguments that they adduced to resist it could scarcely be accepted with justice by a departing Raj, whether they emphasized the need for hostages, or for matching minority populations for exchange in case of need, or for non-Muslim territories to make Pakistan viable economically. The incorporation of the full six provinces in Muslim zones could only have been secured by a British award, and it seems most likely that Jinnah envisaged such an award as a line of advance consistent with Britain's continuing presence in her own interests. In other words, he probably assumed a British withdrawal by stages, at the first of which the Pakistan zones would receive subordinate dominionhood, secured like the princely states by H.M.G.'s continuing control over defence and foreign affairs (as the 1935 Act had stipulated). His reference in October 1938 to a further twenty-five years of imperial rule, the Lahore resolution's emphasis upon all powers 'finally' passing to independent states, his war-time comments, his play for Pakistan dominionhood from December 1946, his reliance on British agency after August 1947, all support such a thesis. His acceptance of the Cabinet Mission's scheme might be seen similarly as evidence of a readiness to postpone full sovereign statehood, provided that the conditions of its eventual emergence were safeguarded, that is Muslim zones and parity in government. He was willing to associate the Muslim nation with central government on the basis of parity but he doubted that such a government could endure. He told Coupland as much:

Assume a 50:50 basis.... The central questions are just those on which Moslems and Hindus must disagree: e.g. (a) Defence: Hindu Ministers will at once want to Indianize in communal proportions.... (b) Tariff: Hindu Ministers will want high protection for industries, which are mainly in Hindu hands, to the deteriment of the Moslems who are more confined to poor agriculturalists than the Hindus.[136]

Such caveats were urged upon Jinnah in May 1946, when he judged the disadvantages of a temporary union to be worth the prize of a safe passage through grouping to an eventual six-province fully sovereign Pakistan.[137]

Jinnah's planning was undermined by the Labour Government's beliefs that Britain's post-war interests would be best served by immediate withdrawal, and that an orderly retreat and sound post-imperial relations with the subcontinent would alike be best achieved by enlisting Congress co-operation. His hopes of obtaining more than a truncated Pakistan depended upon an extended imperial presence of some sort. That they were no mere illusions is revealed by the sympathies of some leading British Conservatives and Liberals. As late as May 1947 Mountbatten's staff and the India Committee of Attlee's Cabinet espoused a scheme that permitted an independent India of many nations while the Chiefs of Staff advised that if Congress rejected Dominion status then Commonwealth membership might be accorded severally to West Pakistan, united Bengal, and even to a maritime state such as Travancore.[138]

Jinnah's readiness to accept, from time to time, quite different constitutional forms as consistent with the Pakistan demand flowed in part from the necessities of a dynamic situation, but in part, too, from the advice proffered by colleagues. In April 1946, 470 Muslim legislators voted for a single sovereign Pakistan of six full provinces; a few weeks later the Working Committee and the Council accepted a scheme for a Union of India; in April 1947 Jinnah endorsed Suhrawardy's plan for a 'Free State of Bengal'; two months later he accepted 'moth-eaten' Pakistan. Yet the essence of the Pakistan demand—the right to a territorial asylum, to the self-determination of the Muslim nation in the north-western and eastern regions of India—was never compromised. Certainly, Jinnah planned that the regions should include virtually the whole of six provinces, whereas in the circumstances of 1947 he was left with a Pakistan defined by religious distribution district by district. Yet that outcome lends no support to speculation that the Pakistan demand was Jinnah's bargaining counter for power in a united India, or that the Partition hoisted him with his own petard.

6
Mountbatten, India and the Commonwealth

It is manifestly important to know why the Indian subcontinent achieved freedom as two separate member nations of the British Commonwealth in August 1947. The transfer of power ended two centuries of empire and a century of Indian unity, presaged the demise of the European empires at large, and inaugurated the multiracial Commonwealth. The partition of India precipitated communal outrage on a massive scale, one of the largest migrations of people in history, and a rivalry between India and Pakistan that was to erupt in spasmodic wars and involve outside powers.

It has been claimed that partition might have been avoided, or at least its immediate evil consequences averted, if the last Viceroy had been in less of a hurry.[1] There has been no lack of concern to correct such conjecture, and the verdict of historians has generally been that India's acceptance of the 3 June plan for dual dominions was a British diplomatic coup. Informed by their direct participation in the historic events from March to June 1947, Alan Campbell-Johnson, V.P. Menon, and Lord Ismay rendered admiring accounts of Lord Mountbatten's achievement.[2] Among later writers, H.V. Hodson and L. Collins and D. Lapierre enjoyed access to the Mountbatten archive and composed eulogies.[3] Hugh Tinker did not enjoy such access for his twentieth anniversary essay on the 1947 'experiment with freedom'. However, he was able to use the official British documents, and he has suggested some important revisions to the Menon version of the evolution of the 3 June plan. He has observed that 'we still await a version of the events of 1945–47 which will describe what happened from within the Congress—and within the Muslim League. So far we see everything through British, official eyes'. Still, of the 3 June plan he concludes: 'It was Mountbatten's capacity for tactical manoeuvre that brought off the final coup'.[4] It was left for Nehru's official biographer, S. Gopal, to suggest an alternative perspective. In essence, Professor Gopal represents Mountbatten's task as 'merely to work out the details and effect the partition demanded by the League and accepted by both the British Government and the Congress'.[5] Before Mountbatten's arrival Congress had reconciled itself to partition. It may be added that Congress had also called for an immediate transfer of power on a Dominion status basis.

With an extensive range of materials now available it is feasible to attempt an analysis in sufficient detail to reveal the roles of the main parties and their principals in the emergence of the 3 June plan. The departures from extant accounts are too numerous to make the correction of them in detail feasible here.[6] In general terms, the analysis suggests that Mountbatten could have neither prevented nor sensibly delayed partition, and that he pursued the object of Commonwealth membership so persistently and with such diplomatic skill that the achievement of dual dominionhood by agreement must be recognized as his personal triumph. Nevertheless, consideration was being given to a Dominion status transfer of power before he went to India, while his contribution to the plans through which dual dominionhood evolved was slight. His grasp of the plans and the fundamentals of established policy to which they necessarily had regard sometimes seemed uncertain, and he was slow to appreciate the essential demands of the Congress. The constructive role of the Congress in the emergence of the 3 June plan has in fact never been understood, and, in particular, the nature and significance of Mountbatten's negotiations with Nehru at Simla have been misconstrued.[7]

I *Mountbatten's Brief*

On 20 February 1947 Clement Attlee announced in the House of Commons that His Majesty's Government intended to transfer power to responsible Indian hands 'by a date not later than June 1948'.[8] Since May 1946 it had been Britain's policy to transfer power to an all-India Union, established by a fully representative Constituent Assembly. By February 1947, however, there seemed little likelihood of the Indian National Congress and the Muslim League agreeing to the broad constitutional principles that the British Cabinet Mission had prescribed for the purpose of bridging the gap between the Congress demand for Indian unity and the League insistence upon a separate sovereign Muslim state. The most contentious principle was that the Constituent Assembly should meet in sections comprising communal groups of provinces. In December 1946 Britain had decreed that each section must make the constitutions for the provinces and the group on the basis of a simple majority vote of provincial representatives. Only after the first provincial elections under the constitution so formed might a province decide to opt out of its group. While this sectional procedure was essential to the League's co-operation with the Cabinet's scheme for an Indian Union, it was accepted by Congress subject to the reservation that the fundamental principle of provincial autonomy must not be violated. In effect, the sectional procedure suspended the principle of provincial autonomy pending the making of the constitution. As the Congress stood by the right of a province—or even part of a province—to exercise a veto within its section, at the end of January the League resolved not to participate in the Constituent Assembly. At the time of Attlee's statement the Assembly was representative of the Congress provinces of British India and some princely states that had agreed to join it. Unless the Assembly became fully representative and worked out a constitution by June 1948, His Majesty's Government would, in Attlee's words, 'have to consider to whom the powers of the Central Government in British India should be handed over, on the due date, whether as a whole to some form of Central Government for British India, or in some areas to the existing Provincial Governments, or in such other way as may seem most reasonable and in the best interests of the Indian people'.[9]

Attlee's statement associated the opening of this new and final phase of British rule with the supersession of the Viceroy, Lord Wavell, by Lord Mountbatten, who was to take over in March. Mountbatten had been approached about the appointment in December but he had reserved his acceptance until he was given an opportunity of commenting upon the statement in draft, together with an intimation of his instructions. He was in favour of a short statement, emphasizing that a new Viceroy was being sent out expressly to terminate the British Raj by a specific date, and presented in the spirit of a 'New Deal'.[10] He had little influence on Attlee's announcement. The draft he saw on 8 February had already been approved by the Cabinet and was not open to variations in substance. Mountbatten did secure the omission of the passage referring to the failure of Indians to agree upon constitution-making machinery and the alteration of the definition of the terminal date for the British Raj from 'the middle of 1948' to 'June 1948'.[11] As for his instructions, Mountbatten had pressed for a formal directive, which Attlee withheld because a fresh viceregal instrument of instructions would require parliamentary approval. They compromised on a letter of instructions. Around 7 February Sir Stafford Cripps produced a draft at short notice as a 'cock-shy' and Attlee asked for Mountbatten's response.[12] Mountbatten redrafted the letter 'without changing the general intention', which was consistent with the February statement.[13] However, he substituted 1 June 1948 for Cripps's 30 June 1948 as the final transfer date, and, most importantly, added a final paragraph:

His Majesty's Government hope that India will remain a free and independent member of the British Commonwealth of Nations. If, however, this does not eventuate, His Majesty's Government is most anxious, after the transfer of power, that there should be the closest and most friendly relations between India and the United Kingdom. A feature of this relationship should be a military treaty. At the appropriate time delegates from the Chiefs of Staff will be sent to India to assist you in framing it.

Whereas Cripps's 'cock-shy' had mentioned neither the Commonwealth nor defence, the instructions that Mountbatten received on 18 March gave clear expression to the objective of Indian membership of the Commonwealth and the need for a defence agreement.

Even after the 20 February statement the British Government still hoped for a Congress acceptance of the sectional procedure in terms sufficiently fulsome to attract the League to the Constituent Assembly. The statement's contemplation of Britain's departure in June 1948 despite the failure of Indians to agree on the constitution of a central authority raised, however, the problem of transferring power to more than one successor. By early March officials at the India Office had concluded that the difficulties of dispersing central functions among the provinces were so great that a plural transfer must mean 'a modified form of Pakistan'.[14] Successor governments and administrations must therefore be set up to receive the central powers. In a memorandum of 4 March the Secretary of State, Lord Pethick-Lawrence, suggested that H.M.G. must decide by June 1947, on the basis of Mountbatten's advice, what course to adopt if the Constituent Assembly was not then fully representative. The planning for successor governments should be begun then, a decision announced in September, legislation passed, and, for climatic reasons, the final transfer arranged in early 1948. He proposed that the India Committee of the Cabinet discuss the matter with Mountbatten. A meeting was set down for 13 March and Mountbatten, together with his senior staff, Lord Ismay and Sir Eric Miéville, were invited to attend.

Another agenda item for the meeting emerged on 10 March, when Gandhi's self-styled 'emissary', Sudhir Ghosh, handed to Pethick-Lawrence a brief draft given him by V. P. Menon, the Viceroy's Reforms Commissioner, on 1 March in Delhi.[15] Menon later claimed authorship of the draft but at the time H.M.G. believed that it was the work of Sir B. N. Rau, Constitutional Adviser to the Constituent Assembly.[16] The draft argued that pursuant to the 20 February statement there was a growing realization that it might be impossible for a constitution acceptable to all parties to be formed by June 1948. A transfer of power might therefore be best arranged by adapting the India Act of 1935 in order to recognize India as a Dominion. As the India Office minuted (and as Cripps had objected when Ghosh showed him the draft on 4 March), the proposal amounted to 'the transfer of full power during the interim period without any concession to the Muslim League point of view'.[17] It meant treating the existing Interim Government over which Nehru presided as a Dominion government, with jurisdiction over unwilling provinces and states. It was consistent with the policy that the Congress espoused in its resolutions of 6–8 March:

> The transfer of power, in order to be smooth, should be preceded by the recognition in practice of the Interim Government as a Dominion Government with effective control over the services and administration, and the Viceroy and Governor-General functioning as the constitutional head of the Government.[18]

At the 13 March meeting, when the transfer of power to more than one authority was considered, Attlee 'thought that, in view of the indications that the Indian leaders were disposed to consider, at least [as] an interim measure, the possible adaptation of the 1935 Act to meet the immediate situation created by the Statement of 20 February, the Act ought to be carefully examined from this point of view'.[19] On 2 May the Secretary of State, now Lord Listowel, who had recently succeeded Pethick-Lawrence, revealed that the examination had resulted in an India Office plan for a transfer of power to more than one authority by means of Dominion status under the 1935 Act. More immediately, the Committee agreed that Mountbatten should 'encourage any moves that might be initiated by Indian leaders in favour of the continuation of India within the British Commonwealth'.[20] If a transfer of power on the basis of unity seemed impossible, Mountbatten was to report by 1 October on the steps to be taken.

II *'Plan Balkan'*

Very soon after his arrival in Delhi on 22 March Mountbatten was seized of the dominant elements in the problem of disengagement. First, as Wavell had been insisting for six months, Britain's capacity to maintain law and order was diminishing daily and a policy initiative was urgently needed in order to avert disaster. On 2 April Mountbatten reported: 'The only conclusion that I have been able to come to is that unless I act quickly I may well find the real beginnings of a civil war on my hands.'[21] Secondly, Mountbatten found that few Indians wanted to sever the British connection entirely. On 24 March the Chancellor of the Chamber of Princes, the Nawab of Bhopal, raised with him the question of states or groups of states being granted Dominion status; soon afterwards he cabled that Jinnah wanted Pakistan to remain in the Commonwealth. Also on 24 March Nehru told Mountbatten that though 'he did not consider it possible, with the forces which were at work, that India should remain within the Commonwealth', nevertheless, 'they did not want to break any threads'.[22] Nehru conveyed 'a direct implication that they wanted to stay in; but a categorical statement that they intended to go out'. He even suggested 'some form of common citizenship'. Mountbatten recorded that 'a formula may have to be found'.[23] Congress had suspected dominionhood as an imperialist device for so long that on 22 January in the Constituent Assembly it had proclaimed its object as the status of an 'independent sovereign republic'. The psychological obstacle to Commonwealth membership was immense.

Mountbatten soon realized that there was insufficient common ground upon which to erect the Cabinet Mission's 'Plan Union'. He saw it as the ideal solution to the Indian problem and he planned to make a final attempt to put it across at a house party of Indian leaders at Simla in May. But within days of his arrival he accepted the need for an alternative approach, which he pursued by combining the elements of a quick decision and Commonwealth membership. In an uncirculated record of a staff meeting on 28 March he

pointed out that, if a decision could be made quickly, it might well be possible to establish some form of Dominion Status in India, which could run experimentally until June 1948. This might consist of a 'Dominion of Pakistan'; a 'Dominion' or 'Dominions' of the Indian states (it was known that the Muslims and the majority of the Princes would be willing to remain within the Commonwealth); and a 'Dominion' of the rest of British India. All these would be autonomous units, but with certain subjects, such as Defence, Foreign Affairs, Finance, Food and Communications, reserved to some form of central Government.[24]

Mountbatten would reserve the right to decide two or three months before the June 1948 deadline whether to recommend a transfer of power to the central government or let the union lapse. As he explained three days later, the idea was a form of partition in May 1947, with the Hindu provinces, including partitioned Bengal and Punjab, the Muslim provinces, and the states forming separate Dominions under a central interim government holding reserved subjects until the final transfer of power. Mountbatten considered the idea of immediate dominionhood and a constitutional viceroy at staff meetings during the first week of April. Ismay and Miéville cautioned him that upon the award of Dominion Status his own powers would become merely advisory and that he would thereby lose control of the armed forces. Mountbatten admitted to vagueness about the means of preserving his powers during an interim period but emphasized the need for an immediate decision in principle, leaving Indians themselves to work out the details. When Ismay and the staff began to draft a plan on 8 April they left the idea of dominionhood out of it.

The essential feature of the new plan became the acceptance of the principle of partition, subject to the operation of provincial—and in Punjab, Bengal, and Assam sub-provincial—self-determination. Though Mountbatten thought the concept of Pakistan 'sheer madness' he became reconciled to it in the course of six interviews with Jinnah from 5 to 10 April. Jinnah, whom he described as a 'psychopathic case', remained obdurate in the face of his insistence that Pakistan involved the partition of Bengal and the Punjab. Early in March 1947 Congress had accepted such partitions as essential to peace in the provinces, and also that any constitution framed by the Constituent Assembly could not be imposed upon unwilling areas. The Assembly's work was essentially voluntary: 'there must be no compulsion either way, and the people themselves will decide their future'.[25] Nehru appreciated that the Muslim areas would ultimately have to choose between a truncated Pakistan and joining the Indian Union, possibly on special terms like a princely state.[26]

The new plan had its genesis in an interview that Mountbatten gave Nehru on 8 April. Nehru 'thought that it would not be right to impose any form of constitutional conditions on any community that had a majority in any specific area.'[27] The provinces and partitioned provinces 'should have the right to decide whether to join a Hindustan Group, a Pakistan Group, or possibly even remain completely independent'. This was no prescription for fragmentation, for 'the whole thing revolved around having a strong Centre, certainly to begin with, and for that reason Pandit Nehru would favour making a statement soon and transferring power to Provinces while there was still time for me to be in charge at the Centre to help in the early stages of negotiations at the Centre'. This was consistent with the Congress's March call for the immediate transfer of power to a Dominion status Interim Government.

Mountbatten noted that 'Lord Ismay is working out further details as the result of these proposals', which he commended as 'perhaps ... the best so far'.[28] He added detail and emphasis to them at a staff meeting on 10 April: the plan would not mention Pakistan as such; power would be demitted to provinces and subprovinces, which would be free to join one or more group assemblies; the states too might join groups as and if they wished; the Interim Government would remain until June 1948; in the North-West Frontier Province, where a Congress government was under challenge from a League civil disobedience movement, there would be a general election. The plan would give 'the greatest measure of self-determination', for it was 'important that the Indian people should take the onus of making a decision' so that 'Britain could not then be blamed after the event'.[29] Ismay commented that it was not intended to transfer power to provinces before June 1948 but to warn them of that outcome if they did not unite in a group or groups. Ismay sent the 'bare bones' of the plan to V. P. Menon on 11 April with a request from Mountbatten for him to add the flesh.[30]

What Mountbatten omitted in his commendation of Nehru's proposals was the insistence that 'the whole thing revolved around having a strong Centre'. Not surprisingly Menon recoiled from Ismay's 'bare bones' and 'insisted on the desirability for granting Dominion status to India immediately if "Plan Balkan" [as it was known, essentially to distinguish it from Plan Union] was brought into operation'.[31] In reply, George Abell, the private secretary whom Mountbatten had inherited from Wavell, insisted that the Governor-General must retain his powers until June 1948. Menon seems to have withdrawn his objection reluctantly. By 14 April, with his help and that of Abell and Miéville, Ismay had completed a draft of the Plan.[32] A meeting of the provincial governors at Delhi accorded it general approval on 15

April. Remarkably, it was presented to the meeting as 'Plan Balkan', 'for ease of reference', and Mountbatten explicitly alluded to the danger of its 'helping towards the "Balkanization" of India and going against everything that Congress stood for'.[33] Ironically, the plan for provincial choice was born of Nehru's own proposals, and Nehru was himself to kill it a full month later because it threatened the 'Balkanization' of India. Though the name 'Plan Balkan' fell out of use later in April (as it became the recommended plan for the transfer of power) it will, for convenience, continue to be used here.

There was also misunderstanding between Mountbatten and Nehru over the Commonwealth. Plan Balkan did not refer to India's adherence to the Commonwealth but Mountbatten believed that the partition of India subject to its provisions would contribute to that end: '... the Indian leaders would have to ask that the Governor-General should stay on with constitutional powers and the right of veto, accorded voluntarily, over the control of the armed forces'.[34] Nehru had himself seemed to grope for a 'formula'. Mountbatten thought the fact that the non-Congress areas wanted Dominion status might allow the Congress to save face on the pretext of bowing to the wishes of the majority. At June 1948 a central organization would be needed to divide the forces and even thereafter to co-ordinate defence. Such assumptions were totally at variance with those of Rau, Menon and the Congress in their plans for Indian dominionhood, extending from an immediate transfer until June 1948. Again, in the 'outline plan' for provincial option that Nehru put to Mountbatten on 8 April he simply assumed that while India might lose some Muslim areas subject to the exercise of self-determination under the Interim Government, nevertheless a strong centre would, with Mountbatten's help, succeed to the rest of India by June 1948 and thereupon leave the Commonwealth. In early April Nehru did not make his assumptions entirely clear and Mountbatten, by his own admission, did not take him fully into his confidence.[35] But it was Mountbatten, not Nehru, who was groping for a formula that would hold India to the Commonwealth.

III *'A Delicate Manoeuvre'*

Mountbatten inaugurated his Commonwealth diplomacy on the very day that he set his staff to work on Nehru's outline plan, 8 April. In an interview with Baldev Singh, the Defence Member of the Interim Government, he pointed out that if India left the Commonwealth the consequent withdrawal of British officers would deprive the armed services of effective leadership. Baldev Singh revealed that he had already proposed that India should remain in the Commonwealth for the sake of defence. The Constituent Assembly's resolution for an independent sovereign republic could be suspended for ten years pending the nationalization of the forces. Mountbatten encouraged Baldev Singh to use his influence as defence member to enlist the support of the minorities' representatives in the Interim Government, Matthai, Bhabha and Jagjivan Ram. They might send a joint letter to their Congress colleagues. Baldev Singh 'seemed quite thrilled at the prospect of playing an important part, and felt that this might be indeed the real solution'.[36] Mountbatten felt sure that the conversation would remain confidential and he was careful to suggest that H.M.G. had little interest in India's remaining in the Commonwealth. Baldev probably approached Nehru after the interview, for Nehru wrote to him the same day of his unconcern about defence.[37] While the British departure would deplete the officer ranks it would encourage self-reliance. Indeed, severance from the Commonwealth would strengthen India's security. The Commonwealth would drag India into Britain's foreign commitments whereas alone she was under no threat from a major power. When Baldev saw Mountbatten next, on 16 April, he disclosed that Bhabha was enthusiastic about Commonwealth membership. Nehru was 'very interested' but wanted 'at least another month or six weeks to think it over'.[38] Mountbatten urged Baldev Singh 'to continue lobbying' and suggested that the 'psychological moment' for putting the matter to the party leaders would be at the Simla house party in mid-May. Meanwhile the fact that Jinnah had made it clear that he wanted Pakistan to remain in the Commonwealth and thereby secure British support was 'a very strong lever for Baldev Singh to use in his discussions with Congress'.

Singh appears to have been over-optimistic towards Nehru's interest in the Commonwealth. Two days earlier Nehru had written to him:

Under no conceivable circumstances is India going to remain in the British Commonwealth whatever the consequences. This is not a question for me to decide or for any few of us to decide. Any attempt to remain in the Commonwealth will sweep away those who propose it and might bring about major trouble in India. We must, therefore, proceed on the assumption which is a practical certainty that India will go out of the British Commonwealth by the middle of next year.[39]

Friendly defence arrangements could be made with Britain but only on the basis of independence. If the British officers leave, 'I shall accept that without losing a night's sleep'. Nehru held to such views despite the counsel of Rajagopalachari, and even that of Brigadier Cariappa, who both thought that Indianization should be spread over five years.[40]

Mountbatten also worked through Sir Chandulal Trivedi, then Governor of Orissa. When Mountbatten had held the South East Asian Command, Trivedi had been secretary of the Defence Department. On 15 April he appealed to Trivedi to discuss India's defence requirements with Nehru. As a ploy, he made much of opposition in Britain to accepting India into the Commonwealth, and quoted the opinion that Sir Archibald Nye, Governor of Madras, had expressed to him the previous day, that the need to defend India against Russia would be burdensome to the Commonwealth, whereas Britain's commercial interests were secured for many years by dint of the sterling debt to India for war-time services.[41] Mountbatten confided to Trivedi that Ismay had told him of adverse Whitehall reactions to the question of dominionhood. As 'India had everything to gain by remaining in [the Commonwealth] and we had nothing whatever to lose by her going out' he feared a negative response to a request for membership.[42] He represented himself as 'one of the very few responsible Englishmen who appeared to be in favour', largely because of his 'sentimental association with the Indian Army in SEAC during the Burma campaign'. Mountbatten must have recorded his next comment with the smile that he had suppressed during the interview:

He asked me whether no one else felt as I did, and I told him in strict confidence that the King had a tremendous sentimental attachment towards India, and in so far as was constitutionally proper I was sure he would recommend accepting any request India made to remain connected with the Commonwealth, or at all events be pleased with any decision made by India not to sever her connection with the Crown.

Mountbatten hoped 'something may come of' this secret discussion. Certainly Trivedi spoke to both Nehru and Vallabhbhai Patel in favour of India's remaining in the Commonwealth for five years for the sake of security and stability.[43]

On 17 April Mountbatten had his most fruitful interview yet—with V. K. Krishna Menon, Nehru's close associate. Menon, noted Mountbatten, said that he was staying in Delhi 'specially in the hope of being of use to me..., to help give me the background of what was going on in Congress circles, and to help me to put over any points that I found too delicate to handle myself directly'.[44] When Krishna asked whether Britain would leave officers with the services as long as India wished Mountbatten explained that they would stay only if India remained in the Commonwealth and they thereby retained the King's commission. Krishna claimed authorship of the phrase 'independent sovereign republic', which he now regretted, and he asked how he might make amends. Mountbatten suggested postponing the implementation of the resolution for five years, thus enabling the officers to stay on for a gradual hand-over, as June 1948 was too precipitate a date. When Krishna protested that the link with the Crown was a symbol of oppression, Mountbatten threw upon him the onus of finding a way to retain it:

I told him that it was up to the Congress to make the first move if they wanted a move to be made. I had no intention of making one, because I had the strictest instructions not to make any attempt to keep India within the Commonwealth ... and I might quite well be shot down by the powers that be ....

He noted in his record of the interview that such remarks were 'made in the way of "tactics"'. They were a gross exaggeration of British opposition to Indian dominionhood. He based them on his knowledge that the pros and cons of Indian dominionhood had been discussed at Whitehall, and on the fact that he had himself been responsible for the inclusion in his instructions of the injunction to attempt to keep India in the Commonwealth.[45] Despite Krishna Menon's plea that he take the first step, Mountbatten was adamant that he would not 'allow any sentimental reasons [to] make me pull your chestnuts out of the fire'. If Congress did not take the first step India would have 'a rotten army' and lose all the benefits of Commonwealth membership, while the rest of the Commonwealth would be spared the expense and anxiety of India's defence.

When Mountbatten now pressed Krishna to suggest a way out of the impasse, the reply brought 'the germ of new plan' into his mind.[46] Krishna suggested that 'if the British were voluntarily to give us now Dominion Status, well ahead of June 1948, we should be so grateful that not a voice would be heard in June 1948 suggesting any change, except possibly to the word "dominion" if that had actually been used up to that date'.[47] Mountbatten expressed willingness to take the step if it were practicable. If the Muslims were prepared to stay in a Union of India he 'would certainly recommend Dominion Status next month'; but as they were not he could not possibly recommend giving Dominion status to the present Interim Government, in which the Muslim League was a permanent minority. Krishna next proposed Dominion status for both India and Pakistan, with the states joining one of the two federations. Mountbatten replied 'Certainly, provided I could retain full powers over defence, since I would have to co-ordinate the use of a single army for both dominions'. Krishna rejected Dominion status without the army as laughable. Mountbatten sent him away to think of 'any solution by which dual dominion status could be granted, with a machinery that would satisfy the Muslim League' as to the army.

During the next few days Mountbatten ruminated on the Commonwealth question at staff meetings. On 18 and 19 April he confided the main points in the 'new plan' that the conversation with Krishna Menon had suggested.[48] There was the problem of who should take the first step: a Congress leader would risk repudiation by his colleagues; H.M.G. would be suspected of imperialism. A solution might be to seize and act upon the Congress's March resolution for a Dominion status Interim Government. Then a means must be found of preventing 'the complete control by Congress of the Muslim League'. Perhaps dominionhood might be granted to Hindustan and Pakistan separately, with a committee of representatives from both sides being set up and the Viceroy holding the casting vote. He rehearsed the objectives of policy: demission by June 1948, with the least strife, the greatest possible unity, and the strongest possible links between Britain and India. The 'most important single problem facing the staff', 'the most urgent question now requiring investigation', was how 'to keep... India within the British Commonwealth, and, in order to achieve this to grant some form of Dominion Status as soon as possible'. On 22 April he pressed his staff on the 'possibility of granting some form of Dominion Status to India as a whole, or, more probably, to the separate parts of India in the near future'.[49] The Governor-General might chair a Defence Council of India and Pakistan, with a casting vote and direct control of British forces. It would be 'a great advantage before the eyes of the world' if Britain were requested by all parties to provide a Governor-General. The staff was enjoined to plan concurrently for the main decision under Plan Blakan and the grant of Dominion status, say by January 1948. To this end, W. H. J. Christie, Joint Private Secretary to the Viceroy, prepared a memorandum on 'a method of transferring power to successor authorities in India which would result in a form of transitional constitution analogous to that of a Dominion'.[50] It was, Ismay advised Mountbatten on 25 April, based on 'what we generally refer to as V. P. Menon's Plan'.[51] As June 1948 would be too early to complete a constitution it preserved the Governor-General's constitutional leadership and permitted a gradual transfer of power. It was not an alternative to Plan Balkan, whereby India would choose between Union and partition, but a corollary to it. It anticipated that the choice would be for partition between at least two successors. Ismay called it a 'long-term plan', for it could not be put into effect until Hindustan and Pakistan possessed authorities ready to work it. While it was developed from the original Rau/Menon plan for Dominion status Interim Government, it reversed the contemplated sequence of events: first partition, then Dominion status. Mountbatten asked for it to be typed out as an appendix to Plan Balkan, which Ismay and Abell were due to take home within a week.[52]

Mountbatten was now aware that practicable machinery could be erected for dual dominions several months before June 1948, and remain until they had made their constitutions. The problem was to sell the scheme to Congress, or rather to induce Congress to offer to buy it. He noted on 28 April: 'I take it V. P. can get Congress to put this request forward when the time comes—but if they don't we can still pin it to their existing request for interim Dominion Status'.[53] But he could not feel confident. When Ismay left for London on 2 May he certainly took Christie's draft of V. P. Menon's Plan but he understood that he was not to reveal it to Cabinet until instructed to do so. The previous day Mountbatten had intimated secretly to the Secretary of State that he was 'working on a very delicate manoeuvre to give Congress an opportunity to come back into the Commonwealth in some form, which might possibly bear fruit, but it is too delicate a matter to write about at present'.[54]

Mountbatten foreshadowed his delicate manoeuvre at a staff meeting on 22 April. He reported that already the Muslim League, the scheduled castes, and some states, in all representatives of about half the population of India, had asked to remain in the Commonwealth. He was considering telling Nehru, through Krishna Menon, of these requests, adding that he could not suppress them and that he believed 'popular sentiment within the rest of British Commonwealth would not allow them to go unanswered'.[55] Later that day he spent two hours with Krishna Menon. He noted, 'we properly let down our hair and discussed every aspect of the plan now being worked on', and especially its relationship to the world situation.[56] He indicated that while he would not support the retention of Pakistan alone in the Commonwealth, if Jinnah appealed to the Commonwealth against expulsion—as he had intimated he would—then there was an 'extreme likelihood of Pakistan being a British dominion'. Pakistan could then call on British officers in all services, secure secret equipment from the Commonwealth, and send its officers to British schools. In short Pakistan would soon have 'armed forces immensely superior to those of Hindustan' and a large Commonwealth naval base at Karachi.[57] Krishna Menon 'absolutely shuddered'. Mountbatten assured him that such an outcome could be forestalled if India were in the Commonwealth, and he went on to sketch the scheme for dual dominions, 'with myself at the head of the Central Defence Council and as Governor-General of both Dominions on a constitutional basis'. Menon was 'rather smitten with this idea' but immediately proposed instead that India should be declared a Dominion consisting of two parts, Hindustan and Pakistan. Menon stressed, too, that Congress was pledged to leaving the Empire and that Nehru and Patel were committed. Nehru, he said, was 'over-working to the point of breakdown' and too absorbed in small matters. He planted the germ of another idea:

He asked me [noted Mountbatten,] if I could not take [Nehru] away for two or three days on a holiday... anywhere restful, so that we could get to know each other—'For', he said, 'between you, you can solve all the problems of India.'

The problem of stirring Congress to take an initiative remained with Mountbatten. Next day, in conversation with Bhabha, he revived his suggestion that the minorities' members of the Interim Government should write to the Congress members seeking a meeting there to express concern at the possiblity of a Pakistan Dominion securing Commonwealth equipment and personnel.[58] To prevent Pakistan stealing the march Congress should be persuaded to ask him to act on its Dominion status resolution. Probably as a result of these interviews, on 26 April the *Hindustan Times* declared that an Indian Union would consider as a 'hostile act' any attempt to conclude with Pakistan any treaty or alliance with military or political provisions. It was Mountbatten's personal conviction that to have part only of India in the Commonwealth would be disastrous. As he told his staff on 1 May, he was merely 'using the Pakistan threat to remain in as a lever to help Congress to "take the plunge" '.[59]

Mountbatten felt it essential to pursue the objective of Indian dominionhood without either himself or his staff raising the matter directly with the Congress leaders. On 1 May he reported that from such intermediaries as Krishna Menon, V. P. Menon, and Bhabha he had learned that Congress were exercised by the Commonwealth question, especially because of the Muslim League's intentions.[60] He counselled H.M.G. to make no pronouncement on the acceptability of only part of India into the Commonwealth, but to leave Congress to ponder the problem. On 1 May Miéville reported that V. P. Menon thought Patel might be disposed to accept an early grant of Dominion status 'for the time being'.[61] It seems certain, however, that Patel still thought in terms of Congress's March resolution for a Dominion status Interim Government pending the making of a constitution, not of post-partition Dominion status for non-Muslim India.

At the beginning of May Mountbatten reposed some hopes in Sir Walter Monckton as a go-between. The two were old friends. Monckton claimed that during his present visit to India, which began late in April, he was more concerned 'to help Dickie' than to pursue his tasks as legal adviser to the Nizam of Hyderabad.[62] After reading Mountbatten's notes of interviews and weekly reports he concentrated on the problem of finding a formula whereby India might remain in the Commonwealth. Mountbatten was saying 'all India or none' in the Commonwealth, but 'a *modus vivendi*, however untidy, must be found', for 'we must not throw everyone out of the family'.[63] His 'general approach [was] that progress [could] best be made by negotiating agreements or conventions all round on specific matters', for example contributions to Central Defence, so as to be able to carry on in a makeshift way after June 1948, 'not worrying too much or too urgently about constitutional logic'. On 1 May Miéville reported to Mountbatten that Nehru had invited Monckton to dine with him on the 3rd to discuss 'some form of continued allegiance to the Crown.'[64] Monckton expected Nehru to insist that '"Dominion Status" stinks in India' though a Commonwealth link might be useful and the independent sovereign republic resolution might be suspended if Indian allegiance to the King-Emperor could be circumvented.[65] Monckton wrote to Ismay, asking that he seek Cripps's guidance on the latter point, and he discussed it with Mountbatten and Krishna Menon on the afternoon of 3 May. This avenue to Nehru disappointed Mountbatten when the dinner conversation that evening failed to get around to the constitutional question. Cripps did pursue

Monckton's inquiry with Hartley Shawcross, the Attorney-General. Shawcross's informal advice, conveyed to Cripps on 9 May, was that the status of members of the Commonwealth was a matter for decision by the members themselves, but that the republic resolution need not prevent India's association with the Commonwealth in some new form, possibly dispensing with allegiance to the Crown as King-Emperor of India while accepting the King as Head of the Commonwealth. While Monckton's intervention served to prepare members of the Cabinet for the emergence of this problem in the longer term, it did not help Mountbatten with his delicate manoeuvre of stimulating a Congress initiative. That he remained hopeful is shown by his strictly confidential intimation to the Deputy Commander-in-Chief, Lieutenant-General Sir Arthur Smith, on 5 May that a Commonwealth formula might be found to enable British officers to stay on after the transfer of power. It seems certain that his decision to take Krishna Menon's advice and invite Nehru to spend a few days away with him was prompted by the need to pursue the matter while Ismay was in London. On 6 May he arrived at Simla with Miéville and V. P. Menon. Krishna Menon and Nehru were to join him at Viceregal Lodge on Thursday 8 May.

IV *'The Alternative Plan'*

Mountbatten had come to Simla for some respite from the gruelling pressures of his first six weeks in India. No suspension of work was intended and he doubtless hoped to achieve Nehru's assent to 'V. P. Menon's Plan', in a form consistent with Plan Balkan. On the basis of his own discussions with the Indian leaders, and from Miéville's account of meetings with Jinnah and Nehru on the eve of Ismay's departure for London, Mountbatten did not anticipate the need to reconsider Plan Balkan itself. At his first Simla staff meeting, however, on Wednesday 7 May, he agreed that an 'alternative plan' must now be prepared, a plan that would meet the political situation as it had developed during the previous week.[66] Since the departure of Ismay and Abell the party leaders' responses to a privileged preview of Plan Balkan had created a new situation. As Ismay was to reflect: 'I had been out of India only seven days, but things had moved so fast that I might have been out of India seven years.'[67] In essence Jinnah's reaction had spurred Congress to define terms for an immediate settlement. The 'alternative plan' that Mountbatten authorized on 7 May resembled those terms closely.

As Ismay had been indisposed with 'Delhi tummy' Miéville had taken Plan Balkan to Jinnah on the morning of 30 April and to Nehru in the afternoon.[68] Though Jinnah did not say definitely that he would reject the Plan he did call for the dismissal of the Constituent Assembly and the transfer of power to the existing provinces. That evening he issued a press statement attacking the scheme for partitioning the Punjab and Bengal as 'a sinister move actuated by spite and bitterness' within the Congress and intended to 'unnerve the Muslims by opening [*sic*] and repeatedly emphasizing that the Muslims will get a truncated or mutilated, moth-eaten Pakistan'.[69] He reiterated the demand for a Muslim state comprising the six provinces of N.W.F.P., Punjab, Bengal, Assam, Sind and Baluchistan. It is likely that Jinnah felt that, as he had won British and Congress acquiescence in the principle of Pakistan, and was well-placed to achieve dominionhood too, the time for hard-bargaining had arrived. In the wake of the February statement's acknowledgement of the possibility of a transfer of power to provinces the League had, by direct action, toppled the coalition government of the Punjab and shaken the Congress government of N.W.F.P. until the British were persuaded of the need for a fresh election, which the League would probably win. Jinnah's 30 April press statement marked the peak of his movement. It was, however, a provocation that caused Congress now to stand absolutely firm and define its position precisely and finally. It brought the situation to crisis point. As it was also a threat to Mountbatten's plans, it precipitated the preparation at Simla of a strategy that would squeeze Jinnah into submission.

When Nehru read Plan Balkan on 30 April he raised only 'comparatively small points'.[70] He did not object to the process whereby Bengal and Punjab would be partitioned on the votes of the members of their legislative assemblies; nor to the provision that provinces and subprovinces should either adhere to the existing Constituent Assembly, or form a second assembly in concert with other provinces, or set up their own separate assemblies. After all, he had himself proposed such a procedure. When, during the mid-April Governors' Conference, Mountbatten had emphasized the danger of the Plan Balkanizing India and suggested limiting the provinces' option to membership of a Hindustan or a Pakistan assembly, Ismay had argued that under the February statement H.M.G. was committed to provincial self-determination and he had retained it in the successive drafts of the Plan. Mountbatten and his staff conveniently assumed that Plan Balkan would yield a dual succession, and Nehru seems to have shared the assumption. His criticism of the 30 April draft was confined to the narrowness of the representation in Baluchistan and, more importantly, to the provision for fresh elections in the N.W.F.P. prior to the polling of its M.L.A.s. In essence his objection, and that of Congress, was to Britain's yielding to the Muslim League civil disobedience movement against the Congress government. This issue would require negotiation. Mountbatten was, however, reassured by Miéville's account of the interview, and also by a letter in which Nehru intimated that the Congress Working Committee accepted the principle of partition by self-determination. The letter was written after a meeting of the Committee on 1 May.[71]

The C.W.C. met at Delhi, with Gandhi in attendance, on Thursday 1, Friday 2, and Sunday 4 May. At a five-hour session on the first day Nehru acquainted his colleagues with the contents of Plan Balkan so that he might refer their views confidentially to Mountbatten and thereby 'avoid any misunderstanding at a later stage'. The Committee, Nehru wrote to Mountbatten, accepted 'the principle of partition based on self-determination as applied to definitely ascertained areas'. This involved 'the partition of Bengal and Punjab', which in any case the recent surge of communalism made 'an urgent necessity'. The Committee prefaced its acceptance of the principle of Plan Balkan, however, with an ominous excursus upon the contrast between the policies of the Congress and the League during the previous year. Congress had accepted the Cabinet Mission scheme in its entirety, pursued the path of peace, and agreed that there should be no compulsion in enforcing a constitution on unwilling parts of India. The League had espoused direct action and since 20 February had 'organized large-scale violent attempts to overpower provincial governments' The Committee insisted:

Every proposal and every change must be viewed in this context. If policy is to be influenced by the kind of brutal and terroristic methods that have prevailed thus far, then the inevitable result will be civil war on an extensive scale. The continuous appeasement of those who employ such methods and a submission to these tactics is the surest way to encourage them.... We can on no account be parties to such a policy.... [This] is the dominating feature of the situation and other matters are secondary.

The Committee then applied its remarks to the present case of the N.W.F.P. where any British proposal to bow to terrorism by holding fresh elections 'must be resisted'.

The broad outlines of Plan Balkan and the Congress response were leaked to the *Hindustan Times*, which on Saturday 3 May carried the headlines: 'Punjab and Bengal must be partitioned. Fresh elections in Frontier opposed. Congress cabinet's decision on Viceroy's proposals'. The story stated that some Congressmen felt that for the first time since he had become Viceroy Mountbatten 'may not be playing fair', mainly because of his policy for the N.W.F.P. The Congress would make the Frontier Province 'a test case'. Any attempt to remove the Congress ministry and hold elections might cause Congress to change its entire attitude towards the British Government. At his Saturday morning staff meeting Mountbatten viewed the leak as an attempt to blackmail him.[72] He was inclined to blame Patel for the leak, though for no apparent reason as any one of the Committee might have been responsible for it. Certainly it was unauthorized. Nehru condemned it in a letter to the Congress president, J. B. Kripalani, in which he lamented that he was no longer able to speak freely in the Committee and must in future discuss major policy matters with only a few trusted colleagues.[73] Gandhi, whose son edited the *Hindustan Times*, was critical of those who accused Mountbatten of dishonesty, and he spoke of bad journalism as 'untruth'.[74] On Sunday 4 May the Committee resolved to warn the paper that its press privileges would be withdrawn permanently if such an incident occurred again.[75]

Mountbatten's response to the N.W.F.P. problem was to propose a referendum. If Plan Union were finally rejected then the voters would be asked to choose between Hindustan and Pakistan. He secured Nehru's agreement and sought a statement from Jinnah that the League would withdraw its civil disobedience movement. On Sunday 4 May Jinnah seemed to agree to the statement provided that it foreshadowed the referendum. However, the publication next morning of a Congress report on violence in the N.W.F.P., and calling for the removal of the Governor, Sir Olaf Caroe, caused him to change his mind. He refused to sign the statement that Mountbatten prepared and sent to him on Monday 5th unless it made clear that elections would follow the referendum, which inclusion Mountbatten had already told him was unacceptable to Nehru. On Tuesday 6th Mountbatten warned Jinnah against making a statement that suggested that any decision had been reached on the N.W.F.P. The plan for the transfer of power was still being considered in London.

On Sunday 4 May, at the conclusion of the C.W.C. series of meetings, Gandhi had a ninety-minute interview with Mountbatten. He remained opposed to the partition of India and appealed for an immediate transfer of power to either a Congress or a League government on a Dominion status basis, with Mountbatten remaining as Governor-General until June 1948. On Monday he told a Reuter correspondent that 'it would be a good thing if the British were to go today—thirteen months means mischief to India'.[76]

At his Monday morning staff meeting Mountbatten alluded to the problems that had arisen since Ismay's Friday departure: 'He had felt all along that Lord Ismay's departure was premature.'[77] The N.W.F.P. problem had blown up. Gandhi had set his face against the partition of India, and Congress and the League were at odds over the partition of Bengal and Punjab. He suggested that when Miéville saw Jinnah later in the day about the N.W.F.P. statement he should seek out Jinnah's real attitude towards the partition of the Punjab and Plan Balkan, and urge the advantages of Plan Union. He himself emphasized in a letter to Jinnah about the N.W.F.P, that 'much as you dislike it, you must realize that the Cabinet Mission plan still holds the field'.[78] He spoke to Nehru in the same terms that afternoon: 'I pointed out that the Cabinet Mission's plan still held the field so far as H.M.G. were concerned and that I proposed to make one more attempt to get it accepted at the meeting with leaders' later in the month.[79]

On Monday night Nehru and Gandhi had a prolonged discussion and next day the C.W.C. met at short notice in an emergency session. Only Gandhi and about half the members attended. The Frontier Province and the general political situation were discussed. A further meeting lasting three hours was held on Wednesday 7th. Though no resolution was taken, from the similarity of documents that were issued independently by Gandhi, Nehru, and Patel within forty-eight hours there is no doubt that an agreement was reached that it was now time to demand an Interim Government on a Dominion status basis for all India. The Constituent Assembly should proceed with constitution-making. The Interim Government would preside over the eventual secession of those areas that rejected the constitution. During the interim period, the minorities would enjoy special judicial safeguards. On Wednesday 7 May Nehru set off for Simla to present these principles as a Congress plan, Gandhi boarded the train for Patna and incorporated them in a letter that he sent to Mountbatten on the Thursday, and Patel remained in Delhi to embody them in a press release that he issued on the Friday.[80]

Mountbatten's response to Jinnah's threatened rejection of the partition of the Punjab and Bengal drew him close to the position that the Congress leadership had assumed. In Mountbatten's Wednesday staff meeting at Simla V. P. Menon predicted that Jinnah would very likely reject Plan Balkan.[81] Though Mountbatten and Miéville had always felt that in the end Jinnah would accept a moth-eaten Pakistan, Mountbatten now accepted the need for a contingency plan. He proposed 'the demission of power under the present Constitution', so that provincial subjects would be demitted to the existing provincial governments and central subjects to the Interim Government. He observed that such a plan might be put into effect together with some form of Dominion status before June 1948. At this moment V. P. adverted to a conversation between Trivedi and Patel about India remaining in the Commonwealth: 'It was . . . Menon's opinion that if the Viceroy approached Sardar Patel on this subject he would get a positive reply. Pandit Nehru would say the same.' Trivedi had suggested dropping the title 'Emperor'. The objects of the Congress would be to secure the Viceroy's help with such problems as the princely states and the tribal peoples, while existing trading links with Britain were also appreciated. Menon argued that it was constitutionally possible for a British Governor-General to have dual responsibility towards two successors, and he could provide a unifying link between them and the states. Mountbatten required Menon to prepare a paper showing how Dominion status might be granted to India by January 1948 on the assumptions, first, of demission to the existing central government under 'the alternative plan' and, secondly, of partition pursuant to Plan Balkan. The 'alternative plan' was put in order and cabled to Ismay on Thursday morning for Cabinet approval in the event of Jinnah rejecting Plan Balkan. It was, in fact, never approved or even considered by the India Committee of the Cabinet. Mountbatten probably had this Simla staff meeting in mind when, in mid-1948, he wrote to Patel to propose Menon for a governorship:

I will never forget the day when V. P. pointed out to me that if I could have power transferred to India on a dominion basis sufficiently early in 1947, you were confident that not only this would prove immediately acceptable but that, in fact, would remove the need for India to sever her connection with the Commonwealth even when the interim period was over.[82]

It must be remembered that at this stage Patel was thinking in terms of a pre-partition Dominion status Interim Government.

V *The Simla Pourparlers*

On Thursday 8 May at 3.15 p.m. Mountbatten's staff opened discussions with Nehru about the N.W.F.P. and the transfer of power. From discussions that he, Gandhi, and the C.W.C. had held with Abdul Ghaffar Khan and Frontier representatives just before he came to Simla, Nehru had reached the conclusion that to hold a referendum at present would be yielding to force. He therefore argued that the referendum should be delayed until after the Constituent Assembly had drafted a constitution. Discussion on the point merged with the general question of transferring power and Nehru presented the following outline, which he called 'The Cabinet Mission's Plan with Modifications':

1. Power should be demitted to the Central Government in June 1947;
2. The Central Government should then be responsible to either the Constituent Assembly or the Central Legislative Assembly;
3. Any suggestion that Pakistan should be created straight away should be ruled out;
4. Provinces should be given the option, as in the Cabinet Mission Plan, of forming groups;
5. This option would later be extended to freedom to leave the Union of India altogether, but this stage would not be reached until after the principles of a new constitution had been worked out. This would be in about three months;
6. At, but not before, this stage the question of the partition of the Provinces would arise.[83]

V. P. Menon argued that the scheme would leave too little time for the detailed work of partitioning provinces and setting up governing authorities in the non-Union areas. Even on Nehru's timetable, which seemed optimistic, the time available between the achievement of a constitutional outline and June 1948 would be a mere eight months. Nehru argued that to allow the principle of partition prior to the transfer of power would open the possibility of 'a Muslim enclave in every province', but if the Interim Government assumed 'the burden of demission' then the Muslim members would remain in it 'at all costs' and would 'face realities'.

Mountbatten was absent from the above discussion but entered the room at this stage. He believed it 'essential to meet Pandit Nehru's views as far as possible' and welcomed his return to the 'Union of India' concept as a step back from the independent sovereign republic resolution. He agreed to cable to London, expressing the hope that sufficient emphasis would be laid in the plan in the Draft Announcement on the 'Union of India'. Provinces adhering to the existing Constituent Assembly should be referred to as 'constituting the Union of India' and those which did not should be referred to as 'contracting out of the Union'.

At the same time he emphasized to Nehru that H.M.G. would not transfer power to any body in which Congress had a permanent majority until those parts of India which did not wish to join the Union had been separated. The only way to transfer power quickly was first to allow those provinces that so wished to contract out of the Union. There could be no transfer to the Interim Government and a referendum must soon be held in the N.W.F.P. if the early transfer that Nehru wanted was to occur. Mountbatten left Nehru and V. P. together to draft a formula for the N.W.F.P. and to discuss the transfer of power. That night Menon brought to him a draft that Nehru had dictated, providing for a referendum with the N.W.F.P. government's concurrence and under the supervision of the Governor-General, in the event of all or part of the Punjab declining to join the Union of India. Mountbatten cabled it to Ismay for Cabinet approval.

At the same time Mountbatten sent a jubilant cable asking Ismay to distribute to the India Committee V. P. Menon's appendix to Plan Balkan. Ismay was to 'inform them that Patel and Nehru have now themselves indicated through V. P. Menon a desire for an early form of Dominion Status (but under a more suitable name) at least until a new constitution has been fully framed, which is unlikely to be for some considerable time after June 1948'.[84] Mountbatten expected to spend the weekend (10–11 May) working out the details with Nehru and obtaining Patel's concurrence. If he succeeded there would be 'a sporting chance' of the main Union of India remaining in the Commonwealth indefinitely, the difficulty of Jinnah's demand for Pakistan to remain in the Commonwealth would be overcome, and a solution to the problem of dissident states would be facilitated. He rejoiced:

I know that at the time you and Abell left it did not seem that this scheme could be pulled off but situation has been completely changed by Patel and Nehru coming forward themselves. This is greatest opportunity ever offered to Empire and we must not let administrative or other difficulties stand in the way.

Mountbatten had sown the seeds of dominionhood by his persistent manoeuvring in April. But it was Congress concern for an immediate transfer of power in order to forestall the spread of direct action and communal disturbances that led the C.W.C. to press the dominion solution during the first week of May. The Muslim League's toppling of the Punjab coalition and undermining of the N.W.F.P. Congress ministry convinced Nehru, Patel and Gandhi that unless power was transferred to a stable central authority at once then problems of national integration would spread like a rash across the subcontinent. A quick transfer under the 1935 Act, with the Viceroy remaining to help with the states, the tribal peoples, and the forces, seemed essential.

The Commonwealth question dominated discussion at the staff meeting on Friday morning, 9 May.[85] Mountbatten wanted a transfer during 1947 and the earliest possible withdrawal of British forces. He expatiated upon the benefits to Britain. She would both terminate her responsibilities and win credit for doing so. An Indian request to remain in the Commonwealth would so enhance Britain's prestige that 'this factor alone was of overriding importance'. It would also enhance the Labour Government's prestige. As for defence, inside the Commonwealth India 'filled in the whole framework of world strategy; a neutral India would leave a gap which would complicate the problem enormously; an hostile India would mean that Australia and New Zealand were virtually cut off'. Mountbatten wanted quick action. Miéville wrote to Monckton:

Things are progressing rather fast, and although we are still in a somewhat vague stage, we are sufficiently far advanced to be sending a telegram this week-end to Pug [Ismay] telling him to warn HMG what is in the wind so that he can get their reactions before he leaves.[86]

Mountbatten realized that Jinnah might resent India securing the advantage of constitutional continuity, a palace, administratively speaking, while Pakistan secured a tent. But he had the 'alternative plan' with which to pacify Jinnah.

Mountbatten felt some insecurity from not having spoken directly with Nehru or Patel about V. P. Menon's scheme, and he cabled Ismay on Friday morning to ask him not to release it to the India Committee for the moment.[87] He was thinking of sending Miéville and Menon down to Delhi to confirm Patel's response. This seemed to become unnecessary when, later that day, Patel issued his press statement advocating an urgent Dominion status transfer.[88] According to

Menon, during a discussion on Friday morning Nehru accepted that if a united Dominion was unattainable then power should be transferred to a Hindustan executive council elected by the Hindustan Constituent Assembly, with the separated areas adopting a parallel procedure, the Governor-General serving both successors, and a joint council handling matters of common concern.[89] Later in the day Mountbatten asked Nehru directly 'what he thought of the plan for transferring power on a Dominion Status basis in 1947'.[90] He emphasized that the matter was up to Nehru, for 'the advantages were almost entirely on his side'. Nehru seemed 'most interested in the plan' but could not rush his supporters on the question of long-term Dominion status. He thought that Menon had the timing wrong, that the new constitution would be framed by September and the new government could be in office by October. He seemed to go back on his acceptance of the need for partition prior to the transfer of power. Accordingly, Mountbatten arranged for Nehru, Miéville and Menon to meet him next morning at 11 a.m.

Before the meeting with Nehru Mountbatten reported to his staff that Krishna Menon had said at breakfast that much of the attraction for Nehru of a Dominion status transfer lay in Mountbatten's influence with the states.[91] V. P. revealed that the previous evening Patel had suggested on the telephone that Nehru must find it difficult to admit to Mountbatten that Dominion status was attractive because of the delays involved in making a new constitution. Mountbatten intimated that he would defer discussion with Patel until he returned to Delhi and that he would not raise the Commonwealth question with Jinnah until the announcement of Plan Balkan, now timed for 17 May. When Nehru arrived at the meeting V. P. Menon explained, at Mountbatten's request, that his plan covered 'the alternative events of there being an united India and of there being two separate states—the Union of India and Pakistan'.[92] Nehru declared for 'a transfer of power as soon as possible on a Dominion Status' basis. Only thus would the processes of continual reference to H.M.G. and party bidding be stopped. He argued for the Cabinet Mission Plan, varied so that provinces might opt out of the Union once the new constitution was formed. 'It was in his opinion wrong to put the process of partition first. The proper thing would be that this choice should come when the broad outlines of the future constitution were decided.' Mountbatten replied that partition could not be postponed. If truncated Pakistan were now conceded it would return to India later, whereas delay would exacerbate agitation. He and V. P.

pressed for the early application of the decision-making process on partition, so that Hindustan could enjoy early Dominion status and Pakistan could follow once the central authority for it was established. At the same time Mountbatten broke the news that the India Committee had refused to amend Plan Balkan in order to recognize the provinces that had entered the Constituent Assembly as representing the Union of India.[93] Correctly speaking the Union did not exist unless all provinces joined it. Nehru was evidently disappointed.

In view of Nehru's comments to Mountbatten and at staff meetings, from his arrival at Simla on 8 May until the morning of Saturday 10th, it is necessary to question V. P. Menon's impression that Nehru was ready to accept Dominion status pursuant to partition. Mountbatten knew that the C.W.C. was exercised by Jinnah's public opposition to the partition of provinces and he assured Nehru that he knew how to deal with Jinnah if he demurred at a truncated Pakistan. He had the 'alternative plan' in reserve, and either he or V. P. may have said enough for Nehru to discern its resemblance to the Congress demand. Nehru may have anticipated that League intransigence would drive H.M.G. into the arms of the Congress. On 10 May, when Patel's demand for immediate Dominion status was widely discussed in the press, and Gandhi's letter in similar terms reached Mountbatten, the unanimity of the big three should have been apparent to Mountbatten. The Congress demand differed sharply from Plan Balkan, the Cabinet's revise of which also arrived on Saturday the 10th. Mountbatten has recorded that he now decided on 'an absolute hunch' to show the revise to Nehru on the Saturday evening.[94] It seems more appropriate to describe his action as dictated by the circumstances. Not only was Plan Balkan at odds with the Congress demand for an immediate transfer to a single Dominion; it was also at odds with dual dominionhood, the basis the Simla pourparlers, and with the concept of the Constituent Assembly representing the Union of India, which Mountbatten had himself accepted.

VI *'Nehru's Bombshell'*

Nehru's explosion when he saw the revised Plan Balkan on the night of 10 May has puzzled historians and has never been satisfactorily explained.[95] Misled by Nehru's own comments, S. Gopal and Sir Cyril Philips have denied that Nehru had seen the full draft on 30 April.[96] On the authority of V. P. Menon, Ismay, and Mountbatten himself, H. V. Hodson has argued that the changes to the plan were merely 'nuances' and that they improved the draft that Nehru had read and seemed to accept.[97] Hugh Tinker accepts this argument and remarks that in a sense the drama that was enacted in May was 'a pageant that was not real life'.[98] He suggests that whereas Patel and the 'organisation men' of the Congress had already accepted the principles of partition and Dominion status, Nehru's bombshell represented the emotional crisis through which he must pass in order to become wholly reconciled to them.[99] Thus, he finds little difference between the draft that Ismay took to London, the Cabinet's revise, and the 3 June plan. Mountbatten speculated that Nehru was so suspicious of H.M.G. that 'the mere fact that the plan had been redrafted in London' provoked his hostility.[100] In fact the 10 May draft differs substantially from that of 30 April. Moreover, Nehru's bombshell must be viewed against the background of the Congress demand as expressed in the March resolution, Nehru's proposals of 8 April, his letter of 1 May, his outline of 8 May, Gandhi's letter of 8 May, and Patel's press statement of 9 May. Thus seen, Nehru's reaction seems appropriate to the circumstances, and important for the formulation of the 3 June plan.

In the first place, on 1 May Mountbatten effected a change in the proposed voting procedure for Bengal that enhanced the likelihood of a sovereign, indeed Dominion status, Bengal.[101] The draft that Nehru had seen provided for the Bengal M.L.A.s to vote first on unity or partition, and only subsequently, in the event of unity being chosen, for independence or association with Hindustan or Pakistan. The amendment, made in response to an intervention by the Governor of Bengal in person, provided for M.L.A.s to vote first on whether, if unity were chosen, they would prefer independence, or association with Hindustan, or with Pakistan; the vote on unity or partition would follow. The Congress had already demanded the division of Bengal and the Punjab if Pakistan were conceded, and Nehru had told Mountbatten that it would regard a separate state of Bengal as a potential addition to Pakistan.[102]

Secondly, as F. F. Turnbull minuted at the India Office:

> To meet the Prime Minister's desire that after the Introduction [to the Plan] there should be an immediate indication of what the object of the whole procedure was, a new paragraph ... has been inserted. This states that the object is to get the different parts of India to decide through elected representatives between three options which were previously set out at a later point in the draft.[103]

Whereas the draft that Ismay took to London laid down a procedure to establish whether it was necessary to demit power to more than one authority, the revise began with the assumption that the Indian parties had been unable to agree upon any form of unified government and went on to prescribe a procedure 'to enable the different parts of India to decide . . . whether their constitution shall be framed: (a) in collaboration with the existing Constituent Assembly; (b) jointly with other parts of India; or (c) separately'.[104] This change extended the principle of full self-determination from those provinces and subprovinces to which the 1 May draft applied it—in effect the non-Constituent Assembly provinces and the N.W.F.P.—to all provinces. Though much the same words were used to describe the three alternative choices, the principle was given greater prominence and universal application. It was even applied to the states. The phrase 'different parts of India' included them too, and the revision of the paragraph on the states was substantial. The draft had merely reaffirmed that when paramountcy lapsed sovereignty would return to the states, which would then be 'free to arrange by negotiation with those parts of British India to which power will be demitted whatever measure of association' they wished.[105] Mountbatten had intended that the rulers should consult their people and 'make a quick announcement about joining the Constituent Assembly (or Assemblies) as soon as the statement of His Majesty's Government has been made', and he certainly gave the states no encouragement on the question of independence.[106] Now the Cabinet's revise offered the states the options of joining the existing Constituent Assembly, 'any other Constituent Assembly that may be established', or 'stand—[ing] out independently, either singly or jointly, as is open to the Provinces'. Ismay explained to Mountbatten that the choice of independence had been deliberately accorded to all parts of India: 'The Cabinet Committee's view has been that there must be a free choice if the scheme is to be consistent and defensible in Parliament'.[107]

The Cabinet's revise thus drew out the tension between the notion of *dual* dominionhood that Mountbatten and Menon assumed in their discussions with Nehru, and the principle of self-determination by the provinces, subprovinces, and states, which contemplated the emergence of several successor nations. At the mid-April Governors' Conference Mountbatten had observed the danger of 'Balkanization' through the full application of self-determination, yet subsequently he spoke and wrote of Plan Balkan as a plan for partition and a dual succession. He utterly overlooked the fact that the draft that Ismay took to London offered the option of independence to N.W.F.P.[108] It is extraordinary that late on Saturday 10 May he could cable home the following passage in an outline of the statement that he planned to make when he put Plan Balkan to the Indian leaders in a week's time: 'I have produced the plan which I am about to read out to you and which His Majesty's Government have approved. It embodies, as far as possible, all suggestions which you have put to me in our individual conversations'.[109] Ismay's confidential remark about Mountbatten on 23 April, when he was drafting Plan Balkan in Delhi, rings true:

We have made almost innumerable alternative drafts... but it is impossible to get Dickie to go through them methodically. He's a grand chap in a thousand ways but clarity of thought and writing is not his strong suit.[110]

Nehru delivered to Mountbatten on Sunday May 11 the letter that became known as his 'bombshell'.[111] He wrote that the Cabinet's revise had produced a 'devastating effect' upon him, for it was utterly at odds with the basis of the Simla discussions:

The relatively simple proposals that we had previously discussed now appeared, in garb that His Majesty's Government had provided for them, in an entirely new context which gave them an ominous meaning. The whole approach was completely different from what ours had been and the picture of India that emerged frightened me. In fact much that we had done so far was undermined and the Cabinet Mission's scheme and subsequent developments were set aside, and an entirely new picture presented—a picture of fragmentation and conflict and disorder, and unhappily also, of a worsening of relations between India and Britain.

The Plan was not consistent with the succession of a Dominion status Interim Government to the central Government of India; nor with the recognition of the provinces represented in the existing Constituent Assembly as the Union of India; nor even with the partition of India into two Dominions.

It is true that from a close reading of Plan Balkan on 30 April Nehru could have seen where the Viceroy's planning was leading. It is equally true that from a close reading of Nehru's letter of 1 May Mountbatten could have recognized the danger signs. While the letter conveyed the Working Committee's acceptance of the principles of partition and provincial option it clearly assumed the unifying context of the Cabinet Mission's scheme. It also revealed that Nehru did not realize that Miéville had acquainted him with 'the full extent of the proposals that Lord Ismay is taking with him to London'. The minds of Mountbatten and Nehru did not meet until 11 May.

Early on Sunday afternoon Mountbatten told Nehru explicitly that if Jinnah rejected Plan Balkan then 'the alternative plan' was to demit power to a Dominion status Interim Government, with safeguards for the Muslims and provision for subsequent partition.[112] Nehru expressed his preference for this alternative but Mountbatten doubted whether H.M.G. would allow its adoption. At a staff meeting at 4 o'clock Mountbatten put it to Nehru that the Cabinet's revise 'did not differ in essentials' from the draft that he had seen on 30 April, and that he was 'extremely surprised' at his reaction.[113] Nehru handed him a long note, the gravamen of which was that

> the whole background of the draft announcement was very different from what he had imagined. He had thought that Provinces were going to be asked to express their wishes on a slight variation of the Cabinet Mission's Plan. This would start on the basis of a Union of India, including the States. In the Cabinet Mission's Plan reference had been made to Provinces being able to opt out from one group to another at a later stage. Congress had now stated the principle of no compulsion and agreed any province which wished to could opt out of the Union completely. But in the present draft of the announcement the concept was not so much of a Union of India but of a large number of successor states to which theoretically power could be transferred and which would then join one group or another.... The approach was different and this became even more evident in regard to the states.[114]

The states were almost invited to stand out and await developments. The draft announcement encouraged people to believe that India was being Balkanized: 'The procedure seemed to be first separation, then a request to join up again. The previous process had been the opposite—first a request for unity and then the option to secede.' Mountbatten agreed that the states should not be encouraged to stand out independently. As for the provinces, he asked Nehru's views on the procedure for allowing Bengal to choose unity and independence, for the revise had applied the principle of it to all provinces. Nehru opposed the separation of Bengal and favoured partition. He sketched outlines for reframing the draft: the Constituent Assembly should be accepted as established, and the option of secession offered to only Punjab, Bengal, Sind, and Muslim-majority Sylhet in Assam. That night Mountbatten cabled to Ismay that in order to meet Nehru's objections 'a very considerable recast both in principle and detail' must be undertaken.[115]

The long note that Nehru submitted at the meeting ran to some 2,500 words.[116] The proposals were condemned as presenting an 'ominous' picture, menacing India and 'the future relation between Britain and India', encouraging 'disruptive tendencies everywhere and chaos and weakness'. They would be totally unacceptable to Congress. They departed from the 'basic factor' of the Cabinet Mission's Union of India subject to the agreement that certain Muslim areas might secede. They rejected the Union as the successor to power and invited the claims of a large number of successor states. The note bears the marks of anxiety and extreme haste. But despite its discursiveness and repetitiveness it is a clear and consistent statement of the confusion into which British constitutional policy had lapsed by 10 May 1947. The British Raj and H.M.G. had come within days of a commitment, in Nehru's words, to 'the theory of Provinces being initially independent successor states', the reversion of 'sovereignty ... to the Provinces', and the emergence of central authority as a 'later step by self-determination'. Britain would depart behind a veil of 'self-determination', thereby absolving itself of responsibility for 'Balkanization', 'civil conflict', 'violence', 'disorder', the 'breakdown of central authority', 'chaos', and the 'demoralization' of India. The theory of the sovereignty of the princely states would encourage at least the major ones to become independent kingdoms, presumably as allies of the British, and to play Pakistan off against the rest of India.

At his staff meeting on Monday morning, 12 May, Mountbatten disclosed that the previous night he had further discussed with Nehru 'the plan which [Nehru] had put forward for the early demission of power to the Interim Government on a Dominion Status basis', which was 'really very similar' to 'the alternative plan with which he [Mountbatten] had previously decided to threaten Mr. Jinnah'.[117] Nehru had argued that neither Mountbatten nor H.M.G. could devise an acceptable solution for India. Any British scheme would be seen as an award and provoke bloodshed. Indians themselves should take the blame, and he 'would be prepared to afford all manner of safeguards and assurances to the Muslim League if power was handed over to the present Interim Government'. Mountbatten suggested to Nehru that this scheme might be made more acceptable to Jinnah if details such as the new capitals of provinces were included before it was put to him. At the staff meeting Miéville saw no prospect of Jinnah preferring this scheme but Mountbatten asked him to cable to

Ismay about it and draft heads of agreement on safeguards. Miéville cabled to Ismay:

The Viceroy is now wondering more and more whether we ought not work on the lines of trying to demit power on a Dominion Status basis with Jinnah being given adequate safeguards in the interim period. What do you think?[118]

Whatever the response, Mountbatten had decided that because of the Indian leaders' suspicion of Whitehall a plan acceptable to Congress must be drafted by his staff in India. He had also decided that the choice of independence must not be accorded to Bengal or any other province.[119]

Ismay's response to Miéville's inquiry was categorical. A transfer of power to the Interim Government prior to partition was unthinkable:

I am all in favour of early Dominion status *provided* both sides get a fair deal. But telegrams suggest Congress leaders have got impression that immediate Dominion status for Interim Government might be alternative to partition plan and that they would then be given a free hand as advocated in Patel's statement to Press on 9th May. I do not see how doing so without successful partition is possible in present circumstances or what adequate safeguards for Jinnah to which you refer would be.[120]

Ismay expressed puzzlement in a cable to Mountbatten, responding to the latter's account of Nehru's 'bombshell'. Nehru seemed to believe that there was 'some alternative plan which would be a substitute for Partition'.[121] This was not the case, for both the V. P. Menon appendix, and the plan for a Dominion status transfer of power that Mountbatten and Menon had discussed with Nehru at Simla from 8–10 May, proceeded 'on the basis of successful partition and cannot be put into effect until that is achieved'. Ismay noted that Patel's press statement of 9 May 'seemed to have forgotten about partition' and envisaged 'a free hand' for the Interim Government. This was 'contrary to assurances by HMG' and could scarcely be what Mountbatten contemplated. 'There must', he wrote, 'be some misunderstanding on the part of the Congress as to the scope of your proposals for early Dominion Status'. Ismay could not know the extent to which Mountbatten had confided to Nehru his predilection for the 'alternative plan'. A colleague of Gandhi's who had discussed his letter of 8 May with Mountbatten had reported: 'He [Mountbatten] was not wholly satisfied with the reactions of His Majesty's Government and was struggling to get them to think along your lines'.[122] W.H.J. Christie was critical of Mountbatten's 'over-trustfulness and impatience' at Simla: 'the "alternative plan" should have remained secret to the last . . . . The Lord needs George [Abell] or Ismay to steady him'.[123]

With Ismay and Abell in London, Miéville 'a bit at sea' in their absence, and Captain Brockman acting as P.S.V. but lacking familiarity with the complexities of the case,[124] Mountbatten had lurched from advocacy of Plan Balkan to near acceptance of the Congress demand—until Ismay's steadying cables reaffirmed H.M.G.'s obligation to the Muslims. Mountbatten's celebrated resilience now came into play, as he recovered his balance to steer Congress towards a transfer of power that was also acceptable to Jinnah—almost immediate dual dominionhood as a final settlement of the problem.

VII *The Deal for Two Dominions*

On Tuesday 13 May Mountbatten brought before his staff a plan that V. P. Menon had drafted the previous day in accordance with Nehru's requirements and in consultation with Patel by telephone.[125] It drew upon Plan Balkan and V. P. Menon's appendix to it. It was a plan for the transfer of power to only two successor Dominions. It might truly be called the Mountbatten-Nehru deal for two Dominions, or, more conveniently, Plan Partition. It arrived in London with Mountbatten's comments in the early hours of 14 May. Mountbatten commended its fundamental departure from Plan Balkan's throughgoing application of self-determination:

> The issues . . . are limited to joining existing Constituent Assembly or joining together in a new Constituent Assembly. I have omitted choice to Provinces of standing out independently . . . . I do not now like the idea of HMG giving them that choice.[126]

No choice would be allowed to the Congress provinces already represented in the Constituent Assembly, except that N.W.F.P. would have a referendum to decide between Hindustan and Pakistan. Mountbatten would tell the premier of Bengal that no provision could be made for provincial independence, but if the Bengal Legislative Assembly passed a resolution in favour of independence then he would 'treat [it] on its merits'. Mountbatten deferred to Nehru in principle and detail. Of the states, he wrote:

> Nehru intensely dislikes passage in Cabinet Committee's draft relating to States. He feels that as drafted it will encourage disruptive tendencies and I

agree. We must preserve the position of the States but at the same time we cannot avoid giving a lead to Princes.'

Menon's draft of Plan Partition observed that H.M.G.'s policy towards the States was unchanged, but it gave the following lead:

Some of the States are already participating in the deliberations of the existing Constituent Assembly. H.M.G. hope that all others will join either the existing Constituent Assembly or the new Constituent Assembly.[127]

Mountbatten indicated that he would clear the draft of Plan Partition with Nehru again, and with Jinnah, 'in order to avoid any further bombshells'.

The India Committee of the Cabinet met at 5.30 on 14 May and Attlee did his best to account for Mountbatten's volte-face: 'In particular the raising at this stage of the possibility of early attainment of Dominion Status by India, or by part of India, seemed to have produced a radical change in the situation.'[128] He declared it unprofitable for the Committee to consider the proposals contained in Plan Partition without first seeking 'further explanations of [the Viceroy's] views and intentions'. At 9 p.m. he recalled Mountbatten to London for consultations.[129] Mountbatten's meetings with the India Committee between 19 and 28 May settled the terms for the final transfer of power in accordance with those of his deal with Nehru. Given the necessity of Pakistan, they enabled India to achieve freedom with the greatest possible unity. They were embodied in the 3 June statement of policy, which formed the basis for the enactment of Indian Independence and Partition well before the end of 1947.

At his first meeting with the India Committee Mountbatten rehearsed the course of his negotiations from the time of his arrival in Delhi on 22 March. He emphasized that a turning point was reached when 'certain Congress leaders' offered to accept partition and Dominion status provided that power was transferred substantially before June 1948 and that India was free to secede from the Commonwealth (though they assured him that 'there would ultimately be no rush to secede from the Commonwealth once Dominion Status had been accepted').[130] Congress had agreed to accept a common Governor-General for both Dominions and wished him to remain for that purpose and as arbitrator, but Jinnah's response to the suggestion was still awaited. The Prime Minister undertook to seek the opposition leaders' co-operation for the rapid passing of legislation to effect a transfer of power by Dominion status. The Lord Chancellor was to pursue the adaptation of the 1935 Act to that end.

Next afternoon, 20 May, Mountbatten informed the Committee that Jinnah was becoming difficult. Suspicious of a Plan that proceeded from the tainted Cabinet Mission scheme, Jinnah was now unprepared to commit himself to the acceptance of power on a Dominion status basis until he had seen the Plan in its final form. Mountbatten undertook to prepare a proposal for dealing with Jinnah if he rejected the Plan. The contingency was a grave one, for Congress had accepted the Plan on the condition that the League agreed to it as a final settlement. Mountbatten emphasized the need for quick action. Power must, he said, be transferred 'not later than the early Autumn of 1947'.[131]

On 22 May Attlee told the Committee that the opposition party leaders had assured him of their support for Plan Partition.[132] Mountbatten helped somewhat to win over Churchill though the key to his assent was India's membership of the Commonwealth. As late as 17 May Listowel was insistent that as the Cabinet Mission Plan was dead H.M.G. was committed to the form of provincial option that had been promised at the time of the Cripps Mission in 1942, that is the option of provincial dominionhood.[133] Churchill, with his usual lack of perspicacity on Indian constitutional matters, was in due course to tell Parliament that the Indian Independence Act was consistent with the central principles of the Cripps offer, for which his government had been responsible, Dominion status and provincial option.

The 22 May meeting settled the strategy for dealing with Jinnah if he rejected Plan Partition, for he was now virulent against the partition of Bengal and Punjab and claiming a land corridor to connect the eastern and western arms of his Pakistan. Mountbatten proposed to frighten him by a policy of isolation: power should be transferred to an Indian Dominion and 'an independent Government outside the Commonwealth for the Muslim majority areas'.[134] Having used Jinnah's initial request for dominionhood to manoeuvre Congress towards the Commonwealth, he would now use the same strategy against the League. The Committee, however, adopted Listowel's proposal that in any event power should be transferred to a Pakistan Dominion, which might secede at once if it wished. It also accepted that Jinnah might be told that 'the consequence of refusal would be a settlement less favourable... than that contained in the announcement', for example a settlement more favourable to the Sikhs.[135] The meeting also authorized Mountbatten to give the princes the 'lead' that he had proposed. He had been insistent that the prospect of direct relations between the Crown and independent states would encourage the 'disintegration of India'.[136] The states 'must be told that their relations with the Crown will have to be through one or other of the Governors-General'. Mountbatten's treatment of the princes prior to the transfer of power was, in effect, authorized by the Committee's acceptance of a note that Mountbatten and Listowel produced.[137] H.M.G.'s 'prime object should be to facilitate the exclusive association of the states with one of the new Dominions'. If H.M.G. admitted the possibility of separate relations with states or groups of states then Congress was 'likely to withdraw its application for Dominion Status'. Listowel added to Mountbatten's drafting a provision that if a state did eventually stand aside from India and Pakistan then H.M.G. would be forced to consider separate relations with it. Nevertheless, the note presaged Mountbatten's large contribution to the long delayed and now miraculously quick mediatization of the states, those monstrous impediments to India's achievement of freedom and unity. On 22 May the Committee also gave Mountbatten 'discretion to settle, without reference to London, points that might arise during the discussions [on the Plan with Indian leaders] provided that he did not depart from the general policy of His Majesty's Government'.

At Mountbatten's last meeting with the Committee, on 28 May, the final policy implication of Plan Partition was resolved, namely, H.M.G.'s attitude to a demand for an independent Bengal.[138] Mountbatten had always been ambivalent over the question. He appreciated the problems that would arise from a divided Bengal, with the eastern part linked with distant West Pakistan, but he also recognized the dangerous precedent that an independent united Bengal would create. He spoke to the India Committee of the viability of a Dominion of Bengal but ultimately he accepted Bengal unity, like the Sikhs, as an inevitable casualty of all-India and Commonwealth exigencies. On 21 May he cabled to Burrows:

> I believe that if Suhrawardy were to renew his request for dominion status for Bengal at this moment it might make Congress leaders chary of agreeing to a united Bengal since they would feel that it would lessen the chances of Bengal coming into the Union at a later date if they had Independent Dominion Status.[139]

The deal with Nehru had given Congress the trump card, and Nehru played it in a press interview on 27 May at Mussoorie, where the Bengali Opposition leader, Kiran Sanker Roy, had come to secure the High Command's blessing for a coalition government with Suhrawardy. 'We can', declared Nehru, 'agree to Bengal remaining united only if it remains in the Union'.[140] Mountbatten advised the India Committee that this development gravely prejudiced 'the prospects of saving the unity of Bengal and securing its establishment as a third Dominion in India'. Only if Jinnah yielded Bengal to India could its partition be avoided. The Committee therefore dismissed as unreal the prospect of a united Bengal Dominion, and as East Bengal was 'clearly not a viable unit', it would 'have to unite with one or other of the Indian Dominions'.

VIII *Conclusion*

Though Attlee's announcement of 20 February 1947 set the transfer of power deadline at June 1948, soon after his arrival in India Mountbatten was seized of the need for a substantial instalment of devolution on a Dominion status basis immediately the Cabinet Mission scheme was finally rejected. A decision in principle upon successor authorities was necessary to counter the civil disorder that uncertainty was breeding. H.M.G. required Mountbatten to report his recommendations by October and enjoined him to encourage Commonwealth membership. Rau, Menon and the Congress had already advocated immediate Dominion status: partly because of the impossibility of drafting an independent constitution by June 1948; partly to prevent national disintegration through Muslim League direct action, dissident movements in the states, and tribal disturbances; partly for reasons of defence. Wavell had long urged the need for quick action (and, at the end, had even recognized the possibility of a Dominion status transfer of power under the 1935 Act).[141] Though as late as March Cripps and Mountbatten still hoped for the acceptance of Plan Union, Jinnah had already dismissed all alternatives to Pakistan and Congress had acquiesced in the principle of partition. Mountbatten's task was to find a formula for partition that was acceptable to the League and the Congress, facilitated a quick transfer of power, and promised co-operation between Britain and the successor nations.

During April and early May the main parties involved in the deepening crisis approached the constitutional problem differently. Congress sought Dominion status for the Interim Government pending the preparation of a sovereign republican constitution by the existing Constituent Assembly. The Interim Government would preside over the secession of any Muslim province or subprovince that might choose separation. With its control of the Interim Government and the Constituent Assembly the Congress might well hope to lure the Muslim areas away from the Pakistan alternative. The approach was contrary to H.M.G.'s past pledges to the Muslims and the Governor of the Punjab believed that it would provoke civil war,[142] though in May Mountbatten toyed with it until he was overruled. Jinnah and the League sought a province-wise division of India, with the Pakistan provinces remaining in the Commonwealth. Their proposed non-partition of Bengal and Punjab provoked Congress hostility, as, in view of the Congress's declaration for sovereign republican status, did the possibility of Britain receiving Pakistan into the Commonwealth. The third approach, unhappily named 'Plan Balkan' by its creators, left the provinces to decide upon partition and to choose between India, Pakistan, and separate independence. Enamoured of the principle of self-determination, mainly as an escape from the odious responsibility for partitioning India, first Mountbatten's staff and then H.M.G. developed a plan that unwittingly encouraged fragmentation, precisely the outcome that the Congress plan was intended to avoid. V. P. Menon's appendix to it provided for Dominion status to be conferred upon the national entities that emerged from the decision-making process, and pending the making of constitutions.

The Simla deal for two Dominions was a negotiated amalgam of the Congress and the British approaches. It was the consequence of the C.W.C.'s determination, in the face of the League's manipulation of direct action and the danger of Pakistan's dominionhood, to secure a final settlement in May 1947. It was the culmination of Mountbatten's brilliant and persistent manoeuvring for a Commonwealth solution, and of H.M.G.'s longstanding policy not to subject an unwilling Muslim League to the Hindu majority. For India it promised to dispose of the prospect of fully independent princely states and of an independent united Bengal. For Britain it avoided the need to decide whether Dominion status should be accorded to only part of the subcontinent, and it offered continuity of arrangements for defence. It promised a measure of Indian unity through the Commonwealth, a joint Governor-General and a joint defence council, albeit, in the event, falsely.

Mountbatten bestowed the inestimable boon of an agreed solution to the Indian constitution problem. He secured from Jinnah acceptance of the partition of the Punjab and Bengal, and from Nehru the acceptance of dual dominionhood as a final settlement of the Indian problem. When the Indian leaders accepted Plan Partition on 3 June Attlee conveyed the whole Cabinet's congratulations. Both he and Listowel acknowledged that the success was due to Mountbatten's personal efforts.[143] Sir John Colville, the senior Governor, wrote from Bombay of 'your wonderful achievement',[144] and Woodrow Wyatt, who had assisted Cripps at the time of the Cabinet Mission, wrote of the agreement as 'one of the finest achievements of any Government that this country has ever had'.[145] Gandhi, of course, opposed partition to the last, yet even he came close to congratulating Mountbatten. On 4 June, alluding to his success in securing the agreement between the Congress and the League, he said, in admonition and admiration: 'You and your magic tricks'.[146]

7
India in 1947: The Limits of Unity

As time gives perspective to the partition of the Indian subcontinent in August 1947, the limits of the unity that were then achieved will probably be related to the history of imperial expansion and control. Apprehensive of external aggression and inconvenienced by unstable indigenous regimes, the British steadily extended their empire to the geographical limits of the subcontinent. At the end of the empire the territories that seceded from British India were (save East Bengal, which could not have seceded alone) among those last annexed—Sind, West Punjab, Baluchistan and the North-West Frontier Province (N.W.F.P.)—while the Pakistan movement itself was first spearheaded from the last of the princely states to be seized, the Kingdom of Oudh. The failure of the Congress national movement to achieve in the dissident areas the dominance that it established almost everywhere else is usually explained simply in terms of the Hindu-Muslim conflict. An analysis of the interaction between the survival of parochial Muslim socio-political structures and the Raj's post-mutiny reliance upon traditional forms of social control is overdue. At the same time, the outstanding problem of national integration around the time of Independence was the assimilation of the princely states, themselves survivals explicable in terms of Britain's need after 1857 to buttress up its direct rule of the provinces with princely alliances.

In the twentieth century the necessities of imperial rule gave the territories of the Muslims and the Rajas a disproportionate importance. During a period of avowed devolution of power upon responsible provincial governments, the princes enjoyed imperial support without obligation to introduce comparable reforms. When modest central reforms unlikely to win Congress support were contemplated, a special effort was made to retain the collaboration of the Muslims by the creation of Sind province, the enhancement of the N.W.F.P.'s status, the perpetuation of communal electorates in the Punjab and Bengal, and the concession of one-third of the seats in the putative all-India federal legislature. The relaxation of imperial control in the provinces, while it remained tight at the centre, enabled Muslim politicians to consolidate their provincial bases without challenge from the national level. Assuredly, Congress strategies contributed to the failure of Britain's two major attempts to set up constitutions for a united India, but under the India Act of 1935 the princes were given a veto on the development of a central government for the subcontinent, and by the Cabinet Mission scheme in 1946 the Muslims were enabled to defeat the creation of a fully representative Indian Constituent Assembly.

Seen thus, the limits of unity that India achieved under the terms of the final transfer of power seem impressive, and the terms themselves acquire particular interest.

I *The Deal for Dual Dominionhood*

The signal for the break-up of imperial India was Clement Attlee's announcement on 20 February 1947. Unless the Constituent Assembly became fully representative and formed a constitution by June 1948, H.M.G. would

> have to consider to whom the powers of Central Government in British India should be handed over, on the due date, whether as a whole to some form of Central Government for British India, or in some areas to the existing Provincial Governments, or in such other way as may seem most reasonable and in the best interests of the Indian people.[1]

The Congress leaders welcomed this irrevocable decision to quit and assumed that in the absence of representatives from the non-Congress areas the Constituent Assembly would proceed to make a constitution that would embrace all areas of India willing to accept it. Nehru was sanguine:

> This may result in the Indian Union being first established for the whole of India except Bengal, the Punjab and Sind. Of course the Union constitution will apply to or rather be open to all; but those Provinces may not choose to adhere to it. If so, the second question that arises is that those parts of Bengal and Punjab which are fully represented in the Constituent Assembly (Western Bengal and Southern Punjab) should be parts of the Union. That means a partition of the Punjab and Bengal. It is unlikely that Jinnah or the Muslim League will agree to this truncated Pakistan . . . . They will thus have to make a choice ultimately between this and joining the Indian Union possibly on special terms. In other words, the position of Bengal and Punjab in such an event approximates to that of an Indian State.[2]

Nehru anticipated the continuation of the Cabinet Mission scheme so that willing areas could form a Union of India. The states would either enter the Assembly and help devise arrangements for joining the federation, or reach 'particular arrangements' with the Union on, he assumed, a subordinate basis.

This was to reckon without the determination that now possessed Jinnah and the League, whose experience during the previous year's unsuccessful negotiations for groups of Muslim provinces within the Union had steeled them to seek security in a separate sovereign nation, however small. Jinnah had called for 'direct action' in August 1946, and the 'Calcutta killing' had ensued. The next month, with the lapse of the Defence of India Rules that suppressed private armies, the ranks of the Muslim League National Guards rapidly rose to some 91,500 men, now subordinated directly to the League's central leadership[3]. The Guards, who were pledged to 'strive for the achievement of Pakistan and for the freedom and glory of the Muslim nation', were, in the words of the Assistant Director of the Intelligence Bureau, 'put... on a war footing'.[4] The Hindu Rashtriya Swayamsevak Sangh (R.S.S.) and the Sikh Akalis were of a similar size. By January 1947 the Guards were parading the streets of Lahore in military uniform, and towards the end of the month the Punjab Coalition (Unionist-Akali-Congress) ministry declared them and the R.S.S. unlawful. When the Guards defied the ban and it was withdrawn the ramshackle coalition of Muslims, Sikhs and Hindus collapsed. On 2 March the Premier resigned. The League's leader in the Assembly was asked to form a government but he could not secure the numbers. As disorder spread and Governor's rule became imminent, Vallabhbhai Patel noted that Attlee's statement 'for the present, has resulted in our losing the Punjab'.[5] Still, like Nehru, he remained confident of eventual unity:

Before next June [1948] the Constitution must be ready and if the League insists on Pakistan the only alternative is the division of the Punjab and Bengal. They cannot have Punjab as a whole or Bengal without civil war. I do not think that the British Government will agree to division .... They will not help the minority in securing or maintaining division, and a strong Centre with the whole of India except East Bengal and a part of the Punjab, Sind and Baluchistan, enjoying full autonomy under that Centre, will be so powerful that the remaining portions will eventually come in.[6]

Early in March the Congress Working Committee passed resolutions that defined its policy in the aftermath of Attlee's statement. They called for the partition of the Punjab between its Muslim and non-Muslim areas. While they hoped for the entry of all provincial and state territories into the Constituent Assembly, they accepted that its work was 'essentially voluntary'.[7] There must be 'no compulsion', and provinces and parts of provinces must be free to accept, by the choice of their own people, whether to join the Union. At the same time, during the transitional period of constitution-making, and pending the transfer of power, the Interim Government must be recognized as a fully responsible Dominion Government with the Viceroy as its constitutional head. Dominion status was to be a device for an interim transfer of power under the existing constitution. Thereby, the Interim Government, with Nehru as Prime Minister and Congress predominant, would preside over the process of constitution-making, the partition of provinces, and the secession of dissident areas. At that moment Congress did not press this demand for full power during the interim period. Lord Wavell's departure was imminent and discussions must be held with Lord Mountbatten as the Viceroy sent out to achieve a 'New Deal' for winding up the Raj.[8] For the moment, too, although the League had launched civil disobedience movements in the N.W.F.P. and Assam, their Congress governments remained in control.

On 8 April Nehru outlined the Congress approach to the transfer of power in an interview with Mountbatten. He emphasized that a constitution should not be imposed on any area against its will and that provinces and partitioned provinces should be free to join Hindustan, Pakistan, 'or possibly even remain completely independent'.[9] This was no prescription for fragmentation, for 'the whole thing revolved around having a strong centre ... and for that reason [he] would favour making a statement soon and transferring power to Provinces while there was still time for [Mountbatten] ... to help in the early stages of negotiations at the Centre'. The reference to a Dominion status Interim Government was clear enough, but Mountbatten regrettably overlooked it when he commended Nehru's principle of partition by self-determination to his staff as the basis of planning.[10] The staff proceeded to work up 'Plan Balkan' which, thus unhappily named, was brought before a conference of the provincial Governors in mid-April.[11] It provided for self-determination by provinces, and the partitioning of provinces, which could be members of Hindustan or Pakistan or independent from both—prior to the concession of Dominion status. The Governors generally approved the Plan. Their discussions suggested that the Plan might yield a very small Pakistan indeed. Though strongly challenged by the League, the Congress government of the N.W.F.P. might still be returned if an election were held in the near future, as the Governor wished, to resolve prevailing tensions. In Bengal, the essentially League ministry had construed Attlee's statement as foreshadowing a transfer of power to an independent province. The Governor preferred that outcome to a partition that would separate out the 'rural slum' of East Bengal, an unattractive prospective partner for West Pakistan. Mountbatten warned of the 'Balkanization' of India by self-determination, but he also spoke of the feasibility of a minimal Pakistan, resembling an Indian state and including only West Punjab and Sind (and with the choice of not taking over the deficit Frontier Province).[12]

In mid-April Mountbatten acheived a minor victory when he induced Gandhi and Jinnah to issue a joint appeal to end the communal violence that was becoming endemic. But the Congress leaders grew increasingly restive at the League's persistent resort to direct action for political advantage. On 20 April, Patel reminded Mountbatten that though he had completed one month in office, 'bestiality' prevailed as the League sought to capture the Punjab, N.W.F.P. and Assam.[13] Soon afterwards he complained that Mountbatten was neither prepared to govern firmly himself nor allow Congress to take over.[14] When 'Plan Balkan' finally issued from Mountbatten's staff at the end of April and Nehru saw that it provided for fresh elections in the N.W.F.P., he called the Congress Working Committee (C.W.C.) into session to take stock. Tension was exacerbated on 30 April by Jinnah's release of a press statement attacking the partition of Bengal and the Punjab as a 'sinister' Congress device and calling for his full six-province Pakistan.[15]

On 1 May the C.W.C. reiterated its acceptance of the principle of partition by self-determination. However, its main emphasis, as expressed in a letter in which Nehru conveyed its opinion of the Plan, was on an orderly transfer of power.[16] The C.W.C. accepted the Cabinet Mission scheme and its Constituent Assembly in their entirety, whereas the League had rejected them and resorted to violence. Since Attlee's statement, the League had attempted by large-scale violence to overthrow provincial governments, even after the Gandhi-Jinnah appeal. 'Every proposal . . . must be viewed in this context.' If policy were to be influenced by terrorism, then the inevitable result would be civil war. Yet in the N.W.F.P. Mountbatten now proposed to yield to violence. The C.W.C. would resist any such proposal to end a duly constituted provincial government and call elections in response to terrorism.

The C.W.C., with Gandhi in attendance, considered the N.W.F.P. and the general political situation on 1, 2, 4, 5, and 7 May. Although no minutes of proceedings are extant, it is clear that the big three, Gandhi, Nehru and Patel, agreed on an immediate showdown. The Congress demand was put by Nehru to Mountbatten personally at Simla on 8 May, by Gandhi in a letter to Mountbatten written on that day, and by Patel in a press release next day.[17] There were individual differences but the approach was essentially the same. Power should be demitted to the Central Government on a Dominion status basis forthwith. The provinces should not be asked to decide their future until the Constituent Assembly had formed a constitution. Then provinces and part provinces should be free to leave the Union and a referendum might be held in the N.W.F.P. The demand was a restatement of the policy that Congress had adopted in response to Attlee's announcement and the unrest that followed it in the Muslim provinces: a strong Indian government at the Centre to preside over the peaceful preparation of an all-India constitution by the Constituent Assembly and the subsequent secession by self-determination of dissident areas.

Much has been made of Nehru's explosion when, on 10 May, Mountbatten showed him the plan for the transfer of power in the form that the British Cabinet had finally approved. There is no doubt that Nehru had seen the full draft of the Plan on 30 April and approved its underlying principle of partition by self-determination—indeed, his own proposals of 8 April had embodied it. However, he did not read the Plan closely enough to realize that the context for the application of the principle had been changed. Instead of a strong Indian Centre presiding over the secession of dissident areas once the Assembly had prepared a constitution, the Plan envisaged that provinces would choose whether to be partitioned, and whether to join Hindustan, Pakistan, or remain independent, prior to the constitution-making process. Moreover, after Nehru had seen the draft Plan, it had been altered by Mountbatten so as to enhance the possibility of an independent united Bengal, and by H.M.G. so as to emphasize the freedom of provinces, subprovinces and states to choose complete independence.[18] Such changes seemed only to encourage the drift towards disunity. The contrasting approaches of Congress and the British only became clear amid the flurry of discussions at Simla and the exchange of cables with Whitehall from 11 to 13 May.

Altough on 11 and 12 May Mountbatten was disposed to accept the Congress scheme for an immediate demission of power to a Dominion status Interim Government, he was pulled up sharp by Lord Ismay, his chief of staff, who had taken the Plan to London. Ismay's cables emphasized that such an approach would be in breach of past parliamentary assurances that the Muslims would not be subjected to the will of the majority.[19] From the wreckage of 'Plan Balkan' and the Congress plan Mountbatten, aided by his Reforms Commissioner, V. P. Menon, now struck with Nehru the deal that was to become the 3 June plan for an immediate transfer of power to two Dominions.[20] For the sake of a final settlement of Muslim claims, the Congress accepted the cession by self-determination of the Muslim majority areas. Congress would lose to Pakistan the areas of Sind, Baluchistan, West Punjab, East Bengal and the N.W.F.P. (despite later backsliding in an attempt to secure its separate independence). But the possible loss of the whole of Bengal was averted and an assurance of Dominion status for the rest of British India within weeks was secured.[21]

Congress had long accepted that unity could not be imposed and that Muslim India must eventually choose to remain in a Union or secede to form Pakistan. It had hoped that, given a favourable sequence of events, the Constituent Assembly might be able to attract the Muslim areas by constitutional concessions. With the deterioration of communal relations in March and April, the possibility receded steadily. At the end of April Nehru still believed that 'sooner or later India will have to function as a unified country', but he recognized that 'perhaps the best way to reach that stage is to go through some kind of a partition now'.[22] At Simla V. P. Menon urged him to accept a quick partition in order to avert the further spread of communal bitterness and to prepare for later reunification.[23] Under the dual Dominions deal there were to be a common Governor-General for India and Pakistan and a Joint Defence Council. Mountbatten himself believed that Pakistan would be scarcely viable, a very poor country with the burdensome Frontier Province and East Bengal, and he expected that it would accept international representation by India or Britain, except in the United Kingdom, the United States and some Muslim countries.[24] The Simla deal averted the fragmentation of British India, drawing the limits of unity by restricting the options of Muslim majority areas to membership of India or Pakistan.

II. *The Problem of the Princes*[25]

Probably the main attraction of the deal to Congress was that it promised to banish the spectre of princely Ulsters. It is likely that the primary significance of the deal will come to be seen as its preparation for the integration of the 562 princely states within the two Dominions, and that Mountbatten's viceroyalty will be assessed mainly in terms of his contribution to that process. On the eve of the deal, the Congress leaders appreciated that as Governor-General of an Indian Dominion, Mountbatten would be most useful in negotiations with the princes.[26] In his letter to Mountbatten on 8 May, Gandhi condemned the 'vicious doctrine' of the 'intransmissibility of paramountcy'—the non-transferability of the Crown's relations with the princes to a successor Indian government.[27] That day, too, Patel was writing of the states as one of the 'outstanding' problems demanding an immediate settlement of 'the shape of things . . . for purposes of transfer of power'.[28] In discussions with V. P. Menon and Krishna Menon at Simla, Nehru revealed that his acceptance of Dominion status rested heavily upon his expectation of Mountbatten's helpfulness with the princes. On 9 May he expressed to V. P. Menon the hope that paramountcy might be transferred in respect of defence, foreign relations and communications.[29]

Policy and protest proceeded from the 'Memorandum on States' Treaties and Paramountcy' that the Cabinet Mission released in May 1946.[30] It was the work of Sir Stafford Cripps, supplemented by some suggestions from Sir Conrad Corfield, Political Adviser to the Crown Representative. It spoke of an interim period between the British Indian parties' acceptance of a plan and the final transfer of power. During the interim period the states might participate in the process of constitution-making by joining the Constituent Aseembly. Whether they did so or not, they would surely wish to strengthen their position by ensuring that their administration conformed to the highest standard and by placing themselves 'in close and constant touch with public opinion in their state by means of representative institutions'. During the interim period, too, they must negotiate with British India over the future regulation of matters of common concern, especially in the economic and financial field. As such negotiations might still be incomplete by the time of the transfer of power, standstill agreements between the states and the new British Indian governments would be necessary. The states were assured that the British Government would not and could not 'in any circumstances transfer paramountcy to an Indian Government'. The rights surrendered by the states to the paramount power would return to the states. When British India became fully self-governing H.M.G. would cease to be able to exercise the powers of paramountcy, which must then lapse:

Political arrangements between the states on one side and the British Crown and British India on the other will thus be brought to an end. The void will have to be filled either by the states entering into a federal relationship with the successor Government or Governments in British India, or, failing this, entering into particular political arrangements with it or them.

Official action pursuant to the Memorandum was the responsibility of Corfield. His predecessor wrote of him:

He is a very able person indeed, but his cast of mind is for these days excessively conservative. He has been all his life in Indian states and has imbibed, perhaps too successfully, the Princely point of view.[31]

His actions reveal a passion for legal correctitude (not always matched in his later reflections by factual exactitude). In mid-December 1946 he called the Residents into conference on the retraction of paramountcy. Although the Cabinet Mission scheme had not secured the agreement of the Indian parties, the Constituent Assembly had met and the princes had set up a Negotiating Committee to discuss terms for the entry of the states. At the same time, an Interim Government with Congress and League members had been formed. Corfield knew and approved of Lord Wavell's 'Breakdown Plan', then under discussion in London, which provided for a full British withdrawal by 31 March 1948, preceded by a phased geographical withdrawal of British civil and military administration.[32] Corfield might well assume that the 'interim period' had begun. On 16 December he told the Residents:

What we contemplated was the gradual reduction of paramountcy intervention *pari passu* with a gradual increase in states' freedom, so that the smallest possible vacuum remained at the end of the interim period when paramountcy would lapse.[33]

The retraction of paramountcy was to be hastened. Residents were to encourage the establishment of states' constitutions that would obviate the need for action by the paramount power.

The conference anticipated Attlee's February statement that during the period up to the transfer of power 'the relations of the Crown with individual states may be adjusted by agreement'.[34] Mountbatten's instructions, too, empowered him to negotiate such adjustments. They enjoined him to persuade rulers 'to progress rapidly towards some form of more democratic government', and to 'assist the States in coming to fair and just arrangements with the leaders of British India as to their future relationships'.[35] On 26 February Corfield furnished Wavell with a memorandum for the Secretary of State on the 'contraction of paramountcy' and proposed a Residents' conference in April to discuss it.[36] The memorandum, which was sent next day, sought the Secretary of State's approval for the contraction of paramountcy so that action could be taken to bring about the maximum devolution by the end of 1947.[37] Thereby, 'alternative arrangements may have a chance of functioning before paramountcy as a system finally disappears.' Lord Pethick-Lawrence agreed to this approach. The December Residents' conference had 'tackled the question in a businesslike and realistic fashion'.[38] Yet while the Viceroy should secure the 'greatest practicable devolution', he should avoid 'any step which would prejudice the future unity of India in regard to defence and communications'. The object was 'to enable states to stand on their own feet to encourage them to stand together but to do everything to encourage them to co-operate to the full with British India.' In particular, negotiation on matters of common concern should be pressed forward to avoid an administrative vacuum at the transfer of power. On 21 March, Pethick-Lawrence followed up with a cautious letter to Mountbatten, fearing that the approved contraction might precipitate the 'premature withdrawal' of political officers.[39] He requested monthly reports from the Political Department on the princes' steps to integrate their rule with the will of their subjects and with the future structure of British India. Corfield advised that the April Residents' Conference would produce a programme of contraction. He added: 'I fear that any tendency to delay withdrawal [of political officers] will defeat the very object at which we are aiming, namely to make the States stand on their own legs.'[40] Only physical withdrawal would stir the princes to action. Moreover, as political officers withdrew, his department would progressively become unable to report as Pethick-Lawrence requested. On 5 April Mountbatten replied to Pethick-Lawrence in these terms.[41] On 8–9 April the Residents' Conference at Delhi concerted a programme for the withdrawal of Political Agents by the autumn and of Residents by the end of the year, and the completion of the Political Department's main duties by March 1948, three months before the transfer of power deadline.[42] In sum, the progressive contraction of paramountcy would mean the substantial transfer of power to the princes some months ahead of the due date for British India.

At the mid-April Governors' Conference, Mountbatten 'handed round' the text of Attlee's instructions to him and unveiled 'Plan Balkan'.[43] The latter provided for the states to become independent on the transfer of power and to negotiate freely with any confederation of provinces that might emerge. In the course of discussion on the wisdom of according provinces the choice of separate independence, Corfield argued that as the states were to have the choice it ought to be extended for the sake of consistency. Ismay argued that the option of independence flowed logically from Attlee's statement. The Plan that Ismay took to London on 2 May reaffirmed that His Majesty's Government (H.M.G.) policy towards the states remained unchanged. Paramountcy would lapse and all rights surrendered to the paramount power would return to the states. They were free to negotiate with the British Indian successors whatever association was in the best interests of their people.

Corfield has written that he was now anxious to clear the programme of contraction with the Secretary of State (Lord Listowel):

> Mountbatten was too busy negotiating with the Congress and Muslim League leaders to give any attention to the States' problem, so I gladly accepted the offer to accompany Ismay to London when he was taking to the cabinet Mountbatten's final plan.... As regards this plan, all I wanted to do was to make sure that the cabinet memorandum of May 1946 was referred to and endorsed.[44]

The Plan did not then refer explicitly to the Memorandum, and Corfield may have feard that Mountbatten would succumb to Congress pressure on the problem of the princes. On 18 April Nehru, as president of the All-India States' Peoples' Conference (A.I.S.P.C.), virtually a Congress subsidiary, attacked the princes for their reluctance to join the Constituent Assembly without assurances on their privileges.[45] Their 'shopkeepers' mentality' would alienate both British India and their own subjects. Those who did not join the Assembly should be regarded as 'hostile' states and be made 'to bear the consequences of being so regarded'. Nehru referred bitterly to the Political Department, which was acting secretly and mysteriously, without the knowledge of the Interim Government, and 'dividing the country not into one or two parts but into one hundred or more'. Patel shared his contempt for the Political Department.[46]

In London Corfield secured a specific reference to the Memorandum in the Plan, which now became far more precise about the states:

> Some may confirm their wish to proceed with framing a constitution in the existing Constituent Assembly. Some may wish to join any other Constituent Assembly that may be established. Some may wish to stand out independently, either singly or jointly, as is open to the Provinces. But, whatever their decision, all will require to enter upon negotiations for new agreements, especially in the economic and financial sphere, on the lines contemplated in ... the Cabinet Mission's Memorandum ....[47]

On 9 May, in a discussion with Listowel on the progressive retraction of paramountcy, Confield won assent to the 'policy of withdrawing first Political Agents and then Residents, leaving by about March 1948 no more than a nucleus at Political Department headquarters'.[48] Corfield 'made it clear that Pandit Nehru disliked this procedure of retraction, and argued that since the structure of paramountcy was built up between the states and the Governor-General in Council, the successor Indian Government[s] should inherit the whole nexus of agreements with the States.' It was 'agreed that this argument was fallacious' for 'the agreements were between *the Crown* and the States'. It was not possible to legislate for the transfer of the Crown Representative's authority to a successor government but only for the abolition of the Crown Representative, thus voiding paramountcy and any agreements between the Crown and the states. New arrangments between the parties were necessary. With the disappearance of the Crown Representative, the British High Commissioner might possibly exercise some residual functions in relation to the states. He would do so as an intermediary not between the states and the successor-governments but between H.M.G. and the states. It was clearly contemplated that some states might decline to join any Constituent Assembly. Corfield returned to India to put the retraction of paramountcy into effect.

Meanwhile the situation underwent a dramatic change. On 10 May, when Mountbatten showed him the Cabinet's revise of the Plan, Nehru alleged that it represented a Balkanization of India. The states were practically encouraged to stand out of the Indian Union, the larger ones to become allies of Britain, playing off Pakistan against the rest of British India. Mountbatten advised Listowel that Nehru intensely disliked the passage in the Plan relating to the states. 'We must preserve the position of the states but at the same time we cannot avoid giving a lead to the Princes.'[49] The deal that Menon drafted and Nehru approved gave the following 'lead':

Some of the states are already participating in the deliberations of the existing Constituent Assembly. H.M.G. hope that all others will join either the existing Constituent Assembly or the new Constituent Assembly [of Pakistan].[50]

Mountbatten's deal with Nehru was for *dual* dominionhood, which involved Mountbatten in exerting his influence to ensure the integration of the states in India or Pakistan. During meetings with the India Committee of the Cabinet in May, he was insistent that the prospect of direct relationships between the Crown and independent states would encourage the 'disintegration of India'.[51] The states 'must be told that their relations with the Crown will have to be through one or other of the Governors-General'.[52] On 24 May the Committee accepted that H.M.G.'s 'prime object should be to facilitate the exclusive association of the states with one of the new Dominions.' However, it also accepted that if a state ultimately stood aside from both then H.M.G. would have to consider separate relations with it.

The 3 June statement as finally issued merely remarked cryptically that the policy of the Cabinet Mission Memorandum 'remained unchanged'.[53] Corfield might feel justified in contracting paramountcy. Yet Mountbatten had authority to 'lead' the princes into the Dominions; he would be in breach of his understanding with Nehru if he failed to do so, and Congress might well refuse to endorse the deal. The relations of the states with the Dominions would depend not upon the execution of a clearly avowed policy but upon the ability of the disputants to impose their interpretations of the flexible Memorandum. The situation produced tensions between Corfield and Mountbatten, the Political Department and the Congress, the princes and Congress, H.M.G. and the Opposition, and even, to a mild degree, between Mountbatten and H.M.G. The reduction pursuant to the 3 June statement of the interim period to ten weeks made this last phase in the long transfer of power the most critical one for Indian unity. The maximization of the limits of unity may be analysed by considering in turn the emergence of policies for, first, the retraction of paramountcy and the negotiation of administrative continuity; secondly, the definition of the states' status in relation to the new Dominions; and, thirdly, H.M.G.'s relations with states that declined association with the Dominions consistently with that definition.

III A de Facto *Policy of Unification*

Nehru had no sooner accepted the 3 June statement than he resumed his attack on the lapse of paramountcy and the Political Department's preparations for it. On 4 June he complained to Mountbatten that the demolition of the Political Department's machinery for regulating relations with the states would provoke administrative chaos.[54] The Department had handled not only the Crown's relations with the Princes but also all-India arrangements between the Government of India and the states, which were vital to the integrity of British India. To confer independence on the states would prejudice the defence and internal administration of India as a whole. Just as the Raj had once articulated relations throughout India essential to its well-being, so too must an Indian Dominion now. On 5 June, at a meeting of the Congress and the League leaders with Moutbatten, Nehru emphasized the need for machinery to co-ordinate the Dominion's relations with the states and complained of the Political Department's sabotage of existing arrangements.[55] On 6 June Mountbatten discussed the complaint at a meeting of Corfield, Ismay, Sir Eric Miéville (Principal Secretary to the Viceroy), and representatives of the states, and he relayed a suggestion of Nehru's that upon the transfer of power representatives of the government of India should be sent out to the residencies to maintain relations on matters of common concern.[56] The meeting was in 'complete disagreement' with the proposal. Some states and groups of states had already arranged to send representatives to the Indian Dominion, and they would no doubt feel that the despatch of central agents to them bespoke the transfer of paramountcy. At a meeting with the Indian leaders on 7 June Mountbatten said that he would write to the states, giving them the choice of sending representatives to the dominions or receiving agents.[57]

On 9 June Nehru urged Mountbatten to set up a department of the Government of India to deal with matters of common concern with the states.[58] The Political Department was 'functioning without any consultation with the Government of India', regardless of paramountcy, the Government was 'concerned with its numerous relations with the states', and it was 'extraordinary and highly improper for the Political Department . . . to liquidate itself and . . . all our relations with the states without reference to us'. Such behaviour was 'unconstitutional' and many things that were being done for the disposal of property, buildings, records and staff were open to challenge in a court of law. The same day C. Rajagopalachari published an article in the same vein in the *Hindustan Times*. He had already sent the gist of it to Cripps: 'Paramountcy came into being as a fact and not by agreement, and on Britain's withdrawal the successor authorities must inherit the fact along with the rest of the context.'[59] Irrespective of relations between prince and Crown, existing relations between the states and British India involved matters of continuing common concern, including civil and criminal administration, railways, posts and telegraphs, currency, defence and external affairs. Cripps disagreed: relations between British India and the states were a function of those between the Crown and the states; they had always been constitutionally distinct from the relations of the executive government of British India, though until 1935 the Crown had employed the Governor-General in Council as its agent. The Cabinet Mission's Memorandum was right and paramountcy must lapse: 'It is a case for co-operation and goodwill on the administrative level in the first instance . . . and cannot be settled on a legalistic basis.'[60] Cripps emphasized that the Memorandum had envisaged standstill agreements as necessary to administrative continuity.

Although there had been no open breach with Mountbatten, Corfield now decided to seek early retirement. He must have felt that they were, in H. V. Hodson's words, 'pulling in different directions'.[61] Whereas he was trying to set the princes on their feet by mid-August, so that they might subsequently negotiate their future relations with the new Dominions from a position of strength, Mountbatten was committed to leading them into a Consituent Assembly by then. On 9 June Mountbatten wrote to Listowel that as Corfield's daughter was to be married in London on 5 August he wished to take leave from 23 July preparatory to retirement.[62] These facts are at odds with Corfield's published account of his departure, which he associated with a conflict over an issue that had yet to arise.[63]

On 10 June Nehru and Patel raised with Mountbatten the validity of the Government of India's existing contractual arrangements with the states after the transfer of power.[64] Mountbatten agreed to raise the question, together with that of standstill agreements, at a meeting of Indian leaders scheduled for the 13th. Nehru also condemned the proposed restoration of power to the princes, and threatened to 'encourage rebellion in all states' that stood out of the Assemblies.

Next day the Standing Committee of the A.I.S.P.C. declared that when paramountcy lapsed sovereignty would reside in the states' peoples. It demanded the transfer of the Political Department and its agencies to the Government of India, or, alternatively, the creation of a new department to receive the properties, records and staff of the Political Department and its Agencies and Residencies.

At the 13 June meeting of Mountbatten, Corfield and the Indian leaders, Nehru charged Corfield with 'misfeasance' (the improper performance of a lawful act) in the progressive retraction of paramountcy.[65] Corfield was on sure ground, for he had acted with the blessing of the Crown Representative and the Secretary of State and consistently with the Cabinet Mission's Memorandum. While Nehru could assert that the document contained no reference to the ultimate independence of a state, Corfield could answer that neither did it require a state to enter a Constituent Assembly; provision was made for 'particular political arrangements', which implied 'autonomy'. In later years Corfield was to argue that while he had thought independence 'impractical' in the long run, the 'threat' of it was a legitimate lever for states to use during negotiations with the successor-governments, which the Memorandum certainly expected to continue beyond the transfer of power into a period of standstill agreements.[66] It might be added that the dual nature of the transfer raised the question of choice for states contiguous to both Dominions and for those with rulers of a different religion from that of most of their subjects. Mountbatten intimated that his plans envisaged the subordination of the states and he produced a document that offered them the choice of sending representatives to a Dominion or receiving agents. When Nehru pressed for a central department, Mountbatten conceded that he could not prevent the Dominions establishing new departments. He proposed the creation of a 'States Department' forthwith. It would have sections for each of the Dominions, which, according to the decision of individual states, would either send or receive agents. The States Department began work on 1 July, with V. P. Menon as its secretary and Patel in charge.[67]

The contentious meeting of 13 June also agreed on the despatch to all Residents of a Political Department letter setting out a formula for standstill agreements.[68] All states (some only after bargaining) accepted agreements covering matters of common concern, especially economic and financial arrangements, with the new Dominions for a period of two years from the lapse of paramountcy, and pending the negotiation of new agreements.[69] Despite the insistence by H.M.G. that all agreements between the Government of India and the states were aspects of paramountcy and must lapse with it, nevertheless the Independence Act, in deference to Congress pressure, provided for agreements to continue until they were denounced by one of the parties or superseded.[70]

The States Department and the standstill agreements ensured administrative continuity, but the status of the states *vis-à-vis* the Dominions remained to be defined. Essentially to accommodate the Muslim provinces, the Cabinet Mission scheme had adumbrated a federation for three subjects only, Defence, External Affairs and Communications. The states might enter a Constituent Assembly on this understanding or, alternatively, enter into 'particular political arrangements' with the Union for such matters. The 3 June deal went further, by opening the way to Dominion governments with wide powers, so that states might well recoil from their Constituent Assemblies. As the deal was to be implemented through the constitutional machinery of the 1935 Act, it is not surprising that the Act should also have been adapted in order to allay princely apprehensions. The Act had provided for the states' incorporation in an all-India federation through the negotiation of an instrument of accession. In June 1947 it was realized that, pending the Dominions' preparation of constitutions, the princes might be invited to accede for only the Cabinet Mission's three Union subjects. Nehru had been contemplating such an interim arrangement since March, and on 9 May he suggested a transfer of paramountcy thus limited. At the beginning of June Sir Walter Monckton (Hyderabad's adviser) was led to believe that Nehru was privately suggesting a limited accession but that he would interpret the three subjects formula widely.[71] On 10 June Mountbatten put it to Nehru and Patel that the princes were understandably frightened off by the departure from the Cabinet Mission's Plan Union, only to be assured by Patel that the central powers would be enlarged only with the princes' consent.[72] On 17 June, when the jurist and constitutional adviser to the Nawab of Bhopal, Zafrullah Khan, voiced the princes' fears at a meeting with Mountbatten, the Nawab and Monckton, Mountbatten himself stated that the Congress would accept the states' accession on the basis of the three subjects only.[73] It was indeed the case that on 6–8 March and 1 May the C.W.C. had resolved upon acceptance of the Cabinet Mission scheme 'in its entirety'. The 3 June deal involved a reaffirmation of the acceptance of the Mission's Memorandum. The three subject accession was thus implicit in the deal, by which Nehru enlisted

Mountbatten's best efforts to effect the transfer of paramountcy 'in every sense except the legalistic' (in Lumby's phrase).[74] Rather too much has been made of Menon's averred conversion of Patel to three subject accession as late as July, and Nehru's subsequent acquiescence.[75] However, they may well have found difficulty in convincing their party colleagues of the wisdom of this apparently generous invitation to the princes, which Patel delivered publicly on 5 July.

Mountbatten construed his role as 'going into battle' with Congress on behalf of the princes.[76] He argued, more as tactics than by conviction, that by holding Congress to the acceptance of a three subject accession he was preserving the internal autonomy of the states. By using his influence as Viceroy to lead them into the Dominions he was securing a better bargain for them than if they were to negotiate individually and from isolation after the lapse of paramountcy, when, as constitutional Governor-General, he would be obliged to accept such action as his ministers found necessary. Nehru had foreshadowed rebellions of the states' peoples against non-acceding princes. The Indian Union 'could never agree' to a state becoming independent,

which means having external relations and the power to declare war or peace and controlling its defence and communications.... The facts of geography cannot be ignored and the dominant power will necessarily exercise certain control over any state which does not choose to come into the Union.[77]

Some princes appreciated Mountbatten's intervention to secure the three subject arrangement as completely transforming their future prospects, which the cruel logic of *realpolitik* threatened to blight.[78] Others saw matters differently. On 11 July the States Department listed the accession scheme on the agenda for a meeting of states' representatives on 25 July, at which Mountbatten would employ his redoubtable talents of persuasion. He was to achieve a diplomatic triumph. But this is to cast ahead, as Mountbatten was casting ahead of H.M.G. in his intimations of the post-paramountcy international status of non-acceding states.

Very early in his viceroyalty Mountbatten learned that some princes wanted the status of separate Dominions, among them Bhopal, Travancore and Hyderabad. Bhopal, Chancellor of the Chamber of Princes, was evidently disappointed when Mountbatten told him on 1 June that Dominion status was not available to any state that sought independence from India and Pakistan. Mountbatten refused, consistently with H.M.G.'s policy of 24 May, to answer or refer questions about H.M.G. entertaining relations with such a state after 15 August. Nevertheless, on 4 June Bhopal declared that he would pursue independence and a week later Travancore and Hyderabad followed suit. In mid-July the learned Diwan of Travancore, Sir Ramaswamy Aiyer, contended that the three-subject accession scheme violated Britain's earlier assurances that state relations with the successor-governments were a matter of negotiation.[79] Accordingly, after paramountcy lapsed, independent Travancore would negotiate with the Dominions about foreign relations, defence, and communications. Junagadh state, in Kathiawar, protested similarly against the 'altogether extraordinary and unexpected' revival of the scheme of federal accession.[80] The states had not been consulted about it and the Cabinet Mission's Memorandum had not mentioned it. The scheme denied states the choice of whether to join a Union or merely seek 'particular political arrangements' with it. Accession during the interim period would cost a state its freedom to stand out once the Dominion's constitution was made.

The main critic and ultimate test of British policy was Hyderabad. Even before Attlee's February statement, Monckton (who was in touch with Jinnah through Bhopal) was testing the possibility of Conservative party support for appeals by Jinnah and the Muslim princes for separate membership of the Commonwealth. In mid-January he was in touch with the chief creator of the 1935 Act, Sir Samuel Hoare (now Lord Templewood), and 'much encouraged' by their measure of agreement. He wrote:

I think what the Muslims would like to know is that if Jinnah came out with a declaration that they want to stay within the Commonwealth—a policy in which the most important Princes would in due course join—they would receive a substantial measure of support from responsible opinion in England. After what you said last night I feel I can give that assurance. Do you think I can assume that RAB [Butler], Anthony [Eden] and Bobbity [Lord Cranborne—later Salisbury] will take the same line?[81]

Templewood's astonishing reply seems to mock the self that had once defied the diehard and Churchillian cries of 'sham' when he toiled indefatigably to bring the putative all-India federation on to the statute book:

I would say [publicly] that our great achievement in India has been the creation of a united and peaceful subcontinent. It has, however, become quite obvious that this unity depended on the British mediatory influence and that, when once this influence is withdrawn, it becomes an artificial sham [*sic*]. This being so, it is better that the fundamental division in India should be recognised in a peaceful and constitutional manner rather than be accepted at the end of a period of chaos and civil war.[82]

He believed such a statement would carry great weight in England and he authorized Monckton to confide his views to Bhopal. He offered to meet Monckton to prepare a campaign before Monckton went out to India in April. In mid-January, too, Monckton was lobbying Lady Mountbatten.[83]

Within days of his arrival in India on 22 March, Mountbatten was approached by Bhopal about dominionhood, which, he confided, was also Jinnah's object for Pakistan. Mountbatten trod warily, offering encouragement in neither case, for although he passionately favoured Commonwealth membership for India, it must be for all of India, and he played his cards astutely to that end. Until the Simla deal he confided doubts about Congress intentions in his reports home, and, in consequence, on 10 May Attlee requested an appraisal by the Chiefs of Staff of the military and strategic implications of Dominion status being accorded to part only of the subcontinent, for example West Pakistan, Bengal, and a seaboard state such as Travancore.[84] On 12 May the Chiefs of Staff reported in favour of Dominion status in all three cases.[85]

Since late in 1945, landlocked Hyderabad had been seeking access to a port.[86] In April 1947 Monckton was in touch with Templewood about the acquisition of port facilities at Marmagao, in Portuguese Goa, with a rail link to be built from the state to the sea. The businessman Sir Alexander Roger was employed as an intermediary, but Monckton himself seems to have visited Portugal in April. He was keeping Templewood informed so that the latter could 'give our enterprise a fair wind when you pay your visit to Lisbon later in May'.[87] However, on 3 May he wrote from Viceroy's House in New Delhi that as the whole Indian situation was 'tense and anxious', Templewood should stay out of the Portuguese negotiations.[88] As a guest and friend of Mountbatten's, he had been shown his notes and plans and been enlisted to help secure the entry of all India to the Commonwealth.[89]

Monckton was chagrined at the dual Dominions deal and the exclusion thereby of separate dominionhood for Hyderabad. On 7 June he wrote a 'Note on the Position of Hyderabad' and on the 9th sent it to Ismay, intimating that he wished to avoid ventilating the grievance through political channels in England.[90] The note acknowledged Mountbatten's success with the British Indian leaders, but criticized his failure to consult Hyderabad's representatives until 3 June. The Congress represented the states as an 'anachronistic heritage to be pressed or cajoled, whether they wish it or not, into the pattern which British India has chosen'. In fact they had a living culture of their own, and were, in many cases, as well administered as the provinces. They accounted for over a third of the area of the subcontinent and a quarter of the population. If they were 'fairly treated', many of them had a 'sounder hope of survival than the brittle political structure of the Congress party after they . . . attained independence'. Hyderabad had a population larger than that of any of the existing Dominions and its area was as large as France; it had been a faithful ally for a century and in two world wars. Yet it was denied association with the Commonwealth except through India or Pakistan. For the Nizam to join India would be political suicide. He wanted to remain in the Commonwealth, whereas Congress would be eager to leave it, and he could not understand Britain's denunciation of his treaties. Monckton concluded: 'I think this is rather a shameful performance. How ready we are to appease our enemies at the expense of our friends.' Yet another letter that he wrote at this time reveals that he remained sanguine of Hyderabad's survival.[91] As Britain would not be present to protect Hyderabad it was necessary not to antagonize the Union of India, but 'if we go warily we shall very likely outlast them'. Jinnah would support Hyderabad if it stood firm, while Corfield, who had 'fought a really noble battle for us', had prepared standstill agreements that could endure for two or three years. If H.M.G. would maintain relations with Hyderabad, then Pakistan would recognize it, as would Egypt and Saudi Arabia. 'Then we can think concretely of U.N.O. and we may well get our Dominion Status in the end.'

For such hopes to have foundation Hyderabad would require direct relations with H.M.G. after paramountcy lapsed. On 14 June, in the wake of the Nizam's declaration of intended independence and amid condemnation of it by Congress leaders, Monckton advised Ismay that he must return home to press the case.[92] On the 17th, when Mountbatten saw Monckton, Bhopal and Zafrullah Khan together, he emphasized that 'Congress would never have accepted the plan [of 3 June] if there had been more than two Dominions; they had even refused to allow Bengal to vote for independence and separate Dominion status to avoid partition.'[93] Nevertheless, Monckton persuaded Mountbatten to recommend that H.M.G. clarify its intended relations with states that joined neither Dominion. Ismay and Miéville drafted a parliamentary question and answer for the purpose. Monckton wrote to R. A. Butler to ask him whether he would put the question to the Under-Secretary of State for India, and Mountbatten, then in Kashmir, surprisingly commended the reply: on the lapse of paramountcy, states were free to join the Dominions of India or Pakistan or become separate autonomous units, and H.M.G. would not refuse direct relations with those taking the latter step.[94] Monckton confided to R. A. Butler, Templewood, Lord Cranborne and Brendan Bracken that Travancore, Bhopal and Jinnah all supported the proposal.[95] He also had in mind the possibility of Hyderabad securing dominionhood if India left the Commonwealth once it had made its constitution. Listowel recognized that the proposed answer went beyond the India Committee's position of 24 May—the discouragement of post-paramountcy relations with the states unless they ultimately became unavoidable. On 26 June the Committee adopted his advice to postpone parliamentary comment until the second reading of the Independence Bill in a fortnight's time.[96] Mountbatten responded to Monckton's evident disappointment by asking Ismay to refer Hyderabad's claim to Mr W. H. Morris-Jones, recently arrived Constitutional Adviser to the Viceroy. Morris-Jones disagreed with Monckton that Hyderabad had a valid claim to the perpetuation of its place in the Empire.[97] Its present place arose solely from its relation with the paramount power. The relationship had been based on political power and the withdrawal of that power would be a political fact. The right of Parliament to terminate paramountcy was beyond doubt. The Independence Act would thus wipe clean the slate of British relations with Hyderabad. The location of Hyderabad precluded the possibility of direct relations without the Indian Dominion's concurrence, for they would be 'most improper' and contrary to the spirit of relations with the Dominions.

On 5 July the India Office cabled to Corfield that during the second reading debate the Government would admit the possibility of a state that did not join a Dominion upon the lapse of paramountcy securing relations with foreign powers through H.M.G. on a temporary basis.[98] Menon cabled the reply: to give any inkling of the possible recognition of the states' independent status would exacerbate the problem of securing their adherence to the Dominions.[99] Now that the Mountbatten-Congress deal over three-subject accession had become public, Menon was on firm ground. On 8 July Listowel told Mountbatten that there would be no statement on the international position of the states during the Commons' debate.[100] The same day Mountbatten impressed on Monckton that Nehru had accepted that Mountbatten himself should undertake the negotiations for the three-subject accession.[101] Next day Monckton sent in a letter from the Nizam protesting against the Independence Bill's repudiation of his treaties and denial of Commonwealth membership unless he joined India or Pakistan.[102] On 11 July Mountbatten commended three-subject accession to a Hyderabad delegation that met with representatives of the Political and States Departments.[103] As Hyderabad was militarily defenceless, completely landlocked and surrounded by the Indian Dominion, H.M.G. would be unable to accept a commitment for its protection. The Nizam must accede to India to enjoy the benefits of Commonwealth membership.

The Government weathered the Commons' debate on 10 July without making an explicit statement on the international status of non-acceding states. Introducing the Bill, Attlee expressed the hope that in due course all states would find their appropriate place in one or other of the Dominions but accepted that until constitutions were framed there 'must necessarily be a less organic form of relationship between them and there must be a period before a comprehensive system can be worked out'. When paramountcy lapsed, the states would 'regain their independence', but he hoped that 'no irrevocable decision to stay out will be taken prematurely'. Monckton was pleased with the Opposition's response.[104] Leading for his party in Churchill's absence, Harold Macmillan referred to the states' right to join a Dominion or enjoy 'independent sovereign authority'. Both he and Sir John Anderson spoke of the need to ensure that no moral or physical 'pressure' should be brought to bear upon states while they were making their choice, and both believed that H.M.G. should enter into independent relations with states that requested them. On 12 July Mountbatten commended to Listowel the States Department suggestion that H.M.G. should announce that it was in the states' own interests to come to an arrangement with an appropriate Dominion over external relations.[105] He added that if he were successful at his meeting with the states' representatives on the 25th, then the question of international status would be 'resolved automatically', and that a prior parliamentary statement might queer his pitch. During the Lords' debate on 16 July, Listowel reaffirmed that on the lapse of paramountcy the states would be

> the masters of their own fate. They will then be entirely free to choose whether to associate with one or other of the Dominion Governments or to stand alone, and His Majesty's Government will not use the slightest pressure to influence their momentous and voluntary decision.... Whatever the future relationship between the new Dominions and the States may be, it will require prolonged consideration and discussion before the final adjustment can be made.

As prompted by Mountbatten, he said that it 'would be in the best interests of their own people, and of India as a whole', that the states should find their appropriate place 'within one or other of the new Dominions'. He went so far as to say: 'We do not, of course, propose to recognise any States as separate international entities.' However, questioned closely by Templewood, he conceded that to cover the contingency of a state failing to enter a Dominion, the question of international recognition would be 'left open to be considered on its merits when such a position arises'. Monckton was delighted by Templewood's 'masterly' leading of Listowel and believed that 'we have got something very valuable in the bag'.[106]

Notwithstanding Listowel's disclaimers, Mountbatten's speech of advice to the state's representatives on 25 July was minatory—'the apogee of persuasion' in Menon's words.[107] He insisted that the three subject accession would leave the states with internal autonomy and all the independence that they could, in reality, manage: '... these three subjects have got to be handled for you and for your convenience by a larger organisation.' Accession by 15 August was urgent in order to avert a chaotic void. He made it seem that Congress's generous offer of limited accession depended upon its immediate acceptance by all states. After 15 August non-acceding states would be isolated internationally and left to fend for themselves. He went further in letters to wavering princes.[108]

Listowel was alarmed at the tenor of Mountbatten's 'advice'. It was right to urge accession but 'we must ... keep balance and not ourselves add to pressure which facts of the situation place in any case on States.[109] He demurred at Mountbatten's intimation that H.M.G. would not continue relations with non-federating states and at his insistence upon accession by 15 August. Parliament had been told that the states might need more time. He did not see how they could be expected to accede by mid-August for even three subjects.[110] It would be better if the Dominions extended external protection to the states pending negotiations for accession. Such a course would be consistent with the Cabinet Memorandum and would relieve H.M.G. of the allegation of imposing pressure. When George Abell (Private Secretary to the Viceroy) put up a conciliatory draft response, Mountbatten minuted in red ink: 'I would like this redrafted to knock these arguments on the head'—after discussion with V. P. Menon.[111] On 4 August, Mountbatten cabled Menon's draft.[112] It explained that the princes could not afford to delay their accession until the Dominions made their constitutions, for after 15 August they would be faced with rebellions of their subjects. There was no question of pressure, merely of commending a good offer:

> I am doing my best while I have bargaining power in my capacity as Crown Representative to see that States get fair offer from Government of India and to induce them to accept it so that conflict which is inevitable if they do not accede should be avoided . . . . I am trying my very best to create an integrated India which while securing stability will ensure friendship with Great Britain. If I am allowed to play my hand without interference I have no doubt that I will succeed. If disintegration is to be avoided we have to act very quickly and should give every encouragement to States to come in and not to stand out.

Succeed he did, and within a few days Listowel cabled: 'We are full of admiration at your success in having overcome the hesitation of so many States about acceptance of the terms of accession offered by Patel.'[113] On the eve of Independence the repentant doubter added:

> I believe that your outstanding ability and fearless determination have saved India from unimaginable disaster and that your achievement will be remembered in time to come as one of the greatest feats of statesmanship in history.[114]

Attlee paid tribute to his 'amazing' skill 'in the successful achievement of a task of unexampled difficulty'.[115]

At 15 August only three of the 562 states were loth to join a Dominion: Junagadh, Kashmir and Hyderabad. Listowel felt 'some sympathy' for Hyderabad, for there were so many considerations in acceding, with a constitution not yet made, even for three subjects.[116] On 28 July, Monckton had told Mountbatten that the Nizam had decided against accession, which would precipitate a Muslim revolt. However, Mountbatten's speech of 25 July must have dimmed the prospect of his obtaining direct international relations with Britain. Monckton now felt 'the association of Hyderabad with the Indian Dominion [to be] inevitable in the interests of both', but it could not be rushed.[117] On 8 August the Nizam wrote to Mountbatten of his difficulty in aligning with India when his ties with Pakistan were numerous.[118] The Dominions might fail to agree on arrangements for defence and external affairs, hostilities might emerge between them, or India might leave the Commonwealth. He must wait and watch events for the moment. On the day of his historic advice to the princes, Mountbatten confided to Listowel his concern about India possibly deciding to leave the Commonwealth at some future time, and on the day that Monckton intimated that the Nizam would not accede, he raised the matter at a staff meeting [119] Morris-Jones was to be asked to consider the possibility of India being accommodated in the Commonwealth permanently, but on a looser basis than Dominion status.[120] Attlee had already in June set up a committee on the question of future relations within the Commonwealth at large.[121] Both the committee and Morris-Jones concluded that India might remain in the Commonwealth even if a republican constitution were adopted. The likelihood might have steeled Mountbatten's resolve to reject the Nizam's offer on 8 August to enter into a treaty with India for defence, external affairs and communications. Hyderabad secured only a two-month extension of the three-subject accession offer.

To all intents and purposes Mountbatten had pursued a *de facto* policy of unification.

IV *The Burden of History*

The Cabinet Mission Memorandum's contemplated sequence of events was: the creation of an Interim Government and the opening of an interim period pending the transfer of power; the rapid establishment of sound administration and representative institutions in the states; the contraction of paramountcy as the states became self-supporting; negotiations between the princes, thus strengthened, and the successor government(s), either by the states entering a Constituent Assembly or otherwise; the making of constitutions; the transfer or power, the lapse of paramountcy, and the operation of standstill agreements until negotiations were complete; the definition of relations in federal terms or under 'particular political arrangements'. Existing relations between the Crown and the states would end at the transfer of power and no new relations were envisaged. Rather, the states would be either subordinated to the new nation(s) federally or by treaty. The failure of the Cabinet Mission scheme created a new situation. From 20 February until about 11 May, H.M.G. and sometimes Mountbatten contemplated the prospect of states becoming Dominions. Under the dual Dominions deal, Congress accepted an immediate partition that maximized the limits of British India by a process of self-determination (modified as necessary by a 'parapolitical' Boundary Award),[122] on condition that there should be no more Dominions. The Dominion constitutions could not now be available for scrutiny by the states prior to the transfer of power and lapse of paramountcy. Standstill agreements were struck, but the contraction of paramountcy was racing ahead of the intended emergence of representative institutions in the states. It was inevitable that it should, probably even under the more leisurely timetable of the Cabinet Mission Memorandum, and that the Crown would thus be returning powers to rulers lacking popular support. The Memorandum, and by implication the 3 June Plan, wishfully imagined reasonable negotiations between harmonious states and the successor government(s). Here was the rub. For the Congess 'nation' could, in reality, undermine or topple a prince by inciting his subjects to rebellion, and then (as the British had once done) intervene in the name of law and order. Ignoring such real prospects, H.M.G. observed consitutional proprieties in Parliament, honestly convinced of its righteousness, while Mountbatten, aware of the tides of history, imposed the *de facto* or para-constitutional solution that the problem demanded.

Mountbatten, Nehru, Patel and V. P. Menon had found the solution to the problem of British India fragmentation in the dual Dominions deal, which blended elements of the 1935 Act and the Cabinet Mission scheme. They found the solution to the problem of the princes in the corollary of the deal, the scheme for three-subject accession, blended from similar elements. A negotiated settlement consonant with political realities emerged, maximizing unity without the deployment of force (though three states achieved a brief 'independence', later to be destroyed by force). Mountbatten certainly used pressure not sanctioned by his instructions and repudiated in Parliament. Certainly, too, the states lost the internal autonomy that Mountbatten, for the sake of tactics, assured them they would enjoy.[123] The alternative was the appearance after 15 August of a rash of unstable regimes, indefensible against external aggression and internally precarious. The situation would invite 'police actions' by the Dominions and, if it persisted long, foreign intervention. This was illustrated by the problems caused by the residue of non-acceding states: Junagadh, Hyderabad and Kashmir.[124]

The residue may be held to reveal a weakness in Mountbatten's policy— say, the lack of a contingency plan, perhaps for accession by plebiscite after 15 August. But after the transfer of power, who was left to administer a scheme that one of the Dominions might find inimical to its interests? Mountbatten and H.M.G. had put their faith in the Commonwealth, operating through a common Governor-General, and in the development of a Joint Defence Council. It is as well that more was not expected of these supra-national agencies. The collapse of the common Governor-General scheme flowed from the fear of the smaller Dominion that the 'advice' of its larger neighbour would prevail in cases of conflict. The collapse of the Joint Defence Council resulted from its lack of military control after the transfer of power, a consequence of Jinnah's concern for immediate military independence. There persisted some hope that over time the geographical unity of the subcontinent would reassert itself. In June 1947 Morris-Jones was asked to evaluate the prospects for joint agencies.[125] His analysis was somewhat pessimistic but not despairing. In the air between Malta and Karachi, after securing the consent of King, Cabinet and Churchill to Mountbatten's remaining as Governor-General of India only, Ismay wrote a paper on problems already solved and those remaining:

Then [he concluded] there is the North West Frontier of India. If India had grasped the elementary fact that ... [it] is just as much their frontier as Pakistan's I should be less disturbed. But as it is I doubt whether they will come to this way of thinking, except after bitter experience.[126]

It seems timely to recall such reflections in the wake of the invasion of Afghanistan in 1979.

In the end, of course, it was not the horrors in the Punjab, or India's police actions to capture the interset territories of Junagadh and Hyderabad, but the Kashmir problem that sundered Indo-Pakistan relations beyond early repair. The underlying logic of the dispute was rooted in the history of British imperialism in India. The plurality of princely autonomy and provincial democracy was responsible for the defeat of the all-India federal solution to the problem of unity in the 1930s. After partition the violent consequences of political and cultural pluralism in Kashmir—a Hindu prince, with Muslim subjects, poised between India and Pakistan—blocked, at least for a generation, the possibility of a subcontinental defensive entente.

Abbreviations used in the notes

A.I.C.C.	All-India Congress Committee
A.I.M.L.	All-India Muslim League
CAB	Cabinet Papers, P.R.O.
CAB 127/57–154	Cripps Collection, P.R.O.
C.O.S.	Chiefs of Staff
C.W.C.	Congress Working Committee
I.O.L.	India Office Library
I.O.R.	India Office Records
L/P & J/10	Pol. Dept. Transfer of Power Papers, I.O.R.
L/PO	Private Office Papers, I.O.R.
L/P & S/12	External Dept. Collections, I.O.R.
MB	Mountbatten Papers, Broadlands Archives (consulted in I.O.R. and cited by file numbers there assigned)
N.A.I.	National Archives of India
N.M.L.	Nehru Memorial Library
P.	Papers
Pol.	Political
P.R.O.	Public Record Office
P.S.V.	Private Secretary to Viceroy
Q.A.P.	Quaid-i-Azam Papers (Pakistan Government Archives)
R/3/1	Papers of the Office of P.S.V., I.O.R.
T.C.	Templewood Collection, I.O.L.
T.P.	Nicholas Mansergh, E.W.R. Lumby, and Sir Penderel Moon (eds), *The Transfer of Power*, 12 vols. (1970–83)
Z.C.	Zetland Collection, I.O.L.

Notes

1 THE PROBLEM OF FREEDOM WITH UNITY

1. M. Gwyer and A. Appadorai (eds.). *Speeches and Documents on the Indian Constitution, 1921–47*, 2 vols. (London, 1957), I, xxvii. Unless otherwise noted, the declarations mentioned in the present chapter may be consulted in this collection.
2. 'Dominion Status and Responsible Government', 4 June 1929, Government of India 100/Notes. N.A.I.
3. *Indian Legislative Assembly Debates*, IV, pt. i, 349.
4. Hailey's memorandum of 27 Oct. 1928, Hailey P., 30, I.O.L.
5. A detailed account appears in my *The Crisis of Indian Unity, 1917–40* (London, 1974), ch. 2.
6. Winterton's diary for 25 Oct. 1929, in *Orders of the Day* (London, 1953), 158.
7. D. L. Keir, *The Constitutional History of Modern Britain, 1485–1937* (London, 1948), 543.
8. *Lords' Debates*, 5 Nov. 1929.
9. *Daily Telegraph*, 12 Nov. 1929.
10. Hoare to Willingdon, 17 Feb. 1935 (cable), Templewood Coll. (hereafter T.C.), I.O.L.
11. Willingdon to Hoare, 31 Jan. 1935 (cable), ibid.
12. *Commons' Debates*, 6 Feb. 1935.
13. Linlithgow to Zetland, 21 Dec. 1939, Zetland Coll. (hereafter Z.C.), I.O.L.
14. The argument of this section paraphrases my *The Crisis of Indian Unity* and 'The Demission of Empire in South Asia: Some Perpectives', *Journal of Imperial and Commonwealth History*, II (1973), 79–94.
15. Cripps's record of a conversation with Liaqat Ali, Dec. 1939, in E. Estorick, *Stafford Cripps, A Biography* (London, 1949), 198. At this time Zetland observed that Jinnah seemed 'to have got back to the position taken up by Minto and Morley thirty years ago' (Zetland to Linlithgow, 22 Nov. 1939, Z.C.).
16. An account of negotiations during the early war months appears below, ch. 3.
17. Gwyer and Appadorai, op cit., II, 484–7.
18. Zetland to Linlithgow, 24 Jan. 1940 (cable), L/PO/252/16, I.O.L.
19. Zetland to Linlithgow, 2 Feb. 1940 (cable), ibid.
20. *Commons' Debates*, 3 Oct. 1939.
21. Zetland to Linlithgow, 2 Oct. 1939, Z.C.
22. Cripps to Nehru, 11 Oct. 1939, in J. N. Nehru (ed.), *A Bunch of Old Letters* (Bombay, 1958).
23. Cripps to Nehru. 16 Nov. 1939. J. Nehru P., N.M.I.
24. Nehru to Mahadev Desai, 9 Dec. 1939, in Nehru (ed.), op. cit.
25. R. A. Butler to S. F. Stewart, 17 Nov. 1939, L/PO/258.
26. Stewart complained that Cripps had unjustifiably claimed his support for the scheme that Cripps took to India in December 1939: 'At best he has been guilty of wishful thinking to the point of crookedness' (Stewart to Laithwaite, 13 Jan. 1940, L/PO/258).

27 Enclosure to Cripps to Stewart, 24 Nov. 1939, L/PO/252/16.
28 Zetland's memo, for War Cabinet, 31 Jan. 1940, WP(G)(40) 37, in L/PO/252/16. For non-official appreciations, arguing the need for urgent action to meet a dangerous situation, see (i) the report by a small sub-committee of the National Labour Organization, 7 Feb. 1940, encl. to M. MacDonald to Zetland, 20 Mar. 1940, L/PO/77; (ii) Guy Wint's letters to Schuster, Mar.-May 1940, L/PO/6/105 d.
29 Amery to Linlithgow, 17 June 1940 (cable), L/PO/6/105 d.
30 Gwyer and Appadorai, op. cit., II. 500.
31 Linlithgow to Zetland, 1 July 1940 (cable), L/PO/6/105 d.
32 Gwyer and Appadorai, op. cit., II, 500–1.
33 Amery to Churchill, 14 July 1940, L/PO/6/105 d.
34 Churchill to Linlithgow, 14 Aug. 1940 (cable), ibid. Certainly Amery was prepared to go further (see, e.g., his letters to Linlithgow, 4 July; Attlee, 21, 23 July; Halifax 23, 30 July; Churchill, 23 July; Zetland, 3 Aug; also Churchill's Cabinet Paper 'remodelling' the already revised draft of the statement that Amery had originally prepared, WP(40) 295, 30 July 1940; all in L/PO/6/105 d. In 1942 Amery was somewhat misleadingly apt to read the germ of the Cripps Mission's offer into the August offer. In particular, he extrapolated the 1942 provision for separate Muslim dominionhood from the 1940 promises: that India would secure Dominion status 'with the least possible delay after the war', and that Britain would not transfer power 'to any system of government whose authority is directly denied by large and powerful elements in India's national life'. In other words, the 1940 offer's insistence upon agreement among the Indian parties was not intended to delay dominionhood. This may have been Amery's own position in 1940 but in view of his difficulty with the August offer it can scarcely be claimed that the Cabinet then contemplated Indian freedom on any basis other than for a single united Dominion. Only in March 1942, when he secured Cabinet approval for the principle of separate Muslim dominionhood, was the precondition of unity waived. See Amery to Linlithgow, 21 Feb. 1942; Amery to Churchill, 25 Feb. 1942; Amery's note,? Apr. 1942; in *T.P.*, i, 163, 181, 681, 838–41.
35 Bevin to Amery, 24 Sept. 1941, Bevin P., Churchill College, Cambridge.
36 G. S. Bajpai to Linlithgow, 1 Dec. 1941, Linlithgow P., F125/130, I.O.L.
37 Cabinet Conclusion 131 of 1941, *T.P.*, i, 6.
38 Churchill to Attlee, 7 Jan. 1942, ibid.
39 Attlee to Amery, 24 Jan. 1942, ibid., 35.
40 Ibid., 79.
41 G. R. Hess, *America Encounters India, 1941–7* (Baltimore, 1971), 36–7.
42 *T.P.*, i, 460.
43 Sir Reginald Coupland, *The Cripps Mission* (London, 1942) 34.
44 Amery to Linlithgow, 21 Feb. 1942, *T.P.*, i, 163.
45 War Cabinet (42) 321, 28 July 1942, L/PO/77.
46 E.g., Memo by Sir E. Villiers on a meeting with Nehru, 5 July 1942, L/PO/6/105 e. Also notes by Graham Spry (Cripps's secretary during his Mission) on his propaganda visit to America, 22 April–30 May 1942, L/PO/6/105 d-f; see esp. note on meeting with L. Currie, executive Assistant to the President, 9 May.
47 A detailed account appears below, ch. 2.
48 *T.P.*, i, 223.
49 D. Monteath's note on a conversation with Sir E. Villiers about his meeting with

Nehru, 13 Aug. 1942, L/PO/6/105 e.
50. Spry's Notes, esp. of meetings with A. A. Berle, Assistant Under-Secretary of State, 11 May; Mr Justice Frankfurter, 13 May; Dr Stanley Hornbeck of the State Department, 13 May; the President, 15 May; all in L/PO/6/105 e-f. Clauson's note on R. I. Campbell to Sir D. Scott, 17 July 1942, L/PO/6/105 e. F. F. Turnbull to A. H. Joyce, D. Monteath and P. J. Patrick, 21 Sept. 1942, ibid.
51. Wavell's attempted initiatives appear in P. Moon (ed), *Wavell: The Viceroy's Journal* (London, 1973); hereafter *Wavell's Journal*. Some Labour opinion also favoured a further war-time initiative (e.g. Labour Party International Department Report No. 265, 'Advisory Committee on Imperial questions: The Indian Deadlock', Mar. 1944, in Bevin P., 2/11, Churchill College, Cambridge).
52. E.g., Eric Stokes, 'Cripps in India', *Historical Journal*, XIV (1971), 427–34.
53. *Wavell's Journal*, 31 Aug. 1945.
54. The point is developed in C. Bridge, 'Conservatism and Indian Reform (1929–39): Towards a Pre-requisites Model in Imperial Constitution-Making?', *Journal of Imperial and Commonwealth History*, IV (1976), 176–93.
55. Quoted in R. Danzig, 'The Announcement of August 20th, 1917' *Journal of Asian Studies*, XXVIII (1968), 31.
56. Birkenhead to Reading, 4 Dec. 1924, In F. W. F. Smith (Lord Birkenhead), *Frederick Edwin, Earl of Birkenhead* (London, 1935), 245.
57. *Indian Statutory Commission Report*, 2 vols. (Cd. 3568–9, 1930), I, para. 460.
58. J. G. Cumming (ed.), *Political India, 1832–1932* (London, 1932), 1–21, see 4–5.
59. Speech of 11 Feb. 1935, in C. H. Philips (ed.) *The Evolution of India and Pakistan, 1858–1947: Select Documents* (London, 1962), 316.
60. D. C. Potter, 'Manpower Shortage and the End of Colonialism: The Case of the Indian Civil Service', *Modern Asian Studies*, VII (1973), 47–73.
61. For Hoare, see Templewood P., XI. 1 (Nov. 1939), Cambridge University Library; Zetland to Linlithgow, 8 Nov. 1939, Z.C.

2 THE MAKING OF INDIA'S PAPER FEDERATION, 1927–35

1. Templewood to Halifax, 7 July 1953, T.C., I.O.L.
2. Halifax to Templewood, 13 July 1953, T.C.
3. For an account of Conservative policy towards implementing the federal provisions of the Act, see below, ch. 3.
4. *The Times*, 12 and 13 Oct. 1928.
5. A note by Lord Irwin on his proposed Dominion status declaration, given to Hoare on 25 Sept. 1929, T.C.
6. Note by Lord Irwin on Dominion status, Nov. 1929, T.C.
7. *The Times*, 26 June 1929.
8. Halifax to Templewood, 1 Sept. 1953, T.C.
9. *Report of the Indian Statutory Commission* (Cd. 3568–9, 1930), vol. ii (Recommendations), paras 24, 30.
10. *Report on Indian Constitutional Reforms* (Cd. 9109, 1918), paras 120, 300.
11. Loc. cit., para 23.
12. Ibid., para 365.
13. Ibid., para 235.
14. Sir W. S. Holdsworth, 'The Indian States and India', *Law Quarterly Review*, xlvi (1930), 407–46, esp. 442–3.

15 *Government of India's Despatch on Proposals for Constitutional Reform*, 20 Sept. 1930 (Cd. 3700, 1930), para 16.
16 Bikaner's press interview of 2 Nov. 1929, in K. M. Pannikar, *His Highness the Maharaja of Bikaner* (London, 1937), 321–2.
17 Sastri to V. S. Ramaswami Sastri, 24 Oct. 1930, in T. N. Jagadisan (ed.) *Letters of the Right Honourable Srinivasa Sastri*. 2nd ed. (London, 1963). 199; hereafter *Sastri's Letters*.
18 Note by Hoare on 'a meeting with Govt. at Downing Steet, Nov. 16th 1930', T.C.
19 Note by Hoare on a conversation with Hailey, 13 Nov. 1930, T.C.
20 Hoare's note of 16 Nov., loc. cit.
21 Cabinet paper circulated on the Prime Minister's instructions, 19 Nov. 1930, T.C.
22 Note by Hoare on a conversation with Simon, 26 Nov. 1930, T.C.
23 Memorandum by Hoare on 'Conservative Policy at the Round Table Conference', 12 Dec. 1930, T.C.
24 *Indian Round Table Conference Proceedings, 12 November 1930–19 January 1931* (Cd. 3778, 1931), 506.
25 *Morning Post*, 5 Feb. 1931.
26 V. S. Srinivasa Sastri, 'The Report of the Simon Commission', *Journal of the East Indian Association*, xxi (1930), 252–80, see p. 253. Cf. Hoare's note of 26 Nov. 1930 (T.C.), recording Simon's view: 'Dominion Status and Responsible govt. with reserves a contradiction in terms.'
27 The Gandhi-Irwin agreement, 5 Mar. 1931, in M. Gwyer and A. Appadorai (eds), *Speeches and Documents on the Indian Constitution, 1921–47*, 2 vols (London, 1957), I, 232.
28 *The Times*, 14 Apr. 1931.
29 *Manchester Guardian*, 19 June 1931.
30 India Office departmental note on communal and minority problems, 25 Sept. 1931, T.C.
31 Memorandum by Sir R. I. R. Glancy on 'Attitude of the Indian States Delegates towards Federation', 1 Sept. 1931, and supplementary memorandum of 29 Oct. 1931, T.C.
32 Hoare to Willingdon, 18 Sept. 1931 (secret telegram), T.C.
33 A. T. Q. Stewart, *The Ulster Crisis* (London, 1967), 21.
34 Message from Baldwin in Hoare to Willingdon, 24 Sept. 1931 (secret telegram), T.C.
35 Hoare's memorandum for Cabinet, 9 Nov. 1931, T.C.
36 Hoare to Willingdon, 19 Nov. 1931, T.C.
37 *Indian Round Table Conference Proceedings (Second Session), 7 September 1931–1 December 1931* (Cd. 3997, 1932), 415.
38 Willingdon to Hoare, 29 Nov. 1931 (telegram), T.C.
39 Willingdon to Hoare, 23 Jan. 1932 (secret telegram), T.C.
40 Sastri to P. Kodanda Rao, 2 July 1932, *Sastri's Letters*, 231–2.
41 'Manifesto' issued by the Liberals, reported in Willingdon to Hoare, 18 Aug. 1932 (telegram), T.C.
42 Ibid.
43 'Manifesto' issued by the Liberals, loc. cit.
44 Issued as *Proposals for Indian Constitutional Reform, March 1933* (Cd. 4268, 1933).
45 Hoare to Willingdon, 6 Jan. 1933 (telegram), T.C.

46 Willingdon to Hoare, 26 Jan. 1933 (telegram), T.C.
47 Willingdon to Hoare, 9 Feb. 1933 (telegram), T.C.
48 Hoare to Willingdon, 16 Feb. 1933 (telegram), T.C.
49 Willingdon to Hoare, 20 Aug. 1933 (telegram), T.C.
50 Willingdon to Hoare, 16 Nov. 1933 (telegram), T.C.
51 Hoare to Willingdon, 28 Nov. 1933 (telegram), T.C.
52 Hoare to Willingdon, 18 Apr. 1934 (telegram), T.C.
53 For an account of the divisions within the Conservative Party over the Indian question see S. C. Ghosh, 'Decision Making and Power in the British Conservative Party: A Case Study of the Indian Problem, 1929–34', *Political Studies*, xiii (1965), 198–212.
54 Hoare to Willingdon, 2 Nov. 1934 (telegram), T.C.
55 Willingdon to Zetland, 1 Sept. 1936, Z.C.
56 Willingdon to Zetland, 24 June 1935, ibid.
57 See below, ch. 3.

3 BRITISH POLICY AND THE INDIAN PROBLEM, 1936–40

1 Attlee's speech on the Government of India Bill, 4 June 1935, in C. H. Philips (ed.), *The Evolution of India and Pakistan, 1858–1947: Select Documents* (London, 1962), 318.
2 Zetland to Willingdon, 22 Mar. 1936, Z.C.
3 Zetland to Linlithgow, 3 May 1937, Z.C.
4 Zetland to Linlithgow, 28 June 1937, Z.C.
5 Zetland to Linlithgow, 25 Sept. 1936, Z.C.
6 Zetland to Linlithgow, 28 June 1936, Z.C.
7 Zetland to Linlithgow, 25 Jan. 1937, Z.C.
8 For Zetland's denial of dilatoriness towards implementing the federal sections of the Act see his *'Essayez'* (London, 1956), 241 ff. Zetland as autobiographer was more fatalistic than as Secretary of State. His account of this question is characteristic of a tendency to emphasize the intractability of the political situation and play down the weaknesses in British diplomacy.
9 Marquess of Linlithgow, *Speeches and Statements, 1936–43* (London, 1945), 200–3; hereafter *Linlithgow's Speeches*.
10 *Commons' Debates*, 21 Feb. 1938.
11 Zetland to Linlithgow, 21 Mar. 1939, Z.C.
12 Zetland to C. Heath, 19 Dec. 1939, Z.C.
13 In Linlithgow to Zetland, 27 Feb. 1940, Z.C.
14 Zetland to Linlithgow, 6 Dec. 1937, Z.C.
15 *'Essayez'*, 247.
16 Zetland to Linlithgow, 13 Dec. 1938, Z.C.
17 Zetland to Linlithgow 22 May 1939, Z.C.
18 Linlithgow to Zetland, 7 July 1939, Z.C.
19 Letter to Zetland, Z.C.
20 Montagu to Asquith, 22 Dec. 1915, in S. D. Waley, *Edwin Montagu* (London, 1964), 82–5.
21 Congress Working Committee resolution, 14 Sept. 1939, Gwyer and Appadorai, op. cit., II, 484–7.

22 Linlithgow's statement of 18 Oct. 1939, ibid., II, 490–3.
23 Zetland to Linlithgow, 2 Oct. 1939, Z.C.
24 Zetland to Linlithgow, 11 Oct. 1939, Z.C.
25 Linlithgow to Zetland, 22 Oct. 1939, Z.C.
26 Linlithgow to Zetland, 27 Nov. 1939, Z.C.
27 Zetland to Linlithgow, 22 Nov. 1939, Z.C.
28 Zetland to Linlithgow, 6 Dec. 1939, Z.C.
29 Linlithgow to Zetland, 21 Dec. 1939, Z.C.
30 Linlithgow to Zetland, 18 Dec. 1939 (telegram), Z.C.
31 Linlithgow to Zetland, 21 Dec. 1939, Z.C.
32 Linlithgow to Zetland, 3 Feb. 1940, Z.C.
33 Linlithgow to Zetland, 6 Feb. 1940, Z.C.
34 Linlithgow to Zetland, 13, 21, 27 Feb., 8 Mar. (telegram), 1940, Z.C.
35 Linlithgow to Zetland, 27 Feb. 1940, Z.C.
36 Letter in Z.C.
37 Linlithgow to Amery, 28 June 1940 (telegram), Z.C.
38 Linlithgow to Amery, 1 July 1940 (telegram), Z.C.
39 Amery to Zetland, 3 Aug. 1940, Z.C.
40 *Linlithgow's Speeches*, 250–2.
41 Resolution of All-India Congress Committee, 15–16 Sept. 1940, Gwyer and Appadorai, op. cit., II, 505–6.
42 Statement of 1–2 Nov. 1941, ibid., II, 518–19.
43 In *'Essayez'* Zetland is less critical of Linlithgow's policy during the early months of the war than one would have expected from the disagreements evidenced by their correspondence (262–85).
44 Linlithgow to Zetland, 25 May 1940, Z.C.
45 Linlithgow to Amery, 30 June 1940 (telegram), Z.C.
46 Linlithgow to Zetland, 27 Feb. 1940, Z.C.
47 Linlithgow to Amery, 30 June 1940 (telegram), Z.C.

4 THE MYSTERY OF THE CRIPPS MISSION

1 Penderel Moon (ed.), *Wavell: The Viceroy's Journal* (London, 1973), 19 Oct. 1943; hereafter *Wavell's Journal*.
2 Lord Glendevon, *Viceroy at Bay* (London, 1971), 232.
3 H. V. Hodson, *The Great Divide: Britain-India-Pakistan* (London, 1969), 103.
4 Eric Stokes, 'Cripps in India', *Historical Journal*, 14 (1971), 427–34, see 431.
5 D. A. Low, 'The Indian Schism', *Journal of Commonwealth Political Studies*, 9 (1971), 158–67, see 167; and review of Glendevon, op. cit., in *South Asian Review*, 4 (1971), 256.
6 A. K. Azad, *India Wins Freedom* (Bombay, 1959), 54–81; Nehru to V. K. Krishna Menon, 13 Apr. 1942, Home Pol. Dept., 225/42, N.A.I.
7 A detailed account of the Mission's antecedents appears in my *Churchill, Cripps, and India 1939–45* (London, 1979).
8 Cabinet Conclusion 131 of 1941, *T.P.*, i, 14.
9 Churchill to Attlee, 7 Jan. 1942, ibid.
10 Sapru to Sir G. Laithwaite, 2 Jan. 1942, ibid., 2.
11 Linlithgow to Amery, 21 Jan. 1942, ibid., 23.
12 See above, ch. 3.

13 *T.P.*, i, 60. See also Attlee to Amery, 24 Jan. 1942, ibid., 35.
14 Ibid., 104.
15 Ibid., 223.
16 Cripps to Churchill, 4 Apr. 1942, ibid., 519.
17 Amery to Linlithgow, 10 Mar. 1942, ibid., 296; and the same, 25 Mar. 1942, ibid., 381.
18 Ibid., 223.
19 D. Dilks (ed.), *The Diaries of Sir Alexander Cadogan* (London, 1971), 440.
20 Amery to Churchill, 5 Mar. 1942, *T.P.*, i, 240.
21 Ibid., 282.
22 India Committee, 9 Mar. 1942, Conclusions, ibid., 283.
23 Ibid., 295.
24 Amery to Linlithgow, 12 Mar. 1942, ibid., 315.
25 Amery to Linlithgow, 28 Feb. 1942, ibid., 196.
26 Amery to Churchill, 7 Mar. 1942, ibid., 291.
27 Ibid., 292.
28 Ibid., 79.
29 Hodson, op. cit., 98; Note by Cripps, 23 Mar. 1942, *T.P.*, i, 368.
30 Notes on Executive Council Meeting, 24 Mar. 1942, ibid., 377.
31 Amery to Linlithgow, 25 Mar. 1942, ibid., 381. See also 499.
32 Note by Advisers to Secretary of State, 6 Mar. 1942, ibid., 254.
33 Linlithgow to Amery 25, Feb. 1942, ibid., 183.
34 Ibid. See also Linlithgow's reference to 'National Government' on 8 Mar. in a cable to Amery, ibid., 275.
35 Memo of Cripps-Linlithgow conversation, night of 25 Mar. 1942, ibid., 384.
36 B. Shiva Rao, 'India, 1935–47', in C. H. Philips and M. D. Wainwright (eds.), *The Partition of India: Policies and Perspectives, 1935–1947* (London, 1970), 413–67, see 428. My italics.
37 Note by Cripps, 27 Mar. 1942, *T.P.*., i, 398.
38 Note by Cripps, 28 Mar. 1942, ibid., 413.
39 Proceedings of Press Conference, 29 Mar. 1942, ibid., 440 (p. 547).
40 Linlithgow to Amery, 25 Feb. 1942, ibid., 183.
41 Ibid., 519.
42 Linlithgow to Amery, 5 Apr. 1942, ibid., 525.
43 Cf. Linlithgow to Amery, 25 Feb. 1942, ibid., 184.
44 Ibid., 530. See also Wavell to Churchill, 5 a.m. 6 Apr. 1942 (received 2.15 a.m.), ibid., 531.
45 D. 3 a.m., 6 Apr. 1942, ibid., 533.
46 Note by Mr Pinnell, 6 Apr. 1942, ibid., 539.
47 Ibid., 532.
48 D. 6 Apr. 1942, ibid., 538.
49 Draft cable, ibid., 536 (para. 3).
50 Amery to Linlithgow, 7 Apr. 1942, ibid., 548.
51 Note by Linlithgow, 8 Apr. 1942, ibid., 553.
52 Linlithgow to Amery, 9 Apr. 1942, ibid., 578.
53 Note by Mr Pinnell, 9 Apr. 1942, ibid., 571.
54 Linlithgow to Amery, 9 Apr. 1942, ibid., 578.
55 Cripps to Churchill, 6 Apr. 1942, ibid., 535.
56 Churchill to Cripps, 10 Apr. 1942, ibid., 582.
57 Azad, op. cit., 61. My italics.

58 Azad to Cripps, 10 Apr. 1942, *T.P.*, i, 587. My italics.
59 Ibid, 604. My italics.
60 Loc. cit. My italics.
61 Sir Reginal Coupland, *The Cripps Mission* (London, 1942), 54–5.
62 Ibid. Also Coupland, *Report*, II, 228–9.
63 Cf. George VI's diary, 28 July 1942, in J. W. Wheeler-Bennett, *King George VI* (London, 1958), 702; A. R. Mudaliar, note of 21 Sept. 1942. *T.P.*, iii, 2.
64 Lord Butler, *The Art of the Possible* (London, 1972), 111. See also *Wavell's Journal*, 29 Mar. 1945.
65 Ibid., 31 Aug. 1945.
66 Amery to Linlithgow, 24 Mar. 1942, *T.P.*, i, 375.
67 Butler to Amery, 6 Mar. 1942, ibid., 255.
68 Butler to Hoare, 6 Mar. 1942, Templewood P., Cambridge Univ. Lib., XIII. 19.
69 Linlithgow to Amery, 21 Jan. 1942, *T.P.*, i, 23.
70 *Wavell's Journal*, 19 Oct. 1943.
71 Speech of 10 Sept. 1942, cited in Tara Chand, *History of the Freedom Movement in India*, IV (London, 1972), 384.
72 Linlithgow to Amery, 23–7 Jan. 1942, *T.P.*, i, 30.
73 Churchill to Attlee, 7 Jan. 1942, ibid., 6.
74 Amery to Linlithgow, 2 Feb. 1942, ibid., 58.
75 Linlithgow to Amery, 21 Jan. 1942, ibid., 23.
76 Amery to Linlithgow, 3 Apr. 1942, with Linlithgow's marginal comments, ibid., 517. D. A. Low notes Linlithgow's 'ferocity' towards Congress in August 1940 and the 'rebuke' that it provoked from the Cabinet (*South Asian Review*).
77 Azad to Cripps, 10 Apr. 1942, *T.P.*, i, 587.
78 Nehru to Menon, 13 Apr. loc. cit. See also Azad to Cripps, 11 Apr. 1942, *T.P.*, i, 604.
79 Azad to Cripps, 10 Apr. 1942, ibid., 587.
80 The author of a proscribed tract presented the whole purpose of the mission as the achievement of a propaganda victory (R. M. Lohia, *The Mystery of Sir Stafford Cripps* (Bombay, 1942), in Home Pol. Dept., 37/16/42, N.A.I.).
81 Cripps to Azad, 10 Apr. 1942, *T.P.*, i, 590.
82 Nehru to Menon, loc. cit. See also Azad's pained and sorrowful letter to Cripps, 11 Apr., loc. cit.
83 Coupland, *The Cripps Mission*, 54–62; *Report*, II, 283–6. Coupland's diary reveals that he knew the inside story (see my *Churchill, Cripps, and India*, passim).
84 C. R. Attlee, *As It Happened* (London, 1954), 181.
85 Attlee's memo of 2 Feb., loc. cit.

5 JINNAH AND THE PAKISTAN DEMAND

1 Sir Penderel Moon, 'Mr. Jinnah's Changing Attitude to the Idea of Pakistan', in A. H. Dani (ed.), *World Scholars on Quaid-i-Azam Mohammad Ali Jinnah* (Islamabad, 1979), 267–70, p. 270.
2 L. Ziring, 'Jinnah: The Burden of Leadership', ibid., 396–408, p. 407.
3 C. H. Philips and M. D. Wainwright (eds), *The Partition of India: Policies and Perspectives, 1935–1947* (London, 1970), 29.
4 N. Mansergh, *The Prelude to Partition: Concepts and Aims in Ireland and India*, The 1976 Commonwealth Lecture (Cambridge, 1978), 26, 59.
5 Viceroy's Personal Report No. 3, 17 April 1947, *T.P.*, x, 165.

6 Mountbatten to Sir Stafford Cripps, 9 July 1947, CAB 127/139, P.R.O.
7 E.g., Clement Attlee's draft memoirs, ATLE 1/13, Churchill College, Cambridge; Mountbatten on Nehru and Patel in letter to Cripps, 9 July 1947, loc. cit.; Moon to J.McL. Short, 2 Sept. 1946, CAB 127/150, P.R.O.; H. V. Hodson, *The Great Divide: Britain-India-Pakistan* (London, 1969), 217–18; L. Collins and D. Lapierre, *Freedom at Midnight* (London, 1975), 101; S. Gopal, *Jawaharlal Nehru: A Biography* I (London, 1975), 257; Tara Chand, *History of the Freedom Movement in India*, IV (Delhi, 1972), 574.
8 K. B. Sayeed, 'The Personality of Jinnah and his Political Strategy', in Philips and Wainwright, op. cit., 276–93, esp. 282.
9 Ibid., 293. Dr Ian Copland more recently observed that Jinnah 'remains an enigma' ('Islam and Political Mobilization in Kashmir, 1931–34', *Pacific Affairs*, 54 (1981), 228–59).
10 E.g. Tara Chand, op. cit., IV, 321ff.
11 See Moon, 'Jinnah's Changing Attitude', loc. cit., for an analysis of such arguments.
12 E.g. S. R. Mehrotra, 'The Congress and the Partition of India', in Philips and Wainwright, op. cit., 188–221, p. 216; A. Seal, 'Imperialism and Nationalism in India', J. A. Gallagher, G. Johnson and A. Seal (eds), *Locality, Province and Nation: Essays on Indian Politics, 1870–1940* (Cambridge, 1973), 1–27, p. 24.
13 For studies of mobilization, see Copland, 'Islam and Political Mobilization', loc. cit., esp. 228–31, 257–9.
14 Cited in H. Bolitho, *Jinnah: Creator of Pakistan* (London, 1954), 70.
15 A. Jalal and A. Seal, 'Alternative to Partition: Muslim Politics Between the Wars', in C. Baker, G. Johnson and A. Seal (eds), *Power, Profit and Politics: Essays in Imperialism, Nationalism and Change in Twentieth Century India* (Cambridge, 1981), 415–54; Moore, *The Crisis of Indian Unity, 1917–40* (London, 1974).
16 Z. H. Zaidi, 'Aspects of Muslim League Policy, 1937–47', in Philips and Wainwright, op. cit., 245–75, esp. 250–7. See also J. A. Gallagher, 'Congress in Decline: Bengal, 1930 to 1939', in Gallagher, Johnson and Seal, op. cit., 269–325, esp. 307–12.
17 Lady Mountbatten wrote to her husband of Miss Jinnah in April 1947: 'Like Mr Jinnah, she has, of course, a persecution mania . . .' (*T.P.*, x, 388). M. L. Chagla, a useful witness, believed that she 'injected an extra dose of venom' into Jinnah's diatribes against the Hindus (*Roses in December* (Bombay, 1973), 119). For recollections of Jinnah see also the works of Kanji Dwarkadas.
18 L. Brennan, 'The Illusion of Security: the Background to Muslim Separatism in the United Provinces', *Modern Asian Studies*, 18 (1984), 237–72.
19 Azim Husain, *Fazl-i-Husain: a Political Biography* (Bombay, 1946), 265.
20 Cited in Bolitho, op. cit., 113–14.
21 See D. Pandey, 'Congress-Muslim League Relations, 1937–39: "The Parting of the Ways"', *Modern Asian Studies*, 12 (1978), 629–54.
22 Brennan shows that in the U.P. 'for the first time since 1909, the Muslim elite seemed to have no leverage in the new institutions of government', 'many of the gains of the past thirty years seemed to be vanishing or at least under threat', and 'the foundations they had fought so hard to build were shown to be straw' (op. cit., 231).
23 Prasad to Patel, 11 Oct. 1938, B. N. Pandey (ed.), *The Indian Nationalist Movement, 1885–1947: Select Documents* (London, 1979), 127–8.
24 Coupland, *Report*, II, 167–78.

25 Jinnah's presidential address to Muslim League at Patna, 26 Dec. 1938, Jamil-ud-din Ahmad (ed.), *Speeches and Writings of Mr. Jinnah*, 2 vols (Lahore, 1960 edn), I, 67–81.
26 Ibid., 80.
27 Ibid., 139.
28 Ibid., 36, 139, 184.
29 Ibid., 116.
30 The earliest X-ray photograph in the Quaid-i-Azam archives at Islamabad (Q.A.P.) is dated Lahore, 26 Oct. 1936.
31 Cripps-Geoffrey Wilson diary of visit to India, 15 Dec. 1939 (in possession of Mr Maurice Shock).
32 Coupland's Indian diary, 1941–42, 17 Jan. 1942, Rhodes House, Oxford.
33 Ibid., 8 Apr. 1942.
34 A. V. Alexander's diary, 4 Apr. 1946, Churchill College, Cambridge.
35 Cited in Hodson, op. cit. 217.
36 The following account of the Karachi conference draws heavily on A. K. Jones, 'Mr. Jinnah's Leadership and the Evolution of the Pakistan Idea: The Case of the Sind Provincial Muslim League Conference, 1938', in Dani, op. cit., 180–92.
37 Gazdar to Jinnah, 10 July 1937, cited in Ziring, 'Jinnah', loc. cit., 406.
38 Alhaj Mian Ahmad Shafi, *Haji Sir Abdoola Haroon: A Biography* (Karachi, n.d.).
39 Address of 9 Oct. 1938, cited in Jones, 'Mr. Jinnah's Leadership', loc. cit., 183.
40 See Jinnah's Osmania University speech, 28 Sept. 1939, Ahmad, *Speeches and Writings of Mr. Jinnah*, I, 87; Cripps-Wilson diary, 15 Dec. 1939; 'Two Nations in India', sent by Jinnah to *Time and Tide* on 19 Jan. 1940 and published 9 Mar. 1940.
41 *Statesman*, 11 Oct. 1938, cited in Jones, 'Mr. Jinnah's Leadership', loc. cit., 186–7.
42 *Statesman*, 14 Oct. 1938, cited in Mehrotra, 'The Congress and the Partition', loc. cit., 207.
43 *Pioneer*, 15 Oct. 1938, cited in S. S. Pirzada (ed.), *Foundations of Pakistan: All-India Muslim League Documents, 1906–47*, 2 vols (Karachi, 1970), II, xix.
44 Zaidi, 'Aspects of Muslim League Policy', loc. cit., 261.
45 Pirzada, op. cit., II, 306–24.
46 Ibid., 321.
47 Ibid., xx–xxi.
48 Shafi, *Haji Sir Abdoola Haroon*, 139.
49 Haroon's correspondence with Aga Khan in Nov.–Dec. 1938, in Shafi, ibid., 137–42. For the Aga Khan's own notion of a 'United States of Southern Asia' see 'Scheme of His Highness Sir Aga Khan as modified by Sir Fazl-i-Husain, January 1936', ibid., 118–21, and Jalal and Seal, 'Alternative to Partition', loc. cit., 445–9.
50 Shafi, op. cit., 150–1.
51 Haroon's introduction to Latif's *The Muslim Problem in India* (Bombay, 1939), v–viii.
52 Ibid.; *The Cultural Future of India* (Bombay, 1938); *A Federation of Cultural Zones for India*, Secunderabad, 20 Dec. 1938; *Statesman*, 30 Mar. 1939.
53 Pirzada, op. cit., II, 153–71.
54 Cited and discussed in Coupland, *Report*, II, 199–201.
55 Hafeez Malik (ed.), *Iqbal: Poet-Philospher of Pakistan* (New York, 1971), appx, 383–90.
56 Ahmad Bashir to Jinnah etc., 22 Mar. 1939, Q.A.P. file 96.
57 Ibid. See also Ahmad Bashir letter to a newspaper, 7 Apr. 1939, ibid.

NOTES

58 Ahmad Bashir to Jinnah, 21 Oct. 1939, ibid.
59 Ahmad Bashir's letters to Jinnah and an account of the Pakistan Majlis appear in Sarfaraz Hussain Mirza (ed.), *Tassawar-e-Pakistan Say Qararadad-e-Pakistan Tak* (Lahore, 1983).
60 Sikandar Hayat Khan, *Outlines of a Scheme of Indian Federation*, Lahore, 30 July 1939. See also Sikandar's speech in *Punjab Legislative Assembly Debates*, 11 Mar. 1941 (in V. P. Menon, *The Transfer of Power in India*, London, 1957, appx I, 451–67). For another Punjabi scheme published in Lahore in summer 1939, see 'A Punjabi' [? Miyan Kifayat Ali] *Confederacy of India*, pub. by Sir Muhammad Shah Nawaz Khan of Mamdot.
61 Ahmad Bashir, 'Sir Sikandar Hayat's Scheme' and 'Sir Sikandar's Federal Scheme', *Civil and Military Gazette*, 5 and 27 Aug. 1939.
62 Syed Zafarul Hasan and Muhammad Afzal Husain Qadri, *The Problem of Indian Muslims and its Solution*, Aligarh Muslim University Press, 14 Aug. 1939.
63 Printed commendation by Amiruddin Kedwaii, Umar Uddin, Zafar Ahmad Siddiqi, Masud Makhdum, Dr Zaki Uddin, Dr Burhan Ahmad Faruqi, Jamil-ud-din Ahmad and Muddassir Ali Shamsee, n.d., but attached to similarly printed address by 'The Authors', d. Sept. 1939, Q.A.P., file 96.
64 Viceroy's statement, 18 Oct. 1939, in M. Gwyer and A. Appadorai (eds), *Speeches and Documents on the Indian Constitution, 1921–47* (London, 1957), II, 490–3.
65 Ahmad Bashir to Jinnah, 21 Oct. 1939, loc. cit. See also extract from his letter to Nehru, 6 Dec. 1939, in S. Gopal (ed.), *Selected Works of Jawaharlal Nehru*, X (New Delhi, 1977), 420 n.
66 Gandhi, 'Opinions Differ', *Harijan*, 11 Nov. 1939, reported in *Statesman* (Delhi), 12 Nov. 1939. Gandhi was replying to a private letter from 'M.A. of Aligarh' (see *Collected Works of Mahatma Gandhi*, LXX (New Delhi, 1977), 332–4).
67 Typescript document, 4 pp., Q.A.P., file 96.
68 'Confidential Note for the President', n.d., ibid.
69 Haroon to Hon. Sec. A.I.M.L., 2 Feb. 1940, ibid.
70 C. Khaliquzzaman, *Pathway to Pakistan* (Lahore, 1961), 223–4. Khaliquzzaman grossly exaggerates his own role, though in March 1939 he had proposed to the Secretary of State a vague scheme for three or four separate federations of provinces and states under a small central co-ordinating body (ibid., 205–7); Marquess of Zetland, *'Essayez'* (London, 1956), 248–9. See also below, pp. 125–6.
71 A.I.M.L. session, 22–4 Mar. 1940, Pirzada, op. cit., II, 325–49.
72 At the time Liaqat Ali Khan rightly said that the term 'territorial readjustments' connoted a Muslim claim to Aligarh and Delhi, an interpretation questioned by Pirzada in the light of later events (ibid., xx–xxi).
73 See above, n. 70, and below, pp. 125–6.
74 See his speech of 11 Mar. 1941 (see n. 60).
75 See Pirzada, op. cit., II, xxii–xxiii; Philips and Wainwright, op. cit., 29.
76 Mansergh, op. cit., 27.
77 Still, the Associated Press of India reported that as Jinnah spoke 'there were many in that huge gathering of over 100,000 people who remembered the late Mohammed Iqbal, the poet of Islam, the animator of the idea of Pakistan' (Pirzada, II, 327). Jinnah later wrote of Iqbal: 'His views were substantially in consonance with my own and had led me to the same conclusions as a result of careful examination and study of the constitutional problems facing India and found expression in due course in ... the Lahore resolution ...' (Malik, op. cit., 384–5).

78 For the discussions, see Gowher Rizvi, *Linlithgow in India: A Study of British Policy and the Political Impasse in India, 1936–43*, (London, 1978), 129ff.; K. Veerathappa, 'Britain and the Indian Problem (September 1939–May 1940)', *International Studies*, VII (1966), 537–67; ch. 3 above.
79 Cited in D. Pandey, 'Congress-Muslim League Relations', loc. cit., 647.
80 Prasad to Nehru, 12 Nov. 1939, B. N. Pandey, op. cit., 137–8.
81 Resolutions of A.I.M.L. Working Committee, 15–17 June 1940, Q.A.P., file 95. See also Coupland, *Report*, II, 243.
82 Sikandar to Jinnah, 31 May 1940, Q.A.P., file 21; Coupland, op. cit., 241.
83 Viceroy's statement of 8 Aug. 1940, Gwyer and Appadorai, op. cit., II, 504–5.
84 Liaqat to Jinnah, 28 July 1941, Q.A.P., file 1092.
85 Allegations of dictatorship remain prominent in Partition historiography (e.g. Collins and Lapierre, op. cit., 103; Tara Chand, op. cit., IV, passim). Hodson wrote that Jinnah 'displayed his authority ... imperiously' in Aug. 1941 (op. cit., 89).
86 E.g., May 1944 speech, Ahmad, op. cit., II, 47–50.
87 Press statement, *Statesman*, 19 Feb. 1941.
88 E.g., Nov. 1940 and Apr. 1941 speeches, Ahmad, op cit., I, 184–5, 259.
89 *Statesman* (Delhi), 18 Feb. 1941.
90 Menon, op. cit., 451–67.
91 Pirzada, op. cit., II, 359–71.
92 Menon, op. cit., 105.
93 Coupland's Diary, 2 Feb. 1942.
94 Ibid., 17 Jan. and 2 Feb. 1942. Coupland assumed these cessions in his own 'Agency Centre' scheme (*Report*, III, 82).
95 Memo. on Pakistan, 21 Mar. 1942, Coupland's Diary, 269–70.
96 Declaration as published, 30 Mar. 1942, *T.P.*, i, 456.
97 Resolution of League Working Committee, 11 Apr. 1942, ibid., 606.
98 See my *Churchill, Cripps, and India, 1939–45* (London, 1979), 88 and n. 4; *T.P.*, i, 380, 392, 393. The Cripps Mission file (802) in the Q.A.P. is 'embargoed'.
99 Coupland's Diary, 185, 214.
100 Ibid., 221–2.
101 Working Committee resolution, 11 Apr. 1942, loc. cit.
102 Ahmad, op. cit., 1, 582–6.
103 For further expressions of the idea, see ibid., I, 383, 409, 477, 567–8.
104 See Richard Casey to Wavell, 11 Sept. 1944, *T.P.*, v, 13, 79; East Pakistan Renaissance Society, *Eastern Pakistan: Its Population, Delimitation and Economics*, Calcutta, Sept. 1944. As early as 11 June 1940 Prof. A. Sadeque, Professor of Economics and Politics at Islamia College, Calcutta, sent to Jinnah a proposal for dividing India into Pakistan, Hindustan and 'Greater Bengal' (Q.A.P., file 106).
105 Pirzada, op. cit., II, xxx.
106 See above, ch. 4, and my *Churchill, Cripps, and India*, 132–5.
107 See my *Escape from Empire: The Attlee Government and the Indian Problem* (Oxford, 1983), 18–31.
108 E.g., interview of 8 Nov. 1945, Ahmad, op. cit., II, 230–3.
109 Pirzada, op. cit., II, 512–13.
110 *T.P.*, vii, 71, 82.
111 Ibid., 126.
112 Ibid., 82.
113 See Ahmad to Jinnah, 29 May 1946, Q.A.P., file 1092.
114 *T.P.*, vii, 303.

115 E.g., M.L. Qureshi (joint secretary of the League's Planning Committee) to Jinnah, 31 May 1946, Q.A.P., file 1092.
116 M.A.H. Ispahani, 'Factors Leading to the Partition of British India', in Philips and Wainwright, op. cit. 330–59, pp. 348–50.
117 Aurangzeb Khan to Jinnah, 19 May 1946, Q.A.P., file 12; Ahmad to Jinnah, 29 May 1946, loc. cit. See also typed lists of 'Advantages' and 'Disadvantages', n.d.; Liaqat to Jinnah, 21 May 1946; Prof. A. B. A. Haleem (Aligarh) to Jinnah, 23 May 1946; all in Q.A.P., file 12.
118 *T.P.*, vii, 469.
119 Jinnah to Wavell, 8 June 1946, ibid., 473.
120 For elaboration see my *Escape from Empire*, 124–44.
121 See, e.g., Jinnah's bitter complaint to Attlee and Churchill, 6 July 1946, *T.P.*, viii, 68.
122 See, e.g., *T.P.*, ix, 153.
123 E.g., Churchill to Jinnah and Simon to Jinnah, both 11 Dec. 1946, Q.A.P., file 21.
124 *T.P.*, x, 229.
125 *Commons' Debates*, 12 Dec. 1946, cols. 1362–70; 20 Dec. 1946, cols. 2341–52. See also K. Dwarkadas, *Ten Years to Freedom* (Bombay, 1968), 195–6.
126 See Sir W. Monckton to Templewood, 15 Jan. 1947 and reply, 16 Jan. 1947, T.C.
127 *T.P.*, ix, 440; x, 105, 165.
128 Ibid.
129 Ibid., 256. See also 276, Annex. I.
130 Ibid., 229. See also 227–8, 264. Cf. the common Pakistani belief that Jinnah saw Suhrawardy's scheme as a heresy (eg. M.A.H. Ispahani, *Qaid-e-Azam as I Knew Him* (Karachi, 1967 edn), 257–8). For relations between Jinnah and Suhrawardy over the scheme from Feb. 1947, see Ziring, 'Jinnah', loc. cit. A draft scheme for a 'Free State of Bengal', d. 4 June 1947, appears in Q.A.P., file 142.
131 See below, ch. 6.
132 See also A. K. Brohi, 'Reflections on the Quaid-i-Azam's Self-Selection as the First Governor-General of Pakistan', and S. M. Burke, 'Quaid-i-Azam's Decision to become Pakistan's First Governor-General', in Dani, op. cit., 289–306. Cf. Mountbatten's simple explanation in terms of Jinnah's vanity and megalomania, and Congress suspicions of Jinnah's fascist intentions (above, nn. 6–7).
133 In May 1949 three of Pakistan's governors, the three chiefs of staff, and 470 military officers, were still British.
134 For Gandhi see his *Autobiography: the Story of My Experiments with Truth* (Ahmedabad, 1927), and S. H. and L. Rudolph, *The Modernity of Tradition* (Chicago, 1967), Pt. II ('The Traditional Roots of Charisma: Gandhi').
135 Appeal for 'Day of Deliverance', 2 Dec. 1939, Ahmad, I, 98–100.
136 Coupland's Diary, 17 Jan. 1942.
137 See, e.g., M. L. Qureshi to Jinnah, 31 May 1946, loc. cit.
138 See below, ch. 6; *T.P.*, x, 387, 416.

6 MOUNTBATTEN, INDIA AND THE COMMONWEALTH

1 The views were held at the time and were argued in, e.g. L. Mosley, *The Last Days of the British Raj* (London, 1961); Chaudhuri Muhammad Ali, *The Emergence of Pakistan* (New York, 1967). That they persisted was revealed in the British and Indian press in the days following the Mullaghmore tragedy of 27 Aug. 1979. See, e.g.

Daily Telegraph, 28 Aug. 1979; *Sunday Telegraph*, 2 Sept. 1979; *Times of India and Indian Express*, 29 Aug. 1979.

2 A. Campbell-Johnson, *Mission with Mountbatten* (London, 1951); V. P. Menon, *The Transfer of Power in India* (London, 1957); Lord Ismay, *Memoirs* (London, 1960).

3 H. V. Hodson, *The Great Divide* (London, 1969); L. Collins and D. Lapierre, *Freedom at Midnight* (London, 1975).

4 H. R. Tinker, *Experiment with Freedom* (London, 1967), esp. 10, 159; and 'Jawaharlal Nehru at Simla, May 1947: A moment of Truth?', *Modern Asian Studies*, 4 (1970), 349–58, esp. 350.

5 S. Gopal, *Jawaharlal Nehru, A Biography*, I (London, 1976), 344.

6 Dr A. K. Majumdar has suggested many corrections (some of them rejected here) in 'Writings on the Transfer of Power, 1945–47', in B. R. Nanda (ed.), *Essays in Modern Indian History* (New Delhi, 1980), 182–222.

7 For subsequent discussion of the negotiations, see Hugh Tinker, 'Incident at Simla, May 1947—What the Documents Reveal: A Moment of Truth for the Historians', *The Journal of Commonwealth and Comparative Politics*, 20 (1982), 200–22, and my 'The Mountbatten Viceroyalty', ibid., 22 (1984), 204–15.

8 M. Gwyer and A. Appadorai (eds), *Speeches and Documents on the Indian Constitution, 1921–47* (London, 1957), II, 667–9.

9 Ibid.

10 Mountbatten to Attlee, 11 Feb. 1947, Mountbatten file 109. I am indebted to the Broadlands Trustees for permission to use Mountbatten's Indian papers (hereafter MB) and to the India Office Records for making their xerox copies available to me. The file numbers cited are those assigned temporarily to the copies by the I.O.R.

11 Minutes of meeting between Attlee, Mountbatten, and Ismay at 10 Downing Street, 11 Feb. 1947, and T. L. Rowan to Ismay, 13 Feb. 1947 (enclosing redraft of the statement), MB, 109.

12 Attlee to Mountbatten, 8 Feb. 1947 (enclosing the draft), MB, 109.

13 Mountbatten to Attlee, 8 Feb. 1947 (enclosing redraft), ibid.

14 India Office Note attached to Memo by Sec. of State for India, 'India, Transfer of Power to More than One Authority', 4 Mar. 1947, L/PO/428, I.O.R.

15 Document handed to Sec. of State by Ghosh on 10 Mar. 1947, ibid.

16 Menon, op. cit., 364; S. Ghosh, *Gandhi's Emissary* (London, 1967), 204.

17 Annexure II to Memo by Sec. of State on proposals brought by Sudhir Ghosh, 12 Mar. 1947, L/PO/428; for Cripps's response see Ghosh, op. cit., 204.

18 Gwyer and Appadorai, op. cit., II, 669–70.

19 L/PO/428.

20 Memo. by Sec. of State, 2 May 1947, ibid.

21 Viceroy's Personal Report No 1, 2 Apr. 1947.

22 Record of Discussion, MB, 191.

23 Viceroy's Personal Report No 1, 2 Apr. 1947.

24 MB, 204.

25 Congress Resolutions of 6–8 Mar. 1947, loc. cit.

26 Nehru to Gandhi, 24 Feb. 1947, in Pyarelal, *Mahatma Gandhi: The Last Phase* (Ahmedabad, 1958), II, 4–5.

27 MB, 191.

28 MB, 191, 108.

29 MB, 204.

30 MB, 108.
31 Viceroy's Staff Meeting, 12 Apr. 1947, MB, 204.
32 Viceroy's Staff Meeting, 14 Apr. 1947, MB, 204. For the draft, see Viceroy's Conference Paper No 28, 14 Apr. 1947, MB, 151.
33 Minutes of Governors' Meeting, 15 Apr. 1947, L/P & J/10/79.
34 Viceroy's Staff Meeting, 10 Apr. 1947, MB, 204.
35 Viceroy's Staff Meeting, 11 Apr. 1947, ibid.
36 MB, 191.
37 Nehru to Singh, 8 Apr. 1947, in Gopal, op. cit., 353.
38 MB, 192.
39 Nehru to Singh, 14 Apr. 1947, in Gopal, op. cit., 352–3.
40 Interviews on 11 Apr. 1947, MB, 191. For the scale of the problem, see C-in-C India to War Office, 30 Aug. 1946, *T.P.*, viii, 225. In May 1947 there were still some 6,000 British Officers in the Indian Armed Forces.
41 MB, 192.
42 Ibid.
43 Trivedi to Mountbatten, 9 May 1947, MB, 40.
44 MB, 192.
45 The history of the Whitehall meeting of the India, Dominions, Foreign, and Colonial Offices to consider India's relationship with the Commonwealth, from Oct. 1946 until Mar. 1947, may be followed in L/P & J/10/122, I.O.L. See also note 57 below.
46 Viceroy's Staff Meeting, 18 Apr. 1947, MB, 204.
47 MB, 192.
48 MB, 204.
49 MB, 40.
50 25 Apr. 1947, ibid.
51 Ismay to Mountbatten, 25 Apr. 1947, MB, 108.
52 Mountbatten's note, 28 Apr. 1947, ibid.
53 Ibid.
54 Mountbatten to Listowel, 1 May 1947, extract in L/P & J/10/79.
55 MB, 40.
56 MB, 192.
57 As a consequence of the independent sovereign republic resolution, the Chiefs of Staff had in March instructed the Commandants of the Inter-Service and Services Staff Colleges, which were attended by Indian students, to exclude western secret information from their curricula. They had also recommended that no further invitations to attend the colleges should be extended to Indian students. See Ismay P., CAB 127/31. The Chiefs of Staff were strongly in favour of India remaining in the Commonwealth, and even, if necessary, of Pakistan alone being welcomed as a member. See Aide Memoire by Joint Planning Staff for Chiefs of Staff Meeting with Ismay, 9 May 1947, and minutes of C.O.S. meeting, 12 May; MB, 152.
58 MB, 193.
59 MB, 40.
60 Viceroy's Personal Report, 1 May 1947.
61 Viceroy's Staff Meeting, MB, 40.
62 Monckton to Ismay, 2 May 1947, Monckton P., Bodleian Library, Oxford. On 14 March Ismay had written to Monckton to say that Mountbatten attached importance to his coming to India as a free-lancer (ibid).

63 Note of 29 Apr. 1947, ibid.
64 Viceroy's Staff Meeting, 1 May 1947, MB, 40.
65 Monckton to Ismay, 2 May 1947, loc. cit.
66 MB, 201.
67 Unsigned typescript, 'India, 18 March 1947–18 July 1947', evidently written by Ismay, 'in the air between Malta and Karachi', W. H. J. Christie P., I.O.L., MSS Eur. D.718/2.
68 MB, 84.
69 Full text of Jinnah's statement of 30 Apr., circulated by India Office, 5 May 1947, L/P & J/10/79.
70 MB, 84.
71 Nehru to Mountbatten, 1 May 1947, MB, 151.
72 MB, 181. Christie noted in his Diary (3 May) that Mountbatten was 'hating the guts of the Congress'.
73 Nehru to Kripalani, 2 May 1947, Rajendra Prasad P., N.A.I., 16-P/45-46-47.
74 *Hindustan Times*, 4 May 1947.
75 C.W.C. Proceedings, 4 May 1947, A.I.C.C. file G43, Part I, 1947, N.M.L.
76 *Hindustan Times*, 6 May 1947; N. K. Bose, *My Days with Gandhi* (London, 1953), 217.
77 MB, 200.
78 Mountbatten to Jinnah, 6 May 1947, in Viceroy to Sec. of State, 6 May 1947 (cable), L/P & J/10/79.
79 Interview with Nehru, 5 May 1947, MB, 193.
80 For Nehru's plan, see below, p. 156. Gandhi's letter appears in N. K. Bose, op. cit., 218–22. Patel's press release (an American Associated Press interview of 9 May) was circulated by India Office, 15 May 1947, and appeared in press, e.g. *Hindustan Times*, 10 May 1947. Patel's thoughts were to some extent foreshadowed in a letter that he wrote to Sudhir Ghosh on 8 May: 'It is time now we settled what the shape of things would be for purposes of transfer of power . . .' (Patel file in Ghosh P., N.M.L.).
81 Viceroy's Staff Meeting, 7 May 1947, MB, 201.
82 Mountbatten to Patel, 19 June 1948, in G. M. Nandurkar (ed.), *Sardar's Letters—Mostly Unknown* (Ahmedabad, 1977), II.
83 MB, 196.
84 Viceroy to Sec. of State, 8 May 1947, L/P & J/10/79.
85 MB, 40.
86 Miéville to Monckton, 9 May 1947, Monckton P.
87 Viceroy to Sec. of State, 9 May 1947, MB, 40. V. P. Menon's scheme was circulated on 10 May.
88 Loc. cit.
89 V. P. Menon to Patel, 10 May 1947, and enclosed note on conversation with Nehru, n.d., but evidently 9 May, in Durga Das (ed.), *Sardar Patel's Correspondence* (Ahmedabad, 1972), IV, 111.
90 MB, 204.
91 Viceroy's Staff Meeting, 10 May 1947, MB, 40.
92 MB, 196.
93 See Viceroy to Sec. of State, 8 May; Memo by Sec. of State on 'Request by Pandit Nehru as to the form of the statement of policy', 10 May; and Sec. of State to Viceroy, 9 May 1947; L/P & J/10/79.

94 Viceroy to Sec. of State, 12 May 1947, L/P & J/10/79.
95 Tinker, 'Jawaharlal Nehru at Simla', surveys the interpretations extant in 1970. See also n. 7 above.
96 Gopal, op. cit., 342–51; C. H. Philips and M. D. Wainwright (eds), *The Partition of India* (London, 1970), 20.
97 Hodson, op. cit., 294–9.
98 Tinker, op. cit., 105.
99 Ibid., 104–14; 'Jawaharlal Nehru at Simla'. But see Nehru's letters to K. P. S. Menon and Cariappa, 29 Apr. 1947, cited in Gopal, op. cit., 344–5; and Patel to K. Dwarkadas, 4 Mar. 1947, in Nandurkar, op. cit.
100 Viceroy's Personal Report. No 7, 15 May 1947.
101 Viceroy's Staff Meeting, 1 May 1947, MB, 201; successive drafts of Plan Balkan to 1 May in MB, 151; record of Mountbatten's meeting with Burrows, 1 May 1947, MB, 196; Mountbatten to Burrows, 2 May 1947, MB, 118.
102 Miscellaneous Meeting, 22 Apr. 1947, MB, 196.
103 Turnbull to Croft and Monteath, 7 May 1947, L/PO/428.
104 Draft Announcement, Revised 10 May 1947, L/P & J/10/79. The successive stages of revision may be traced in this file.
105 Text in Viceroy to Sec. of State, 1 May 1947, ibid.
106 Viceroy's Personal Report No 4, 24 Apr. 1947.
107 Sec. of State to Viceroy, 10 May 1947, L/P & J/10/79.
108 Viceroy to Sec. of State, 10 and 11 May, and Sec. of State to Viceroy, 10 May, ibid.
109 Viceroy to Sec. of State, 10 May 1947, L/P & J/10/79.
110 Ismay to Lady Ismay, 23 April 1947, in R. Wingate, *Lord Ismay* (London, 1970), 153. Christie's Diary records similar criticisms of Mountbatten in relation to the paper, 'The Administrative Consequences of Partition'.
111 Viceroy to Sec. of State, 11 May 1947, L/P & J 10/79.
112 MB, 196.
113 Ibid. Miéville made it absolutely clear that the document that he had shown Nehru on 30 April was the full draft of the whole plan.
114 The quotation is drawn from the record of Nehru's statement at the meeting, not the note itself (see below).
115 Viceroy to Sec. of State, 12 May 1947, L/P & J/10/79.
116 Note by Pandit Nehru dated 11 May 1947, ibid.
117 MB, 203.
118 Miéville to Ismay, 12 May 1947, R/3/1/153, I.O.L.
119 Viceroy's Staff Meeting, 12 May 1947, MB, 119.
120 Ismay to Miéville, 12 May 1947, R/3/1/153. See also India Committee Minutes, 14 May, L/P & J/10/79.
121 Sec. of State to Viceroy, 12 May 1947, L/P & J/10/79.
122 Pyarelal, op. cit., II, 175.
123 Christie's Diary, 14 May 1947. Though the India Committee had never considered the 'alternative plan', Listowel, Ismay, and Abell had rejected it from the outset. See Memo by Sec. of State and covering note, 9 May 1947, L/P & J/10/79.
124 Ibid., 3 May 1947.
125 MB, 196. See Menon, op. cit., 370–1.
126 Viceroy to Sec. of State, 13 May 1947, L/P & J/10/79.
127 Plan of 13 May, ibid.
128 Ibid.

129 Sec. of State to Viceroy, 14 May 1947, ibid. It has been wrongly claimed that Mountbatten was given the alternative of receiving a Cabinet Minister (Hodson, op. cit., 309), though Ismay reported to him that the Cabinet Committee had considered that possibility (Ismay to Mountbatten, 15 May 1947, MB, 153).
130 L/P & J/10/79.
131 Ibid.
132 Ibid.
133 Memo by Sec. of State on Draft Statement of Policy, 17 May 1947, ibid.
134 Note by Sec. of State covering note by the Viceroy, 21 May 1947, and 'Notes for [sic] the Sec. of State for the India Committee', n.d., ibid.
135 L/P & J/10/79
136 Sec. of State to Viceroy, 20 May 1947, ibid.
137 Note by Sec. of State on relations between H.M.G. and the Indian States after the transfer of Power, 24 May 1947, ibid. See below, ch. 7.
138 L/P & J/10/79.
139 Sec. of State to Governor of Bengal, 21 May 1947, ibid.
140 Extract from *News Chronicle* of Nehru's interview with Norman Cliff, 27 May 1947, ibid.
141 Note by Joint Planning Committee, 31 Jan. 1947, with Viceroy to Sec. of State, 3 Feb, 1947, L/P & J/10/77.
142 Sir E. Jenkins at Viceroy's Staff Meeting, 11 May 1947, MB, 196.
143 Prime Minister to Viceroy, 4 June 1947, MB, 209; Listowel to Mountbatten, 5 June 1947, MB, 44.
144 Colville to Mountbatten, 4 June 1947, MB, 44.
145 Wyatt to Attlee, 4 June 1947, Attlee Coll., Bodleian Library, Box 7.
146 MB, 193.

7 INDIA IN 1947: THE LIMITS OF UNITY

1 M. Gwyer and A. Appadorai (eds). *Speeches and Documents on the Indian Constitution* (London, 1957), II, 667–9.
2 Nehru to Gandhi, 24 Feb. 1947, in Pyarelal, *Mahatma Gandhi, The Last Phase* (Ahmedabad, 1958), II, 4–5.
3 C. P. Scott memo, 'Volunteer Organizations/Private Armies in India', 12 Apr. 1947, MB, 117.
4 'Rules of the All-India Muslim League National Guards', 1 Oct. 1946, and E. J. Beveridge's Secret Minute, 8 Nov. 1946, Home Dept. (Pol), 28/4/46, N.A.I.
5 Patel to K. Dwarkadas, 4 Mar. 1947, G. M. Nandurkar (ed.), *Sardar's Letters—Mostly Unknown*, II (Ahmedabad, 1978), 209.
6 Ibid.
7 C.W.C. Resolution of 6–8 Mar. 1947, Gwyer and Appadorai, op. cit., II, 669–70.
8 Mountbatten's own phrase in letter to Attlee, 11 Feb. 1947, MB, 109.
9 MB, 191.
10 MB, 191, 108.
11 Minutes of Governors' Conference, 15–16 Apr., L/P & J/10/79. For 'Plan Balkan' see Viceroy's Conference Paper No 28, 14 Apr. 1947, MB, 151.
12 On the evening of 15 April, Sir Francis Mudie (Governor of Sind) suggested to Mountbatten the feasibility of a Pakistan that included only Sind and West Punjab. It would be no threat to Indian unity and might be seen as a large state that

declined to join the Constituent Assembly. Mountbatten noted: 'This opens up a new vista.' On 12 April Patel suggested to him that a decision to partition Bengal and Punjab might cost Jinnah the support of Muslims in these provinces, and that if Jinnah could secure only Sind and West Punjab then the Muslim League might revolt against the idea of Pakistan (MB, 192).

13 Patel to Mountbatten, 20 Apr. 1947, in Durga Das (ed.), *Sardar Patel's Correspondence* (Ahmedabad, 1972), IV, 22–5.
14 A. Campbell-Johnson, *Mission with Mountbatten* (London, 1951), 72.
15 In L/P & J/10/79.
16 Nehru to Mountbatten, 1 May 1947, MB, 151.
17 For Nehru's plan see record of 8 May meeting, MB, 196; for Gandhi's letter, Pyarelal, op. cit., II, 171–2; for Patel's statement, *Hindustan Times*, 10 May 1947.
18 See drafts of 1 and 10 May, L/P & J/10/79; Viceroy's Staff Meeting, 1 May, MB, 201; as Turnbull to Croft and Monteath, 7 May 1947, L/PO/428.
19 Ismay to Miéville, 12 May 1947, R/3/1/153; Sec. of State to Viceroy, 12 May 1947, L/P & J/10/79.
20 Viceroy to Sec. of State, 13 May 1947, ibid.
21 India Committee meetings of 19, 20, and 28 May, ibid.
22 Nehru to K. P. S. Menon, 29 Apr. 1947, in S. Gopal, *Jawaharlal Nehru*, I (London, 1976), 343.
23 Menon to Patel, 10 May 1947, Durga Das. op. cit., IV, 111–16.
24 Viceroy's Staff Meeting, 6 June 1947, MB, 100.
25 An assessment of the literature on this subject appears in J. Manor, 'The Demise of the Princely Order', in R. Jeffrey (ed.), *People, Princes and Paramount Power* (Delhi, 1978), 306–28.
26 Viceroy's Staff Meeting, 10 May 1947, MB, 40.
27 Loc. cit.
28 Patel to Sudhir Ghosh, 8 May 1947, Sudhir Ghosh P., N.M.L.
29 Enclosure by Menon to Patel, 10 May 1947, loc. cit.
30 *T.P.*, vii, 262.
31 Sir Francis Wylie to Mountbatten, 12 Aug. 1947, R/3/1/40. Corfield thought Wylie 'unsympathetic to the rulers'. Corfield, 'Some Thoughts on British Policy and the Indian States, 1935–47', in C. H. Philips and M. D. Wainwright (eds), *The Partition of India* (London, 1970), 527–34.
32 Penderel Moon (ed.), *Wavell: The Viceroy's Journal* (London, 1973), 384.
33 Minutes of Residents' Conference, 16–17 Dec. 1946, Pol. Dept. 113–P(S)47, N.A.I.
34 Loc. cit.
35 Attlee to Mountbatten, Mar. 1947, in H. V. Hodson, *The Great Divide* (London, 1969), 545–7.
36 Corfield's Secret Minute, 26 Feb. 1947, Pol. 27 R(S) 1947, N.A.I.
37 Crown Rep. to Sec. of State, 27 Feb. 1947, ibid.
38 Sec. of State to Crown Rep., 5 Mar. 1947, ibid.
39 Ibid.
40 Corfield's draft, 31 Mar. 1947, ibid.
41 Ibid.
42 Minutes of Residents' Conference, 8–9 Apr. 1947, Pol. 1–R(S)47, N.A.I.
43 Loc. cit. Yet Corfield, who was present, later disclaimed any recollection of seeing Mountbatten's instructions (letter mentioned in T. Creagh Coen, *The Indian Political Service* (London, 1971), 125).

44 Corfield, 'Some Thoughts', loc. cit., 531. Cf. Corfield, *The Princely India I Knew* (Madras, 1975), 152.
45 In L/P & J/10/79.
46 Patel to Ghosh, 8 May and 29 June 1947, Ghosh P.
47 Revise of 8 May 1947, L/P & J/10/79.
48 Note of Discussion on Retraction of Paramountcy on 9 May 1947, d. 12 May 1947, L/P & J/10/79.
49 Viceroy to Sec. of State, 13 May 1947, ibid.
50 In Viceroy to Sec. of State, 13 May 1947, ibid.
51 Sec. of State to Viceroy, 20 May 1947; ibid.
52 Listowel's note on 'Relations Between H.M.G. and the Indian States after the Transfer of Power', 24 May 1947, pursuant to India Cttee decision of 22 May, and enclosing 'Revised Draft Statement', ibid.
53 Changes to the states paragraph of the 'deal' (in Viceroy to Sec. of State, 13 May, loc. cit.) were suggested by Listowel (memo. of 17 May, in L/P & J/10/79) to avoid 'impression of pressing the states to enter these Constituent Assemblies, at any rate at this stage'. For Corfield's comments see Viceroy to Sec. of State, 21 May, ibid.
54 Nehru to Mountbatten, 4 June 1947, MB, 142.
55 Miscellaneous Meeting, 5 June 1947, MB, 196.
56 Interview, 6 June 1947, MB, 84.
57 Miscellaneous Meeting, 7 June 1947, MB, 196.
58 Nehru to Mountbatten, 9 June 1947, R/3/1/136. and B. N. Pandey (ed.), *The Indian Nationalist Movement, 1885–1947, Select Documents* (London, 1979), 241–2. Far more than the destruction of records was at issue (Cf. Manor, op. cit., 318).
59 Rajaji to Cripps, 8 June 1947, R/3/1/136.
60 Cripps to Rajaji, 23 June 1947, CAB 127/146. Rajaji to Cripps, 2 July 1947 and reply. 8 July 1947. ibid.
61 Hodson, op. cit., 359.
62 Viceroy to Sec. of State, 9 June 1947, MB, 142.
63 The issue was three subject accession (see below). See Corfield in 'Some Thoughts', 533, but he is more specific in *Princely India*, 159. The earlier date of Corfield's decision to depart rends the fabric of such appraisals as Paul Scott's (*Times Lit. Supp.*, 16 July 1976) but is not sufficient to vitiate Scott's judgement of Corfield as a man of firm opinion and principle.
64 MB, 193.
65 MB, 196. V. P. Menon gives a full account of the meeting (*Integration of the Indian States* (London, 1956), 85–90). See also, Corfield, *Princely India*, 155–7, where (as Manor notes, op. cit., 327, n. 52) Nehru is said to have alleged 'malfeasance' (evil-doing, or official misconduct in public affairs). Yet W. H. J. Christie's Diary for 19 June 1947 (I.O.L. D718) records that Corfield told him that Nehru had said he 'should be impeached for misfeasance'. Corfield 'was not pleased by H.E.'s apparent lack of support'.
66 Corfield, 'Some Thoughts', 532; see also *Princely India*, 157.
67 Summary of conclusions of meeting in Political Adviser's Room, 28 June 1947, Pol. 18 PR/47, N.A.I.
68 Pol. Dept. to Residents, 14 June 1947. Pol. 46 R(S)47. Pt I. N.A.I.
69 Consolidated statement of states' reactions, 15 July 1947, Pol. 46R(S) 47 Pt. II, N.A.I.

70 See R/3/1/138, I.O.L.
71 Monckton to J. C. P. Brunyate [beginning of] June 1947, T.C., I.O.L.
72 MB. 193.
73 Ibid.
74 E. W. R. Lumby, 'British Policy Towards the Indian States, 1940–7', in Philips and Wainwright, op. cit., 95–103, p. 103.
75 Menon, *Integration*, 94–9; cf. Hodson, op. cit., 366–9.
76 E.g. in interview with Bhopal and Indore, 4 Aug. 1947. MB. 194.
77 Nehru to Ismay, 19 June 1947, MB, 210, also in Pandey, op. cit., 243–4.
78 E.g. Gwalior and Jodhpur in interviews of 12 and 14 July 1947, MB, 194.
79 Aiyer to Resident for Madras States, 10 July 1947, Pol. 46R(S)47, II, N.A.I.
80 Note by Govt. of Junagadh, 20 July 1947, ibid.
81 Monckton to Templewood, 15 Jan. 1947. T.C.
82 Templewood to Monckton, 16 Jan. 1947; ibid. For Churchill and the 'sham' federation, see my *Churchill, Cripps, and India, 1939–45* (London, 1979), 1–4, 23n., and above, ch. 2.
83 Monckton to Templewood, loc. cit. It seems that Monckton knew that Mountbatten was to become Viceroy three weeks before Wavell was told of his dismissal, and a month before he was told of his successor.
84 Attlee to Maj-Gen. Sir Leslie Hollis, 10 May 1947, MB, 152.
85 Meeting of Chiefs of Staff Cttee, with Ismay and A. V. Alexander, 12 May 1947, ibid.
86 See L/P & S/12/1081.
87 Monckton to Templewood, 18 Apr. 1947. Sudhir Ghosh believed that Roger was paid ten thousand pounds for his efforts, and that on the Portuguese side Dr Antonio Bastroff, and on the British side Sir William Barton (Resident of Hyderabad, 1925–30), were also involved. Ghosh to Patel, 26 Aug. 1947, Ghosh P. But on Barton, see Menon, op. cit., 388–9.
88 T.C.
89 Monckton's Note of 29 Apr. 1947, Monckton P.
90 MB, 70.
91 Monckton to Brunyate, [beginning of] June 1947, T.C.
92 MB, 70.
93 MB, 193.
94 Monckton to Butler, 19 June 1947, T.C.; Listowel's memo of 24 June 1947, 'Proposed Parliamentary Question about Policy towards the States', L/P & J/10/81.
95 Monckton to Templewood, Butler, Salisbury, Bracken and Strauss, 25 June 1947, T.C.
96 India Committee Meeting, 26 June 1947, L/PO/431.
97 Memo. of 28 June 1947, commenting on Monckton's 'Hyderabad Note', 27 June 1947; MB, 70.
98 Patrick to Corfield, 5 July 1947, MB, 143.
99 Menon to Patrick, 7 July 1947, ibid.
100 Sec. of State to Viceroy, 8 July 1947, R/3/1/138.
101 Interview, 8 July 1947, ibid.
102 Monckton to Miéville, 9 July 1947, and enclosure, n.d., MB, 212.
103 MB, 196.
104 H. Gordon (Monckton's personal assistant) to Templewood, 12 July 1947, T.C.
105 Crown Rep. to Sec. of State, 12 July 1947. MB 144.
106 Gordon to Templewood, 21 Feb. 1947, T.C. For Listowel's 'anxious moments in

the Lords', see his 'The Whitehall Dimension in the Transfer of Power', *Indo-British Review*, VII, 3 and 4, 22–31, p. 30.
107. Menon, op. cit., 108. For the speech, see Mountbatten, *Time Only to Look Forward: Speeches* (London, 1949), 51–6.
108. E.g., to the Maharaj-Rana of Dholpur, 29 July 1947, in Corfield, *Princely India*, 183–5.
109. Sec. of State to Viceroy, 1 Aug. 1947, MB, 144.
110. Listowel to Mountbatten, 2 Aug. 1947, MB, 176.
111. Abell's draft of 2 Aug. 1947, R/3/1/139.
112. Viceroy to Sec. of State, 4 Aug. 1947, MB, 144.
113. Sec. of State to Viceroy, 9 Aug. 1947, MB, 176.
114. Sec. of State to Viceroy, 14 Aug. 1947, L/PO/18.
115. Attlee to Mountbatten, 14 Aug. 1947, ibid.
116. Sec. of State to Viceroy, 9 Aug. 1947, MB, 176.
117. Monckton to Mountbatten, 28 July 1947, MB, 70.
118. Nizam to Mountbatten, 8 Aug. 1947, MB, 73.
119. Mountbatten to Listowel, 25 July 1947, MB, 176; Meeting of 28 July 1947, MB, 203.
120. Morris-Jones's paper, 'Position of India and Pakistan within the Commonwealth', 5 Aug. 1947, MB, 213, discussed at Staff Meeting, 5 Aug. 1947, MB, 41. See also B. N. Rau to Abell, 1 Aug. 1947, and Morris-Jones's 'Note on Right of Secession', 11 Aug. 1947, R/3/1/152.
121. Meeting of Ministers, 9 June 1947, MS Eur D714/81, I.O.L.
122. H. R. Tinker's phrase to describe Sir Cyril Radcliffe's 'solution to the problem of the Sikhs' (in 'Pressure, Persuasion, Decision: Factors in the Partition of the Punjab, August 1947' *Journal of Asian Studies*, XXXVI, 4(1977), 695–705, p. 696).
123. These allegations were the gravamen of Corfield's case against Mountbatten: 'Some Thoughts', 531–2; *Princely India*, 158–60; Creagh Coen, op. cit., 125.
124. See Menon, op. cit., 124–50, 314–415.
125. Morris-Jones's 'Note on Joint Organizations', n.d., but seen by Miéville on 9 July 1947, MB, 93.
126. Undated and unsigned typescript, 'India: 18 March 1947–18 July 1947', evidently by Ismay, in W. H. J. Christie P., D718/2, I.O.L.

Index

A.I.S.P.C., *see* All-India States' Peoples' Conference
Abdul Ghaffar Khan, 156
Abell, George, 141, 147, 150, 157, 167, 198
Afghanistan, invasion of, 201
Aga Khan, 39, 51, 66, 72, 114
Ahmad, Dr Burhan, 116
Ahmad, Jamil-ud-din, 129
Aiyer, Sir Ramaswamy, 192
Akalis, 176
Alexander, A.V., 111–12
Ali, Rahmat, 115
Ali, Shaukat, 112
Aligarh scholars, 116, 118, 120, 122, 125, 132
All-India Muslim Conference, 49–50, 108–9
All-India Muslim League, *see* Muslim League
All-India States' Peoples' Conference (A.I.S.P.C.), 184, 189
All-Parties Conference, 39
All-Parties Muslim Conference, 39–40
Amery, L. S.
    Cripps Mission and, 27–31, 88–91, 94–101, 103–4
    India Committee of the War Cabinet member, 88
    Linlithgow and, 21, 23–4
    mentioned, 22, 25
    war-time negotiations, 3–4, 80–3
Anderson, Sir John, 30, 88, 196
Assam, 117, 125, 128, 140, 151, 164, 177–8
Atlantic Charter, 25
Attlee, Clement
    Cripps Mission, 26, 30, 90, 102–4
    India Committee of the War Cabinet member, 88
    India policy, 5–8, 23, 75, 87–8
    India's war role and, 18–19
    mentioned, 24–5, 68
    Pakistan issue, 130
    transfer of power negotiations and, 1, 3, 135–8, 168–99 *passim*
Aurangzeb Khan, Mohamed, 114, 129
Azad, Abul Kalam, 21, 30, 87, 94, 96–8, 101

Bahawalpur, 52
Baldev Singh, Sardar, 142–3
Baldwin, Stanley, 11, 41–2, 53
Balfour declaration, 12–14, 27–8
Baluchistan, 15, 39, 115, 128, 151–2, 174, 180
Bashir, Ahmad, 115–16, 118–20
Bengal
    government of, 109, 178
    political development, 15–16, 33, 39, 65, 68, 116–80 *passim*, 193, 195
    terrorism, 56
    see also East Bengal
Benn, Wedgwood, *see* Stansgate, Viscount
Berar, 116
Bevin, Ernest, 25–6, 30, 35, 87
Bhabha, C. H., 143, 148–9
Bhopal, 60, 191–2
Bhopal, Nawab of, 50, 139, 190, 193–5
Bikaner, Maharaja of, 44, 52
Birkenhead, Lord, 12, 34, 42
Bombay, 109, 112
Bracken, Brendan, 195
British Government
    Cabinet Mission scheme, 1, 5, 128–9, 132, 135, 152–92 *passim*, 199–200
    commercial interests, 15, 27, 32, 35–6, 53, 61
    Cripps Mission, 2–4, 26–31, 86–105, 126–7, 169
    defence issues, 2–3, 5–6, 15, 27, 31, 35, 93–8, 100, 158, 193
    transfer of power negotiations, 135–73, 177–201

transfer of power plan (Plan Balkan), 130, 141–2, 147–84 passim
transfer of power plan (Plan Partition), 167–70, 173
War Cabinet, 30, 75, 80, 88–91, 97, 103–4
Brockman, Capt R. V., 167
Burma, 88
Burrows, Sir Frederick, 170
Butler, R.A., 4. 20, 99–100, 192, 195

'Calcutta Killing', 176
Campbell-Bannerman, Sir Henry, 100
Campbell-Johnson, Alan, 134
Cariappa, Brig. K. M., 144
Caroe, Sir Olaf, 153
Ceylon, 31
Chamber of Princes, 41, 52, 59, 63, 139, 191
Chamberlain, Sir Austen, 42, 62
Chamberlain, Neville, 38, 77
Chintamani, C. Y., 57
Christie, W. H. J., 146–7, 166–7
Churchill, Winston
   Act of 1935 and, 3, 34, 38
   Cripps Mission, 26–31, 89–90, 93–7, 99–101, 103–5
   his Government's Indian policy, 23–5, 87
   India Committee of the War Cabinet member, 88
   mentioned, 35, 37, 42, 62, 66–7, 77, 81, 85, 201
   Pakistan issue, 4–5, 130
   Plan Partition, 169
civil disobedience, 22, 24–5, 31–3, 40, 42, 56, 58, 141, 152–3
Clauson, Miles, 30
Collins, L., 134
Colville, Sir John, 173
Congress, Indian National,
   Cabinet Mission scheme, 128–30, 152, 178, 190
   constitutional negotiations, 1–3, 5–7, 14–23, 32–84 passim, 131–3, 174–5
   Cripps Mission, 29–31, 86–7, 89, 93–4, 97, 100–2, 105, 126–7

Muslims and Muslim League, 21–2, 110–11, 114, 122–3
transfer of power negotiations, 135–42, 149–61, 163–73, 177–81, 184, 187, 190–1, 193–4, 200
Working Committee, 16–17, 23, 33, 35, 100, 110, 163, 176–9, 190
Corfield, Sir Conrad, 181–9, 194–5
Coupland, Sir Reginald, 1, 3–4, 7–8, 27, 98–9, 102, 111, 125–6, 132
Cranborne, Lord, 192, 195
Cripps, Sir Stafford
   1942 Mission, 1–4, 26–31, 86–105, 126–7, 169
   Cabinet Mission, 128
   constitutional negotiations, 10, 19–21, 76
   India Committee of the War Cabinet member, 88
   Jinnah and, 111
   Krishna Menon and, 19
   mentioned, 35, 138, 149–50
   Nehru and, 19, 75
   private tour of India, 20, 26
   transfer of power negotiations, 137, 171, 173, 181, 188
Curzon, Lord, 34, 67–8

Dawson, Geoffrey, 41
Defence of India Rules, 176
Delhi, 116–17, 125
Derby, Lord, 61–2
Dholpur, 52
Dominion Conferences, see Imperial Conferences
Dominion status, 2–8, 10–51 passim, 74, 78, 81–2, 133–81 passim, 191, 193–5
Durrani, Ubaid Ullah, 116
dyarchy, 33, 42–3, 108

East Bengal, 180; see also Bengal
East India Association, 48
Eden, Anthony, 192

Faringdon, Lord, 26

INDEX

Fazl-i-Husain, Mian, 50–1, 108–9

Gandhi, Mohandas Karamchand
  arrest of, 56, 58
  civil disobedience and, 59
  Cripps Mission, 30–1
  launches his Quit India movement, 69
  Linlithgow and, 18, 22–3, 75, 77–80, 83
  mentioned, 21, 33, 76, 78, 100, 131
  Muslim issue, 116, 120–1, 127
  Round Table discussions, 49–51, 53–7, 65
  transfer of power negotiations, 152–4, 156, 158, 160–1, 173, 178–9, 181
Gandhi-Irwin Pact, 32
Gazdar, M. H., 112
Glancy, Sir Reginald, 52–3, 64
Glendevon, Lord, 86
Gopal, S., 134, 160
Ghosh, Sudhir, 138
Government of India Acts
  1919 Act, 1–2, 10–14, 32, 41
  1935 Act, 1–3, 9, 13, 16–18, 33–4, 37, 67–118 *passim*, 158, 169, 171, 175, 190, 200
Grigg, Sir James, 30, 88

Hailey, Lord, 10–11, 20, 45, 61
Halifax, 1st Earl of
  Dominion Status proposals, 11–12, 41, 43
  Federation discussions, 2, 34, 63, 66, 69–70
  Gandhi and, 32, 49
  India tour, 20
  mentioned, 19, 24, 39, 56, 67–8, 76–7
  Simon Committee, 40–1
  Round Table discussions and, 41–4, 65
  views on Churchill, 37–8
Haq, Sir Fazlul, 112, 115, 118
Haroon, Sir Abdoola, 112–15, 117, 132

Harriman, W. A., 26
Hasan, Syed Zafarul, 116, 118
Hindustan, 5, 116, 127, 146–8, 153, 160–1, 167, 176, 179
Hoare, Sir Samuel, *see* Templewood, Lord
Hodson, H. V., 86, 134, 161, 188
Holdsworth, Sir William, 43
Hydari, Sir Akbar, 45
Hyderabad, 31, 60, 116, 125, 191–6, 198–9, 201

Imperial Conferences, 10, 12
India Committee of the Cabinet
  Cripps Mission, 26, 30–1, 89–91, 95–7, 103
  established, 88
  mentioned, 56, 133
  transfer of power negotiations, 137, 155, 157, 160, 168–70, 195
  Wavell's proposals, 33
Indian National Congress, *see* Congress
Indian States Committee, 14, 41
Indore, 52
Inskip, Sir Thomas, 18
Interim Government
  Dominion status, 141, 146–7, 154–5, 163–6, 171, 177, 180
  formed, 182
  mentioned, 6, 157, 185, 199
  negotiations, 128–30, 142, 172
Iqbal, Sir Muhammad, 50, 114–15, 120, 132
Irwin, Lord, *see* Halifax, 1st Earl of
Ismail, Mirza, 45
Ismay, Lord, 130–66 *passim*, 180, 184, 187, 194–5, 201

Jagjivan Ram, 143
Japan, 61, 87–8
Jayakar, M. R., 57–8
Jinnah, Mohammad Ali
  background and characteristics, 106–12, 131, 140
  Cabinet Mission, 128–30, 132
  constitutional activities, 39, 110–33, 176

Cripps Mission, 28, 93, 126–7
  illness, 113
  Linlithgow and, 23, 73, 75–8, 80
  mentioned, 21, 33, 40, 50, 66, 150, 158, 201
  Nehru and, 110
  Pakistan issue, 3–7, 106–7, 131–3, 139, 143, 148, 151, 157, 175, 193
  prestige and power, 106–7, 111–12
  transfer of power negotiations, 130–1, 139–40, 151, 153–4, 164–9, 171, 178, 192, 195
Johnson, Col. Louis, 30, 95–6, 103
Joshi, P. C., 57
Junagadh, 192, 198, 201

Karnatic, 116
Kashmir, 7, 115–16, 198, 201
Khaliquzzaman, Choudhry, 4, 112, 117, 125–6
Kripalani, J. B., 153

Lapierre, D., 134
Latif, Dr Syed Abdul, 114–16
League of Nations, 10
Liaqat Ali Khan, Nawabzada, 17, 21, 28, 112, 114–15, 117, 122–3
Linlithgow, Lord
  characteristics, 68–9
  commits India to war, 17
  constitutional negotiations, 18–19, 22–5, 33, 68–85, 116, 118–19, 122
  Cripps Mission and, 3, 29–31, 86–101, 103–4
  criticism of, 2, 38, 69
  mentioned, 21, 35, 63
  Pakistan issue, 84–5
  Round Table Conferences, 13
Listowel, Lord, 138, 169–70, 173, 184–5, 188, 195–9
Lloyd George, David, 11–12
Lloyd, Lord, 23
Low, Anthony, 86

MacDonald, Ramsay, 11–13, 40–1, 45–8, 53, 55, 57, 61, 65

Macmillan, Harold, 196
Mahmudabad, Raja of, 112
Maine, Sir Henry James Sumner, 34
Majid, Shaikh Abdul, 113
Malabar, 116
Mansergh, Nicholas, 106, 120
Marmagao (Portuguese Goa), 193
Matthai, Dr John, 143
Menon, V. K. Krishna, 19, 98, 101, 144–50, 159, 181
Menon, V. P., 134, 138–200 *passim*
Miéville, Sir Eric, 137, 140–1, 149–52, 154–5, 158–9, 164–7, 187, 195
Minto, Lord, 68
Monckton, Sir Walter, 149–50, 158, 190, 192–9
Montagu declaration, 10–11, 13–14, 34, 36, 65, 67, 74
Montagu-Chelmsford ('Montford') reforms, 1, 9, 14–15, 32, 42, 47, 68
Moon, Sir Penderel, 106
Morris-Jones, W. H., 195, 199, 201
Mountbatten, Lady, 193
Mountbatten, Lord
  Gandhi and, 153–4
  Jinnah and, 106–7, 112, 130–1, 139–40, 153–4
  Nehru and, 135, 139–42, 150, 153–4
  Pakistan issue, 106–7, 140
  recalled to meet India Committee, 168–71
  transfer of power negotiations, 6–7, 134–73, 177–81, 183–201
  transfer of power plan (Plan Balkan), 130, 141–2, 147–84 *passim*
  transfer of power plan (Plan Partition), 167–70, 173
Mudaliar, A. R., 99
Muslim League
  Cabinet Mission, 128–30
  Committee of Writers, 129
  constitutional negotiations, 3–6, 14–17, 21–3, 34, 39, 44–5, 49–51, 71–80, 83–5, 176–7
  Cripps Mission, 27, 86, 97, 101, 105
  Foreign and Inland Deputations Sub-committee, 114, 117, 125

Muslim nationalism and, 28, 106, 111, 113, 122
  separatist objectives, 80, 107, 112–27, 131–3, 175
  transfer of power negotiations, 134–87 *passim*
  Working Committee, 112, 114, 117, 123–5, 128–9, 133
Muslim League National Guards, 176
Mysore, 60

Nazimuddin, Sir Khwaja, 114
Nehru, Jawaharlal
  Cabinet Mission, 176
  Commonwealth membership issue, 142–4
  Cripps Mission, 30, 87, 95–7, 101–2
  Jinnah and, 110
  mentioned, 7, 19, 21, 89, 97, 100, 112, 148
  Monckton and, 149
  Pakistan issue, 130
  transfer of power negotiations, 135, 139–42, 150–68, 170–1, 173, 175, 177–81, 184–91, 200
Nehru, Motilal, 45
Nehru Report (1928), 15, 39, 41, 48, 64
Nizam of Hyderabad, 19, 72, 149, 194, 196, 198–9
Noon, Sir Firoz Khan, 99
North-West Frontier Province
  government of, 178–9
  political development, 15, 39, 55, 65, 68, 109, 115, 128, 141–80 *passim*
  terrorism and violence, 152–3, 177
Nye, Sir Archibald, 144

Oudh, 174

Pakistan
  demand for and viability of, 1, 4–8, 17, 23, 80, 84–5, 106–86 *passim*, 193
  Jinnah's definition of, 124
  mentioned, 73, 167

name coined, 115
officially conceded, 33
see also West Pakistan
Pakistan National Movement, 115
Patel, Sardar Vallabhbhai, 144, 148, 153–5, 158–61, 167–91 *passim*, 200
Patiala, Maharaja of, 52, 61
Pattani, Sir P., 52
Peel, Lord, 12
Pethick-Lawrence, Lord, 137–8, 183
Philips, Sir Cyril, 106, 160
Prasad, Dr Rajendra, 75–6, 110, 122
princely states and princes
  1935 Act and, 1–2, 68
  constitutional negotiations, 4–5, 9–76 *passim*, 110, 130
  transfer of power negotiations, 136, 170, 174–201
Punjab
  government of, 109, 158, 176, 178
  political development, 6, 15–16, 33, 39, 65, 68, 115, 126–77 *passim*, 201
  see also West Punjab

Qadri, Dr M. A. H., 116, 118
Quit India movement, 31, 33, 69

R.S.S., *see* Rashtriya Swayamsevak Sangh
Rajagopalachari, C., 144, 188
Rao, B. Shiva, 92, 98
Rao, Raghavendra, 20, 76
Rashtriya Swayamsevak Sangh (R.S.S.), 176
Rau, Sir B. N., 138, 142, 171
Reading, Lord, 11–12, 41–2, 44, 47
Reed, Sir Stanley, 20
Roger, Sir Alexander, 193
Roosevelt, Franklin Delano, 88
Round Table Conferences, 13, 16, 32, 40–60, 64, 66–7, 108
Roy, Kiran Sanker, 171

Salisbury, Marquess of, 59, 62
Sapru, Sir Tej Bahadur, 45, 57–8, 82, 87–9

Sastri, V. S. Srinivasa, 45, 48, 54, 57, 59
satyagraha, *see* civil disobedience
Sayeed, Khalid Bin, 107
Schuster, Sir George, 20, 25
Setalvad, Sir Chimanlal, 40, 57
Sethna, Sir P., 57
Shafat Ahmad Khan, 50
Shawcross, Hartley, 150
Sikandar Hayat Khan, Sir, 112, 114–17, 122–3, 125
Sikh Akalis, *see* Akalis
Simon, Sir John, 2, 11–13, 23, 30, 34, 40–2, 46, 77, 88
Simon Commission, *see* Statutory Commission
Sind
  government of, 112
  political development, 15–16, 33, 39, 55, 65, 68, 109, 115, 128, 151–80 *passim*
Sind Provincial Muslim League Conference, 112–13
Smith, Lt. Gen. Sir Arthur, 150
Snell, Lord, 20, 76
Sorensen, R. W., 20
Srivastava, Sir J. P., 99
Stanley, Sir George, 61
Stansgate, Viscount, 20, 32, 40–1, 43, 65
Statute of Westminster, 14, 18
Statutory Commission, 1, 11–14, 32, 39–44, 46, 48, 54
Stewart, Sir Findlater, 20
Stokes, Eric, 86
Stubbs, William, 34
Suhrawardy, H. S., 131, 170–1
Swaraj Party, 60

Templewood, Lord
  constitutional negotiations and, 2, 5, 17, 35, 44, 46–8, 53–65, 192–3, 195, 197
  his memoirs, 37–8, 63, 66
  mentioned, 13, 45, 67–8, 77
Tinker, Hugh, 134, 161
Travancore, 60, 133, 191–3, 195
Trivedi, Sir Chandulal, 144, 155
Turnbull, F. F., 30, 161

Udaipur, 60
Uddin, Dr Zaki, 116
Unionist Party (Punjab), 108–9
United Party (Sind), 112
United Provinces (U.P.), 56, 109–10
United States, 25–6, 30, 32, 36, 88, 96

Versailles Peace Conference, 10

Wavell, Lord, 3, 6, 31, 33, 93–5, 97, 99, 105, 124, 130, 132, 136, 139, 171, 177, 182–3
West Pakistan, 193; *see also* Pakistan
West Punjab, 174, 178, 180; *see also* Punjab
Willingdon, Lord, 13, 32–3, 37–8, 53–63, 65
Winterton, Lord, 12, 71
Wyatt, Woodrow, 173

Zafrullah Khan, Sir Muhammad, 190, 194
Zetland, Lord
  background, 68
  Dominion status issue, 3, 18
  India tour, 20
  Linlithgow and, 21–2, 69, 71, 73–9
  mentioned, 19, 62, 72, 80, 82–3
  princes issue, 34, 70
  Willingdon and, 63
Ziegler, Philip, 7
Ziring, Lawrence, 106